100 Years
of Reimagining Flight

100 Years of Reimagining Flight

GE Aviation

Rick Kennedy

Wilmington, Ohio

ISBN 978-1939710-994
Copyright©2019 GE Aviation

No part of this publication may be reproduced in any material form (including photocopying or storing in any medium by electronic means and whether or not transiently or incidentally to some other use of this publication) without the written permission of the copyright holder except in accordance with the provisions of the Copyright, Designs and Patents Act 1988.

Published for GE Aviation by:
Orange Frazer Press
P.O. Box 214
Wilmington, OH 45177
Telephone: 937.382.3196 for price and shipping information.
Website: www.orangefrazer.com

Book and cover design: Alyson Rua and Orange Frazer Press

Cover photograph of GE90 fan blade by John Oakes

Back photograph by Rob Butler

Library of Congress Control Number: 2018967011

Printed in China

First Printing

To my late father, Charles Kennedy, who relied on GE turbosuperchargers during his missions over Europe as a US Army Air Corps B-17 bombardier during World War II. Among his last words, "You've got to do that GE book."

Acknowledgments

Writing this book was a labor of love. During my thirty years at GE Aviation, co-workers from the factory floor to the executive offices instilled in me a fascination for the company's amazing success, resulting from the heroic work of thousands of people. I am grateful for my long friendships with Richard Ostrom, Robert Conboy, and the late Jim Stump, three GE veterans who never viewed the old, yellow-brick factory buildings at Evendale as anything less than magical.

GE Aviation President David Joyce, a formidable company historian in his own right, endorsed this project immediately and provided valuable resources and insights. My dear friend Dwight Weber hired me into the company's media team in 1988, and, thirty years later, served as the book's critical and pesky editor. Tim Morison, another longtime GE associate who embodies the company's special culture, encouraged and advised me throughout the writing process.

Current and former GE leaders gave personal insights that made these pages come alive. Special thanks to Muhammad Al-Lamadani, Colleen Athans, Michael Benzakein, Ed Birtwell, Jonathan Blank, Chip Blankenship, Vic Bonneau, Hank Brands, Brian Brimelow, Tom Brisken, Bill Brown, Bruce Bunch, Chuck Chadwell, Chaker Chahrour, William (Bill) Clapper, Thomas Cooper, Sanjay Correa, Eric Ducharme, Mohammad Ehteshami, Mearl Eismeier, Bill Fitzgerald, Chet Fuller, Klaus Huber, the late Henry Hubschman, Jeff Immelt, Freeman James, Michael Kauffman, Brian Keith, Thomas Lodge, Jean Lydon-Rodgers, Robert McEwan, James McNerney, Gary Mercer, Tim Meyers, Greg Morris, Brad Mottier, Harry Nahatis, Brian Ovington, Alan Paxson, Jamie Regg, Jeannie Rosario, the late Brian Rowe, Jan Schilling, Gary Sheffer, Russ Sparks, Lloyd Thompson, Robert Turnbull, and Glenn Varney.

From GE Aviation's communication team, Janet Flaherty, Nick Hurm, and Miles Vaught assured the project became a reality. Rob Butler shot most of the book's best photographs, and organized the rest.

Recognition is due for the historical insights and support of my thirty-year colleague Jamie Jewell, longtime journalist and friend Guy Norris, and ace historians David Carpenter and Russell Nash. Thanks also to Kim Lovins, David Wilson, Rich Gorham, Shane Wright, Lindsay Keegan, Dan Meador, Tomas Kellner, Shannon Thompson, Peter Prowett, Jennifer Villarreal, Marcy Hawley, John Baskin, Sarah Hawley, and Alyson Rua.

I wish to offer a heartfelt thanks to my children, Kip and Natalie Kennedy, and especially my wife, Jane, for enduring my distracted mind and many late-night hours on the computer during the creating of this book.

A special shout-out goes to the staff of the Friendly Stop Tavern, in the shadow of the GE Aviation world headquarters, where some of this book's best copy was inspired.

Following a tradition...

This book recognizes the work of many people who carefully preserved GE's aviation history over many years. The late Bill Schoneberger led the editorial and research team for the company's first comprehensive history, *Seven Decades of Progress*, published in 1979. Eric Falk led the editorial team for the follow-up book, *Eight Decades of Progress*, published in 1990.

Three GE Aviation giants each wrote insightful and candid memoirs before their deaths: Gerhard Neumann's *Herman The German* was published in 1984 and was followed by Brian Rowe's *An Engineer's Life* in 2005. Jack Parker published *Have We Done Everything We Came Here To Do?* in 2011.

An expert on the company's early years, David Carpenter, has written several books on GE engines, most notably, *Flame Powered: The Bell XP-59A Airacomet and the General Electric I-A Engine*. In 1998, the late Robert Garvin authored *Starting Something Big: The Commercial Emergence of GE Aircraft Engines*. In 2016, CFM International published the joint company's definitive history, *CFM: The Power of Flight*, written by Guy Norris and Felix Torres, and orchestrated by Jamie Jewell.

Organizing the 100-year history of a complex and fast-growing company is daunting. I formatted this book as a year-by-year chronology in order to serve as both a historical narrative and convenient reference book. My hope is this makes the detailed content more accessible for readers, especially for young GE Aviation employees as they add new chapters to this remarkable story.

US Army pilot John Macready prepares for another record-breaking, high-altitude flight in a GE "turbo-supercharged" biplane in 1921.

Contents

Foreword page xvii
Prologue page xxi

1892–1940 • Into Rarefied Air page 2
- **1892** Iconic inventor establishes GE
- **1893** Lynn River Works expands
- **1903** Hiring an engineering genius
- **1917** An America at war turns to GE
- **1918** A mountaintop experience
- **1919** GE's aviation business born over the Dayton skies
- **1920s** Chasing the "altitude ceiling"
- **1930s** Turbine research continues
- **1935** A "Flying Fortress" on the horizon
- **1937** The genesis of jet engines
- **1939** "Prized" turbosupercharger
- **1940** War spawns mammoth Ohio factory

1941–1964 • Fast Jets page 26
- **1941** The "Hush Hush Boys" & the I-A engine
- **1942** Lifting the US into the Jet Age
- **1943** GE's dramatic wartime advances
- **1944** First US operational fighter jet
- **1945** Welcome to "Turbo Town"
- **1946** Aviation's most-produced jet engine
- **1948** "Magnificent seven" come to Ohio
- **1949** A brilliant woman in a man's world
- **1950** J47 power over Korea
- **1951** LaPierre: Turbojets will rule the skies
- **1952** GE's "Mach 2 engine"
- **1953** GE's aviation roadmap
- **1954** Thinking small to create something big
- **1955** "Proving Ground" in the Ohio hills
- **1956** Passenger jetliners shrink the world
- **1957** Changing the helicopter landscape
- **1958** Pioneering the "turbofan" engine
- **1959** The little engine that could

1960	The J85 goes commercial
1961	"Herman The German" era begins
1962	Engine building block for the future
1963	Birth of the cool: The Lear Jet
1964	Heading straight up with lift fans

1965–1986 • Chasing Jetliners page 80

1965	GE changes jet propulsion forever
1966	GE's secret "stealth" propulsion
1967	GE tackles helicopter challenge
1968	GE's bold return to the airline industry
1969	Powering the first Airbus jetliner
1970	Core values: GE F101 engine
1971	Beginning of a beautiful friendship
1972	Turboshaft engine for the ages
1973	Franco-American engine heats up in Iceland
1974	CFM International is born
1975	Lynn's ubiquitous fighter engine
1978	CF6 engines score the big twins
1979	Launch saves CFM International
1980	Refueling tanker fuels CFM
1981	A victory changes the competitive landscape
1982	New CFM showdown brews in Europe
1983	CFM's new competitor
1984	The "Great Engine War"
1985	Military engines roll down the line
1986	The revolutionary UDF engine

1987–2006 • Big Fans page 130

1987	New leaders in jetliner power
1988	Powering the regional jet revolution
1989	The high-thrust workhorse
1990	Brian Rowe's bold vision
1991	GE military engines: ecstasy & agony
1992	Powering a super-sized Hornet
1993	CFM's next engine for new Boeing 737
1994	F-16 fighter engine leadership
1995	Regional jets take a growth step
1996	The unique engine alliance
1997	GE's buying spree in engine services
1998	The Engine Alliance pursues the A380

1999	GE90: The comeback kid
2000	The offspring replaces iconic parent
2001	GE commits to a shaken industry
2002	China and Middle East breakthroughs
2003	One for the record books
2004	Unveiling the GEnx
2005	Memorable year for the big fans
2006	Revamped GE Engine Services strategy

2007–2018 • Wider Horizons page 190

2007	Beyond the jet engine
2008	Game On: CFM "LEAPS" to 2040
2009	A LEAP to China
2010	GE electrifies aviation's birthplace
2011	The LEAP Summer of Love
2012	A technology epiphany
2013	World's biggest jet engine gets bigger
2014	GE's manufacturing renaissance
2015	Challenging a turboprop dynasty
2016	GE's future military engines
2017	All eyes on the LEAP engine
2018	CMCs: GE's bold technology odyssey

Epilogue page 245

The GE Aviation Propulsion Hall of Fame Members page 247

Endnotes page 263

Bibliography page 271

Index page 273

Foreword

Since the first time GE Aviation took to the skies a century ago, we have been inspired by the possibilities of powered flight. That challenge has ignited a burning passion for invention in each succeeding generation and fueled a will to achieve that defines the unique culture at the heart of our business.

Our technology has kept our men and women in uniform safe, taken commercial passenger travel to new heights, and propelled economic development around the world. At any moment of the day, hundreds of thousands of people in the sky depend upon the remarkable reliability of our engines and aircraft systems. We embrace this responsibility with an intense commitment to our mission and to the safety of those placing such trust in us.

As the CEO for the last decade—and an employee for almost forty years—I have had the privilege of building a career at GE Aviation. I have been blessed with rich relationships and experiences that shaped our business. I often tell our teams that we stand on the shoulders of giants who made courageous decisions to assure a strong future for the next generation. Reading the pages of this book, you will be struck by how our greatest achievements often occurred while persevering through our greatest headwinds.

As a young engineer, I listened to leaders recount the challenges involved in inventing the first "high-bypass turbofan" and the Herculean team effort required to enter commercial aviation. Only later did I fully appreciate those efforts when we developed the GE90 turbofan. Its very survival and remarkable success epitomized the courage and conviction of so many. Today, we can't imagine our company without this game-changing engine or without our many airline customers.

Our military teams fought for years to secure positions for GE engines, and, once successful, went on to make the aircraft they powered more capable than ever imagined, distinguishing our technology with military customers around the world.

CFM International, our joint company with Safran Aircraft Engines in France, exists today because leaders on both sides of the Atlantic Ocean refused to quit pursuing a vision that ultimately changed the landscape of jet propulsion.

Every generation at GE Aviation shares similar experiences: moving mountains for customers, winning high-stakes competitions, battling adversity through tough industry cycles, and overcoming major challenges to advance technology. When I meet retirees (many of whom I've worked with), they proudly recall the first test of a new engine in the morning fog at our remote facility in Peebles, Ohio, or designing engines now powering the world's airline fleets, or supporting airlines and military deployments during challenging times. They were willing to coach and teach, to "pay it forward," to make sure their experiences would provide the necessary lift to the generation of leaders guiding the business today. Leaders who exude the same passion and drive continue to make our company and customers successful.

You see, we believe a single sentence has encapsulated the pride, passion, and purpose of the people at GE Aviation for generations. We invent the future of flight, lift people up, and bring them home safely. Now, after 100 years of innovation and learning, GE Aviation is poised to begin the next century with the experience, enthusiasm, and confidence to tackle the challenges of an aviation industry operating on an unprecedented scale.

Our classroom has been the development of powered flight, and our teachers have been the pioneers whose legacy is the library of knowledge and accomplishment that are the foundation of our future. Our pioneers knew the importance of building a business that succeeds with great purpose. They put learning at the center of their imperatives as the universal quality that extends across all disciplines and transcends generations. Our pioneers created a culture of excellence that defines the standard of performance for our business and is a source of inspiration for all of those who join us. And they created a culture in which we care for each other and for the communities in which we live and work.

These pioneers are as present today at GE Aviation as they have been for the past century, exhibiting the same pride, passion, and purpose. We invent the future of flight, lift people up, and bring them home safely. I know that single sentence inspires the leaders of GE Aviation today, and I'm confident it will do the same in the future as we begin our second century of business.

It has been a privilege to be a part of something so significant in the history of aviation and so essential to the growth of our modern world. I can't imagine a career anywhere else or a more exciting time to be at GE Aviation, delivering for our customers today and shaping the future. What a wonderful tradition to bring into a new century.

David Joyce
GE Vice Chairman
President & CEO of GE Aviation

Prologue

The GE Aviation of today was unimaginable back when GE's experimental turbosupercharger, attached to the piston engine of a US Army biplane, first lifted off a grass runway on July 12, 1919, in Dayton, Ohio. Launched a century ago by the goateed inventor Sanford Moss and his handpicked team of engineers and machinists in Lynn, Massachusetts, GE Aviation is now among the most successful companies in aviation history.

Headquartered near Cincinnati, Ohio, GE Aviation operates a global network of more than eighty sites with more than 40,000 employees. The engines from GE and its partner companies powering civil and military aircraft are fast approaching 70,000—the largest engine fleet in the sky since the dawn of the Jet Age.

The company's technical achievements include America's first turbojet (generally called a "jet engine") and turboprop engines, turboshaft engines for helicopters, turbojets for record-breaking Mach 2 and Mach 3 combat aircraft, and the most popular high-bypass turbofan engines for small and large passenger jetliners, which continue to make air travel affordable for billions of people.

GE Aviation's future is equally promising. The company's recent breakthroughs include record temperatures and pressure ratios for jet engines, unique applications for ceramic matrix composites and additive manufacturing, and bold advances in electrical power extraction. These achievements, combined with the company's industrial backlog of products and services exceeding $200 billion in 2019, assure that GE Aviation will continue to advance air travel far into the future.

While recognized within the aerospace community, GE Aviation's 100-year heritage as an aviation innovator is less well known to the general public. During much of its history, GE's aviation division (which has changed names several times) has been a small piece of the parent General Electric Company's industrial and financial services portfolio. Needless to say, the GE that brought "good things to life" with consumer appliances and light bulbs was far more recognizable than the one advancing powered flight. Indeed, without the corporation's support, the aviation division would not have gone airborne.

The promising GE Aviation of tomorrow will operate in a culture defined by the company's proud history of determined visionaries. While the grass runways, open cockpits, and smoky turbojets have been replaced by quiet, clean, and efficient aircraft that race above the clouds almost unnoticed, the GE Aviation mission will always be the same: invent the future of flight every day.

100 Years
of Reimagining Flight

1892-

100 YEARS OF REIMAGINING FLIGHT

1940

Into Rarefied Air

1892–1940

- ✈ **As the Wright Brothers** in Dayton, Ohio, master powered flight, industrial giant General Electric Company (GE) develops turbines and compressors to generate power for electrical products.

- ✈ **These very technologies** will eventually lead to GE's entry into the fast-evolving aviation industry.

- ✈ **Two global wars** create an urgent challenge for military airplanes: The need to fly higher than their piston engines can take them.

- ✈ **GE is approached** for a solution. Boosted by GE turbosuperchargers, early military airplanes soar to unprecedented heights in the early 1920s.

- ✈ **Twenty years later**, the same GE technology influences the outcome of World War II.

- ✈ **This technology** will propel GE into the brave new world of jet propulsion.

1892

In the beginning: Thomas A. Edison.

1940

1892
Iconic inventor establishes GE

The rise of Thomas Edison: Son of a hardscrabble saloon operator and land speculator, Thomas Edison is born in Milan, Ohio, in 1847 and grows up in a large family living mostly in Port Huron, Michigan. He is a frail child, hearing-impaired and with little formal education. But he is a passionate reader educated mostly by his mother, a former schoolteacher.

In his teens, Edison becomes a traveling telegraph operator in several American cities. Through his travels, the young man evolves into a confident salesman and obsessive tinkerer. He combines both traits to earn a small fortune by inventing telegraphic devices.

In 1876, Edison creates an industrial research laboratory in Menlo Park, New Jersey. He is all of twenty-nine years old. The next year, he gains world fame when his phonograph machine reproduces sound by using tinfoil on a grooved cylinder. He files patents for electric lights and an electric lamp using a carbon filament.

In 1880, he establishes Edison Illuminating Company and constructs electrical generating stations. In 1883, he refines a phenomenon in which an electric current can flow through an evacuated space from a filament to a plate in an incandescent bulb. He patents the discovery, later known as the "Edison Effect." It is the basis for the vacuum tube, predecessor of the transistor. During the decade, he folds his businesses into a single company, Edison General Electric.

On April 25, 1892, General Electric Company (GE) is established through a merger, orchestrated by New York banker J.P. Morgan, between Edison General Electric and a competitor, Elihu Thomson's Thomson-Houston Electric Company, an electrical innovator in Lynn, Massachusetts.

GE is headquartered at Edison General Electric's complex in Schenectady, New York. The company produces large industrial machines to generate and distribute

The massive Lynn "River Works" in the 1890s.

electricity, such as steam turbines and electrical generators, and consumer products such as light bulbs and appliances. In 1897, GE pursues turbine power for generating electrical energy. By 1903, GE develops large centrifugal compressors and installs the world's largest steam turbine generator in Chicago, Illinois.

1893
Lynn River Works expands

At the original Thomson-Houston Electric Company operations, the first set of large factory buildings of Lynn River Works is completed under the newly established GE. Easy access to transportation along a major railroad line, motor highway, and the Saugus River makes Lynn River Works perfectly suited for heavy manufacturing. The river also provides needed cooling water for foundry products, steam turbines, and large generators.

By the early 20th century, the mammoth Lynn factory complex, with its steel and iron foundries, is integral to GE's industrial empire. Lynn produces everything from trolley motors to large steam turbines to centrifugal air compressors.

1903
Hiring an engineering genius

Hiring Sanford Moss: As a teenager working for $6 a week in a dusty machine shop in San Francisco, California, Sanford Moss is fascinated by motors and air compressors. The experience influences his decision to earn degrees in mechanical engineering from the University of California.

In 1903, he receives a doctorate from Cornell University in Ithaca, New York, with a thesis on gas turbine technology. In the school laboratory, he is among the first Americans to power a turbine with combustion gas by burning fuel in a chamber under pressure to operate a turbine. Like Edison, Moss is a tinkerer who believes all red-blooded engineers should be drawn to take apart their pocket watches simply to marvel at the inner workings.[1]

Upon his graduation, Moss joins GE's growing Steam Turbine Department in Lynn. He eventually collaborates with legendary GE technologists Elihu Thomson and Charles P. Steinmetz. GE allows Moss to experiment with his gas turbine concepts. However, without high-temperature metals and efficient compressors and turbines, his early gas turbine designs are not commercially viable. Nevertheless, his centrifugal compressors influence future industrial applications. By 1907, Moss designs centrifugal air and gas compressors. GE's Lynn plant produces compressors for blast furnaces, conveyors, and other machines.

Sporting his trademark Van Dyke goatee, the brilliant and eccentric Moss helps to establish the Turbine Research Department in Lynn. With the outbreak of global war in 1914, the department works on submarine detectors and centrifugal machine guns.

In the years ahead, he will draw upon his lifelong experiences in compression and turbine technology with eyes toward the sky.

The dashing Sanford A. Moss, age 22, in 1894.

1917

An America at war turns to GE

GE turbosupercharger: With air superiority as an urgent objective, a revolutionary form of warfare emerges during World War I (1914–1918) in the skies over Europe.

Combat and surveillance airplanes, mostly designed in Europe, improve dramatically through better aerodynamics and materials, along with more powerful piston engines. Yet the engines struggle to maintain power in oxygen-thin altitudes above 15,000 feet.

France pursues a "turbosupercharger" designed by French inventor Auguste Rateau, which is flight-tested while attached to the piston engine. He bases his design on a 1910 patent by Swiss engineer Alfred Büchi.

The device has a centrifugal compressor (impeller) attached by a shaft to a turbine wheel. The piston engine's hot exhaust gas is directed into the device's turbine, thereby turning the compressor. Its fast-rotating impeller squeezes the thin air fed into the compressor, thus creating a higher air density and an oxygen level closer to sea-level pressure. The "turbosupercharged" air is fed into the piston engine's carburetor.

After the US enters the war in 1917, the French government shares its turbosupercharger research. The US National Advisory Committee for Aeronautics (established by US President Woodrow Wilson and forerunner to the National Aeronautics and Space Administration) hires a Rateau-sponsored team to build three devices. However, during ground tests, the turbine wheel continues to overheat and fail.[2]

Enter Dr. Stanford Moss. The committee seeks GE's expertise in turbines and centrifugal compressors to develop turbosuperchargers. In an important wrinkle to the story, Committee Chairman William Durand, a former Cornell engineering professor, vividly recalls Moss's gas turbine

Professor William Durand, recalling the noisy gas turbine experiments of Sanford Moss, brings GE into the aviation industry.

research. In fact, Durand's old Cornell office is above the laboratory where Moss would run his noisy tests.³

GE embraces the government's wartime request, and Moss leads the secret project. He assembles a small team in a secured building in Lynn to begin developing a turbosupercharger.

After the US enters World War I, the city of Dayton, Ohio, becomes the nation's hub for military aviation. In 1917, the Aviation Section of the US Signal Corps (later named the US Army Air Service) establishes Wilbur Wright Field as a flight training center staffed with American and French flight instructors, and nearby McCook Field as the nation's first aviation research center.

Wilbur Wright Field is east of Dayton at Huffman Prairie, the open field where Wilbur and Orville Wright tested their historic aircraft earlier in the century. McCook Field is west of Wright Field and a mile north of downtown along the Great Miami River.

During 1917–1918, the government constructs an airfield, hangars, laboratories, and barracks at McCook Field. Here, military pilots and engineers play a central role in collaborating on GE's turbosupercharger. By 1927, McCook's operations are consolidated at Wright Field, which, in 1948, becomes Wright-Patterson Air Force Base.

1918

A mountaintop experience

Pikes Peak testing: Boom! In July at McCook Field, GE and Army Air Service technicians test a Moss turbosupercharger attached to a Liberty piston engine. Surrounded by sandbags, the test rig runs at full throttle when the fuel and air mixture ignite prematurely. The piston engine's sparkplugs explode like rockets off the contraption.

The Army test report concludes: "When using the [Moss] supercharger with the Liberty engine, it was difficult to make many tests with the supercharger operating. Even when only subjecting the engine to a small amount of supercharge at this low altitude, the sparkplugs failed and numerous other difficulties developed."[4]

But Moss has a trick up his sleeve: "The stage was reached where nothing more could be done except run at high altitude," he writes.[5] McCook officers and the Moss team trek to remote Pikes Peak, Colorado, the highest US altitude reachable by a drivable road. By railroad car, GE transports a truck packed with a portable

Dr. Moss, center, with US Army and GE personnel at Pikes Peak in 1918.

test laboratory (including the engine test mount, fuel tanks, instruments, and a small machine shop) to nearby Colorado Springs.

The team drives twenty-eight miles up the steep and winding road to the top. For weeks, they test the turbosupercharger on a Liberty engine at 14,109 feet to replicate flying conditions. Moss likes to say that the turbosupercharger tricks the piston engine into thinking it is running at sea level. After tests on the mountain in September and October, the team calls it quits on October 17 due to bitter weather.

In the rarefied air, the Moss device benefits from GE's expertise with fast-rotating steam turbines and high-temperature metallurgy. Its prime advantage over the Rateau design is the introduction of cooling air into the casing of the turbine wheel, which revolves more than 20,000 times per minute in exhaust gases up to 1,500 degrees Fahrenheit. At high-altitude, the air's low density reduces the device's capacity for heat absorption. As a result, the turbine actually requires more cooling surface at high altitude than at sea level.[6]

At Pikes Peak, the GE turbosupercharger boosts the Liberty engine to reach 356 horsepower at high altitude, compared to 230 horsepower without it. GE is

GE's portable test laboratory at Pikes Peak. The men manually start the Liberty engine (far left). The turbosupercharger is installed on top.

awarded its first US military aviation contract to test the device on an airplane. However, World War I ends the following month, and US military contracts are suspended. GE's turbosupercharger is in peril before it ever leaves the ground.

1919
GE's aviation business born over the Dayton skies

The first flight: The Power Plant Laboratory at McCook creates a post-war technology roadmap to reinstate certain projects cancelled after the Armistice. Viewing issues with the Rateau device as insurmountable, the Army Air Service collaborates exclusively with Moss and his team on GE's turbosupercharger design.[7]

On the Saturday of July 12 on the McCook runway, Army Major Rudolph "Shorty" Schroeder (who's actually six feet four inches tall) climbs into the open cockpit of a French-designed, Packard-built Lepère biplane for the maiden flight of GE's turbosupercharger. It is attached to the forward end of a 400-horsepower, US-designed Liberty engine. The flight occurs about one year after the failed ground tests at McCook.

The impact is immediate. Schroeder flies without the assistance of oxygen in the cockpit and quickly takes the biplane in rapid ascent to more than 16,000 feet. The engine comfortably sustains power. His initial checkout flight with the Moss device includes cruising above airspace circled by the Wright Brothers in 1904–1905 at Huffman Prairie while mastering practical airplane flying. "A very good showing was made from the first flight," Moss writes.[8]

While a milestone day for GE, the flight is overshadowed by three deaths in four days from separate experiments at McCook. The day before, an officer is killed in a parachute test. Two days after Schroeder's flight, two more officers perish when an airplane (without the Moss device) nosedives shortly after takeoff. McCook aviators are a fearless bunch.

Within two weeks, the Army Air Service goes public with its secret GE turbosupercharger experiments in Dayton. (Declining post-war budgets for military aviation likely influence the timing.) Syndicated columnist Charles M. Ripley is given the scoop, and he writes a detailed account, published in newspapers worldwide, about the turbosupercharger and the McCook flights. He declares that the turbosupercharger will "do for the physicist desiring to study the upper regions of thin air what the telescope did for the astronomer in permitting him to study the planets and the fixed stars!"[9]

The Army's turbosupercharger contract with GE calls for a Liberty engine to sustain 400 horsepower (its sea level rating) at 20,000 feet. Using new metal alloys to handle the device's high temperatures, GE and the Army Air Service advance American metallurgical capabilities.

To further promote aviation advances at McCook, the US Army organizes several high-profile flight demonstrations. On August 2, Schroeder climbs back into the GE-boosted Lepère biplane and sets an altitude record of 18,400 feet. By September, he is approaching 30,000 feet. Looking back on those heady days in Dayton, Moss writes, "A flight record of some kind or another was broken at every flight."[10]

Dr. Moss (right) next to the US Army's Lepère biplane with his turbosupercharger attached above the Liberty engine, at McCook Field, Dayton, Ohio. The 1919 flight demonstrations put GE in the aviation business.

1920s
Chasing the "altitude ceiling"

More altitude records: On February 27, 1920, Schroeder miraculously survives a perilous flight at McCook that captures the nation's imagination. He pilots the GE-boosted Lepère biplane to his third altitude record of more than 30,000 feet. Yet the ensuing drama resembles a scene from a silent movie.

Schroeder climbs steadily for one hour and forty-seven minutes. At peak altitude, he removes his goggles to change oxygen tanks used to breathe in the thin air. At -55 degrees Fahrenheit, his eyeballs and eyelids freeze together, and he loses consciousness. He apparently falls on the control stick, because the biplane goes into a five-mile dive. At about 3,000 feet and barely conscious, he pulls the biplane out of its plummet and glides home to McCook. Details of his "chasing the altitude ceiling" and his surviving to tell about it prompt large newspaper headlines worldwide.[11]

The chase upward continues. The next year, another McCook pilot, Lieutenant John Macready, surpasses 34,000 feet. Meanwhile, in France, famed French pilot Joseph Sadi-LeCointe surpasses 35,000 feet with an aircraft boosted by a Rateau turbosupercharger. US newspapers eagerly follow the daring, high-altitude competition between the US and France.

The stage is set for Macready's ultimate flight. On September 28, 1921, he pilots the GE-boosted Lepère biplane to an estimated 40,800 feet at which point the piston engine finally stalls. He glides the powerless airplane back to McCook. The fearless pilot, complaining only of slight numbness, promptly climbs out of the plane and poses for Dayton news photographers. "Human nerves and human brains both triumphed in this instance," the US wire services report. "Two inventors of science, the GE Moss Supercharger, and the Caldwell high-pitch propeller, accomplished the unheard of."[12]

Advertising the feat in trade magazines, GE claims its turbosupercharger reaches the highest speed ever achieved by any commercial machine. Macready makes fifty flights over 30,000 feet with the GE turbosupercharger.

Bombing demonstration: In July 1921, Army General Billy Mitchell drops bombs at 15,000 feet with a piston-powered MB-1 bomber aircraft boosted by the GE turbo-supercharger. He sinks two target battleships (both captured German vessels from World War I), which have been towed 100 miles off the Virginia coast. Mitchell contends that bomb-carrying aircraft are more effective than surface guns in sinking naval ships. His bombing demonstration sets the stage for the high-altitude bombing missions of World War II.

Internal superchargers: Despite the high-profile flight demonstrations and altitude records set with GE turbosuperchargers, US Army enthusiasm for high-altitude flying fails to gain momentum during peacetime.

Government-sponsored research with GE continues, but no substantial production contracts for the Moss device are

Left to right: Lieutenant John Macready, Dr. Moss, Captain George Hallett, and "Doc" Berger (McCook engine laboratory) in front of the Lepère biplane after Macready pilots the aircraft above 40,000 feet for another world record.

forthcoming for many years. As the 1920s economy booms, GE focuses on electric power generation, lighting, and home appliances.

Meanwhile, the small Lynn aviation team under Moss produces thousands of impellers and diffuser plates for geared superchargers in air-cooled piston engines produced by Pratt & Whitney (P&W) and Wright Aeronautical, America's two leading piston engine producers for aircraft. The subcontract work continues into the 1940s.

1930s
Turbine research continues
US Army collaboration: The Army Air Corps, now consolidated in Dayton at Wright Field, collaborates with GE on technology for turbosuperchargers and general gas turbine concepts.

In 1931, GE receives the first of several research contracts to refine and test turbine blades and nozzles. It leads GE to create its first high-temperature test stand. Modest military R&D funding with GE continues during the decade. These small contracts, combined with the steady subcontract work from the piston-engine manufacturers, enable GE to maintain a toehold in the aviation industry during many lean years.

1935
A "Flying Fortress" on the horizon
Boeing Model 299: In the mid-1930s, at the height of the Great Depression, a new Boeing bomber prototype provides GE's opportunity to secure a more prominent place in aviation.

Nicknamed the "Flying Fortress" by a Seattle reporter, the new Boeing Model 299, powered by four piston engines, rolls out to the public, and is hailed as the world's fastest, longest-range bomber. During flight tests in 1935, the aircraft completes a nonstop flight from the Boeing factory in Seattle, Washington, to the Army Air Corps' Wright Field in Dayton, Ohio.

The next year, the US government orders thirteen aircraft, with the designation YB-17. While the airplane demonstrates range and speed, specifications also demand high-altitude capability above 20,000 feet in order to more safely conduct bombing missions. During 1937-1938, the aircraft's piston engines are fitted and

The Boeing 299 prototype is developed years before its production version, the B-17, will blanket the skies over Europe during World War II.

tested with upgraded GE turbosuperchargers, both a technical coup and a business boost for the Lynn team.[13]

✈ Also in 1935...

Fighter plane application: Army Air Corps flight tests begin for the Consolidated PB-2A two-seat fighter plane, powered by a Curtiss piston engine boosted by a GE turbosupercharger. The PB-2A is the only single-engine, two-seat monoplane fighter to enter operational service between the two world wars, though the production run is under a hundred aircraft.

1937
The genesis of jet engines

Running the first jet engines: By the early 1930s, gas turbine engines for airplanes (called "turbojets" or "jet engines") are actively studied in Europe and the US, including research papers by GE engineers for the Army Air Corps at Wright Field. However, as US studies continue on paper, the Europeans move ahead toward practical applications.

In 1937, England's Frank Whittle and Germany's Dr. Hans von Ohain will work independently of each other in ground testing the first turbojet engines.

A turbojet is a type of gas turbine in which air is compressed, and passes into a combustion chamber where fuel is burned. The resulting hot air both turns the turbine driving the compressor and provides forward thrust to the aircraft and engine.

As a 23-year-old Royal Air Force (RAF) flight officer in 1930, Whittle files the world's first turbojet patent application, which is published internationally. Facing disinterest within the Royal Air Force and British government, however, the young RAF officer allows the patent to expire.

Whittle's fortunes change in 1935 when the London investment house of O.T. Falk & Partners bankrolls his commercial venture called Power Jets Ltd., which enables his jet engine design work to resume. In addition, the RAF allows the young flight officer to work part-time on his propulsion experiments. In 1937, Power Jets begins running Whittle's turbojet design in a test cell with varying success.

In Germany, von Ohain patents a turbojet design in 1935 as a 24-year-old post-graduate aerodynamics student at the University of Göttingen. The Heinkel Aircraft Company in Germany hires him to advance turbojet engine designs for future aircraft. In 1937, he ground tests an improved version of his turbojet.

The historic Whittle and von Ohain jet engine tests set the stage for dramatic advances in aviation propulsion during World War II. They also steer the future course of GE's budding aviation enterprise. But first, GE establishes a thriving turbosupercharger production business.

TWA's Northrop Gamma with pilot D.W. "Tommy" Tomlinson in 1937. The aircraft's "over the weather" flying bolsters GE's prospects for the turbosupercharger.

✈ *Also in 1937...*

High-altitude momentum: On the heels of Boeing's YB-17 flight tests in 1937, aviation designer Jack Northrop and Trans World Airlines (TWA) organize flights that further demonstrate how the GE turbosupercharger keeps aircraft flying safely above the weather.

The timing is perfect for GE. During several publicized flights, a Northrop-designed, all-metal Gamma monoplane routinely surpasses 30,000 feet powered by a GE-boosted, Wright Cyclone piston engine. TWA promotes its Northrop Gamma as an "over-weather laboratory airplane."[14] Former Navy flying ace D.W. "Tommy" Tomlinson pilots the smooth flights above the storm clouds. One flight in 1937 from Kansas City, Missouri, to Wright Field is heralded as one of the first "over the weather flights between two distant cities."[15]

Perhaps more importantly for GE, the TWA flights further encourage Army Air Corps funding of the high-altitude Boeing YB-17 bomber. High-altitude flying capability becomes increasingly crucial as the world becomes unstable.

The Air Corps awards GE with a contract to produce 230 of its "Type B Turbosuperchargers" to enable a 1,000-horsepower piston engine to maintain full power to 25,000 feet. The contract takes GE out of the realm of limited "experimental" work and gives rise in 1937 to the creation of the GE Supercharger Department in Lynn.

That December, GE gives Moss a special retirement dinner in Dayton, Ohio. GE selects Dayton because of his work at McCook after World War I. Not surprisingly, Moss soon comes out of retirement to serve as "technical advisor" for the new Supercharger Department. After all, GE finally has a large production program that Moss spent two decades working to establish.

First Turboprop: GE submits a technical paper to Wright Field called "Gas Turbine Power Plants for Aeronautical Applications," which refers to propellers driven by gas turbines. A concept is brewing. Two years later, Moss proposes a gas turbine-driven propeller engine (turboprop) to GE management.

1939
"Prized" turbosupercharger

GE-boosted B-17 flight: On August 1, 1939, to commemorate the thirtieth anniversary of the Army's first aircraft order with Dayton's Wright Brothers, a production B-17 Flying Fortress flies from California to New York in nine hours and fourteen minutes, the fastest transcontinental flight by a US military airplane.

The airplane's four Wright Cyclone engines are boosted by what the Army Air Corps calls its "prized and secret turbosuperchargers" from GE.[16] During most of the flight, the B-17 flies above 25,000 feet and at times beyond 33,000 feet to avoid storms. Reminiscent of the early 1920s, GE technology helps to recapture the public's fascination with high-altitude flying.

By 1940, the GE Supercharger Department in Lynn is managed by veteran technologist Reginald Standerwick, an Englishman who joined GE's Lynn operations in 1909. He creates a team of young, talented

engineers in the Supercharger Department, including future GE jet pioneers Donald "Truly" Warner and Joseph Alford, whose 66-year career as a GE propulsion engineer and consultant touches nearly every GE jet engine over the next half-century.

1940

War spawns mammoth Ohio factory

Wright Aeronautical in Lockland, Ohio (before GE): With the Nazi German invasion of Europe and the Imperial Japanese Army invasion of China and the Pacific islands, US President Franklin D. Roosevelt calls on the nation's industrial machine, slowed for years by the Great Depression, to flex its muscles.

On Memorial Day weekend of 1940, US industrial and government leaders gather in Washington, D.C., to initiate the National Defense Program. After the meeting, Wright Aeronautical commits to deliver more than 1,000 Cyclone radial

The Boeing B-17 high-altitude bomber provides critical production for the GE turbosupercharger.

engines per month from a new government-financed factory complex to be built for defense purposes between the Appalachian and Rocky Mountains.[17]

On July 27, the US Department of Defense announces rural space on the edge of Lockland, Ohio, a northern industrial suburb of Cincinnati, as the site for a massive Wright Aeronautical factory to produce Wright engines for military airplanes supporting the Allied effort. America's entrance into the war is still more than a year away.

Wright Aeronautical cites the "fine vocational training programs of the Cincinnati public schools and the concentration of machine tool builders in the city, and the abundance of experience in metal working among workers" as key factors in the selection.[18] The complex, established on 320 rural acres with thirty-five acres of factory floor space, becomes the largest industrial operation in the Cincinnati area, with a payroll more than twice as large as any other area employer.

Inside the Wright Aeronautical plant in Lockland, Ohio, 1941. Among the largest US factories during World War II, the Wright factory produces piston engines until 1945.

The Lockland complex will cost the government about $40 million. It includes enormous manufacturing buildings for a machine shop and engine assembly, an aluminum cylinder head foundry, and seventy-two test cells. Designed by Albert Kahn Associated Architects and Engineers of Detroit, Michigan, the Lockland complex is among the largest, most sophisticated US factories of the World War II era.

The "Center Machine Shop" building (today's Building 700) is heralded as the world's largest single-story structure: 1.5 million square feet of floor space unbroken by supporting walls and large enough to accommodate 100 building lots, 100 by 150 feet. Much of the roof is comprised of glass skylights to allow sunlight to illuminate the shop floor and thus reduce electric lighting.

An expanded, two-mile highway is constructed to support traffic flow to the new plant. Cutting through the neighboring town of Lockland, this track

Uniformed female workers monitor the dials outside the magnesium foundry at Wright Aeronautical in Lockland, Ohio, 1941.

Aviation icon Orville Wright examines a Wright Cyclone piston engine at the Lockland factory in 1941. The plant's formal dedication is briefly delayed because Wright, a guest of honor, is wandering about the assembly line. *(Cincinnati Enquirer)*

of highway, incorporated decades later into Interstate 75, utilizes part of the original Miami-Erie Canal bed from the 1840s. (The town's name is derived from the canal locks once situated there.)

In early 1941, plant excavation is briefly delayed when a three-foot tusk (mastodon or mammoth) is unearthed.[19] Engine production begins in April with the first finished engine parts rolling off four long lines of machines. The plant's foundry, touted the world's largest, is capable of manufacturing 20,000 castings per month.

On June 12, six months before the US enters World War II, the Wright complex is formally dedicated. Aviation pioneer Orville Wright from nearby Dayton attends as the special guest. In Building 700, the 69-year-old Wright, sporting a Panama hat, wanders through the massive production line and briefly delays the ceremony.

While the elderly Wright marvels at the factory's sheer size and production capability, he is also troubled by its reason for existing. "Wilbur and I never envisioned the plane as a terrible engine of war," he tells a group of reporters at the Wright plant dedication. "That always has been my answer when people ask whether we would have attempted our early experiments had we been able to foresee all of this terrible destruction."

Over the next four years, the Lockland plant produces Wright engines for many critical World War II aircraft, including the C-47 transport, the B-17 Flying Fortress, the B-25 Mitchell, the B-29 Superfortress, and the B-32 Dominator.

At peak production, the factory operates around the clock, employing more than 30,000 people and producing more than 3,000 radial engines a month. When operations are suspended on August 17, 1945 with the end of World War II, 27,000 employees work in the complex. Final paychecks are issued a week later, and the massive plant is mothballed.

The property continues to be owned by the federal government. Electric Auto-Lite Corporation eventually acquires the factory buildings, and some space is leased to other companies. The complex is mostly empty for years.

In 1948, GE's aviation enterprise will begin to breathe new life into the sprawling Lockland plant. But more about that later. ✈

1941-

100 YEARS OF REIMAGINING FLIGHT

−1964

Fast Jets

1941–1964

- ✈ Introduced in Europe during World War II, the jet engine becomes one of the century's most significant inventions. The US military must play catch-up with Europe, and GE will help to even the aviation playing field.

- ✈ After introducing America's first jet engine, GE advances military air power with several innovative turbojet engines at the height of the Cold War. GE turbojets incorporate several breakthroughs from variable stator vanes to air-cooled turbine blades.

- ✈ In an era where speed is everything, GE turbojets power the world's fastest fighters and bombers. And even business jets.

- ✈ GE extends its jet propulsion prowess into land and marine applications, and creates a remarkable turboshaft and turboprop engine franchise for helicopters and smaller fixed-wing aircraft.

1941

A turbojet invented by Hans von Ohain powers the world's first jet aircraft, the Heinkel He 178 from Germany. It flies secretly for the first time on August 27, 1939.

1941
The "Hush Hush Boys" & the I-A engine

America's wake-up call: As every major military conflict since World War I has accelerated aviation innovations, the onset of World War II sparks the first flights of turbojet-powered aircraft in Europe. The Jet Age has arrived.

In August 1939 in Germany, the highly-secret Heinkel He 178 experimental aircraft with Hans von Ohain's engine is the first plane to fly with turbojet power. Days later, Nazi Germany invades Poland and throws Europe into full-blown war.

In August 1940 in Italy, inventor Secondo Campini's piston-based "turbojet" powers a Campini Caproni aircraft. The piston engine powers a variable pitch fan that directs air through a pipe fitted with a variable-area nozzle. Fuel fed into the pipe mixes with the compressed air, and the mixture ignites to produce thrust. The Italian government publicly promotes the aircraft, which is erroneously considered the world's first jet airplane due to the secrecy of the German program.

In May 1941 in England, Frank Whittle's turbojet powers the Gloster E.28/39 aircraft. Two years earlier, the British Air Ministry awards a contract to Whittle's Power Jets to develop turbojets for the Gloster aircraft. From 1937 to 1941, Whittle overcomes technical challenges in the test cell, including turbine failures and engine explosions. Nevertheless, his centrifugal-flow turbojet leads to the deployment of the first jet aircraft by an Allied nation toward the end of WWII. (In 1944, the German Luftwaffe deploys the first operational jet fighter with the Messerschmitt Me 262.)

These developments are a wake-up call for the US. Up to this point, many US scientists and engineers believe gas turbines for aircraft are overweight and consume too much fuel for the power they generate. In April 1941, General H.H. "Hap" Arnold, Deputy US Army Chief of Staff for Air, personally reviews England's jet propulsion advances, including the Gloster aircraft and its Whittle turbojet. He forms a different opinion.

British jet engine inventor Frank Whittle. His early turbojet designs embraced by the US Army Air Corps will lead GE into the Jet Age.

Arnold initiates a US jet propulsion program and engages GE to produce America's first turbojet using Whittle's design. His selection of GE is based on the company's innovative impellers, turbines, turbosuperchargers, and compressors, which are developed mostly in GE's Lynn and Schenectady operations. Arnold's contract with GE is expressed in one sentence. He says: "Consult all you wish and arrive at any decision you please, just as long as General Electric accepts a contract to build fifteen of them."[1]

Arnold does not invite leading US aircraft engine producers P&W and Wright Aeronautical to compete for the jet engine contract. For one, he needs them mass producing piston engines for Allied aircraft. Also, the Whittle turbojet design is radically different from piston engines. Selected over Allis Chalmers and Westinghouse, GE is the logical choice. The GE turbosupercharger and the Whittle turbojet have similarities, including advanced impellers and turbines operating in harsh environments.

In 1941, GE's Supercharger Department in Lynn receives a Whittle W.1X turbojet in crates, as well as drawings for an upgraded version, called the Whittle W.2B. (The W.1X is flown from Scotland concealed in the bomb bay of a B-24 Liberator.) A handpicked team in Lynn, nicknamed "The Hush-Hush Boys," will rebuild the Whittle design, designated the I-A engine. The Supercharger Department employees are denied access to the secret project. Many believe a new, giant turbosupercharger is being created.

✈ Also in 1941...

GE develops America's first turboprop: GE's Steam Turbine division in Schenectady proposes the TG-100 turboprop engine, later designated the T31, to the US National Advisory Committee for Aeronautics. The design work begins in July. The Steam Turbine division uses experience gained in developing a gas turbine-powered locomotive.

1942

Lifting the US into the Jet Age

Flying the I-A: Donald "Truly" Warner, a top engineer in Lynn's turbosupercharger department, leads the top-secret I-A program. His team reconfigures Whittle's W.2B design to American production standards with several improvements, including a more robust impeller, an automatic control system, and improved metal alloys for more durable turbine blades. The I-A, a centrifugal flow design with a two-sided impeller, is similar in many ways to a GE turbosupercharger.

After initial challenges firing up the engine, the GE Lynn team successfully runs the I-A on April 18 in a concrete test cell dubbed "Fort Knox." Engine exhaust in the test cell is ducted into a sixty-four-foot chimney. (The test cell, with eighteen-inch walls and a distinctive smokestack, will become a historical monument.)

The first test run occurs about six months after Lynn receives drawings for the upgraded Whittle W.2B engine—a remarkable and patriotic feat by the team. A sentence in the team's secret logbook for April 18 says it all: "Everyone worked like beavers but all felt well repaid."[2]

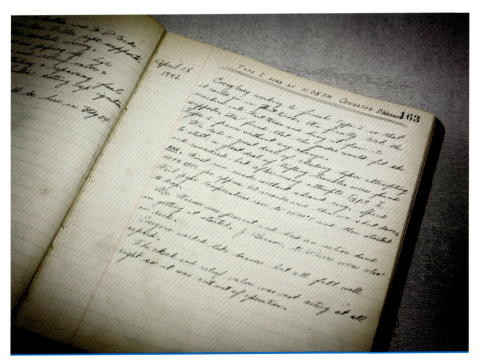

The Lynn test logbook page for April 18, 1942, captures the first I-A jet engine run. "Everyone worked like beavers but all felt well repaid," the diary happily records. *Rob Butler photo.*

Lynn team runs one of its first turbojets.

In June, RAF officer Frank Whittle arrives in Massachusetts to lend a hand for several weeks. He helps to tackle issues with excessive gas exhaust temperatures. His clandestine stay involves checking into the Hotel Statler in Boston under "Mr. Whitely" and demanding a telephone installed in his room that is not connected to the hotel switchboard. He also insists the same bellhop deliver his room service. Then, several days later in the dark of night, he moves into the Marblehead, Massachusetts, home of GE's Standerwick, a fellow Englishman whose wife is not told the inventor's true identity. "He [Whittle] had a small moustache and thick brown hair, and he seemed so lonely," she tells *The Boston Globe* years later.[3]

While testing the engine, GE also works on the XP-59A jet aircraft in tandem with aircraft designer Larry Bell of Bell Aircraft. In August 1942, GE personnel under armed guard load I-A engines, labeled "Type I Superchargers" for security reasons, into a boxcar in Boston for shipment to Bell Aircraft in Buffalo, New York. From there, the engines and aircraft head to Muroc in southern California. To protect the engines' bearings and shafts during the cross-country train ride, a small gas-driven compressor turns the engine shafts continuously. In September, the aircraft, engines, Bell and GE personnel, and ever-present armed guards arrive in Muroc for flight tests.

On October 1, two I-A engines, each rated at 1,250 pounds of thrust, power the first low-altitude flights of the Bell XP-59A Airacomet at Muroc Dry Lake (today's Edwards Air Force Base). Bell test pilot Bob Stanley pilots the first flights; the second pilot is Army Colonel Laurence C. Craigie, the first US military pilot to fly a jet-powered airplane. On October 3, Stanley flies the XP-59A to 10,000 feet. The XP-59A is flight-tested almost one year from the day that the US Secretary of War approved the program contract. The production run for the I-A engine is thirty engines.

Army General B.W. Chidlaw, XP-59A program director, assesses the milestone's importance: "We wished to start this project primarily in a fighter configuration as a fighter prototype test bed hoping that we can expedite the translation from the experimental test plan into a useable superior performance fighter, capable of being produced in quantity for our Army Air Force fighter units."[4]

However, the XP-59A will not become an operational fighter aircraft. Rather, it will serve as a trainer for the forthcoming GE-powered Lockheed P-80 Shooting Star, America's first operational fighter jet. The XP-59A flight program is not revealed to the public until early 1944, when some newspapers call the I-A turbojet a "supercharger that has grown up."[5]

Despite all the wartime seriousness, the test flights have some lighthearted moments. When the aircraft is parked, it is fitted with a wooden propeller to deceive potential foreign agents, while entertaining those in the know. One Bell test

US Army Air Corps flight tests in 1942 at Muroc Dry Lake, California, with the XP-59A powered by the I-A engine. GE team members (left to right) Frank Burnham, Ed Tritle, Roy Shoults, Ted Rogers, and Angus McEachern.

pilot keeps a gorilla mask in the cockpit, and Army Air Corps pilots observe a plane with no propeller flying past them at incredible speed piloted by a gorilla who waves to them.[6]

1943
GE's dramatic wartime advances

First production jet engines: After delivering a small production run of handmade I-A turbojets, the Lynn team quickly assumes a major role at the vanguard of jet propulsion technology. A flurry of new US aviation requirements drives a hurried effort to meet or surpass jet propulsion advances in Europe.

More powerful turbojets are demanded, and the Lynn team pursues higher-thrust I-A turbojet derivatives, the I-14 and I-16, later designated the J31. The J31 powers the Bell P-59 aircraft, which reaches a maximum altitude of 46,700 feet. The J31 becomes the first US turbojet produced in meaningful quantity with 241 engines delivered between 1943 and 1945.

J33 for a Shooting Star: However, the US has even greater ambitions. The Army Air Corps specifies a turbojet capable of 4,000 pounds of thrust. Even as the J31 rolls off the production line, GE immediately creates a higher-thrust successor

Lynn's R.G. Standerwick with an I-40 cutaway engine. Later called the J33 "Superjet," it is the last GE turbojet designed with a centrifugal-flow compressor.

called the I-40 "Superjet." Later designated the J33, it is GE's first turbojet of its own design and the last with a centrifugal-flow compressor.

The J33 will power the innovative P-80 Shooting Star developed by a Lockheed team led by legendary designer Kelly Johnson. A turbojet from de Havilland of England powers the first P-80 prototypes while the Lynn team races to complete the J33, which further incorporates metallurgical advances from GE turbosuperchargers.

Lynn meets the ambitious timetable. In 1943, the J33 achieves 4,200 pounds of thrust during ground tests, which is more than three times as powerful as the Whittle-designed I-A turbojet. It is believed to be the highest thrust achieved by any turbojet to date. A young Neil Burgess, soon to become one of GE's greatest propulsion engineers, is on the J33 team.

Yet GE falls victim to its own success. While GE is designing innovative turbojets, the US government worries that the demands of turbojet production may disrupt critical turbosupercharger deliveries. "It has become one of the most important focal points in America's war effort," *Popular Science* writes in describing GE's turbosupercharger. "No effort or expense is being spared to push its mass production."[7]

After GE produces 300 J33 turbojets, the government hands the drawings and tooling to Allison Engine Company, a division of General Motors, in Indianapolis, Indiana. Allison manufactures the J33 until 1959, delivering more than 7,000 engines.

Axial flow wins over centrifugal flow: As early turbojets are developed, the industry chooses between two compressor designs: A centrifugal compressor whirls incoming air in a circular casing using an impeller, compressing the air by forcing it to the outside of the casing.

An axial flow compressor moves air parallel to the engine centerline and uses stages of blades mounted on a rotating shaft combined with stationary blades mounted in the casing to compress air as it moves straight through from the front to the back of the engine.

In addition to being more efficient, axial-flow engines are smaller in diameter and more aerodynamically attractive to aircraft designers by the mid-1940s. The larger diameters of centrifugal designs create more air resistance and drag. To grow its thrust, a centrifugal-flow engine must increase in diameter, thus creating challenges for aircraft designers.

GE's TG-100 (T31 military designation), America's first turboprop engine, is successfully ground tested. It is the first GE engine to adopt an axial-flow compressor, and the company will never look back. At the same time, GE's Schenectady operation begins the longer-term development of an axial-flow TG-180 turbojet, later designated the J35.

✈ Also in 1943…

Booming turbosupercharger production: As the Allied air campaign expands, GE turbosupercharger production swells. By 1943, about 100,000 GE devices power US and Allied aircraft. GE promotes its technology marvel in newspapers as a "fire-eating machine that takes its power from the red-hot exhaust and uses that power to cram fresh air down a big engine's windpipe fast enough to give it full military power at almost any altitude!"[8]

The device is produced at GE facilities in Lynn and Everett, Massachusetts, in Fort Wayne, Indiana; at the Allis Chalmers plant in Milwaukee, Wisconsin; and Ford Motor plant in Detroit, Michigan. In addition to the B-17, the device is installed on other aircraft, including the Lockheed P-38, the Consolidated B-24, the Republic P-47, and the Boeing B-29.

1944
First US operational fighter jet

J33 in operation: The US Army Air Corps flies its first operational jet fighter, the J33-powered Lockheed P-80 Shooting Star. The Army Air Corps claims to smash speed records exceeding 550 miles per hour with an altitude ceiling above 40,000 feet. The P-80 is billed as the fastest, highest-flying, and most powerful fighter jet in aerospace history.

J33 turbojet benefits also include reduced pilot fatigue due to lower aircraft vibration. The engine can be removed in twenty minutes compared to the hours involved in removing a piston engine. In addition, the J33 readies the Shooting Star for takeoff thirty seconds after the engine starts.

While the low-wing, all-metal P-80 is highly anticipated and promoted (publicly revealed with great fanfare on July 31, 1945), the aircraft sees limited action in the final months of World War II. It reappears as the modified F-80 in the Korean War several years later.

The J33 powers America's first operational jet fighter, the Lockheed P-80 Shooting Star. Eager to catch up with European aviation, the US Army Air Corps touts the P-80's many speed records.

Testing the J35: GE's turbojet design comes into its own when ground tests begin for the J35 prototype. Its axial-flow design produces higher airflow and greater pressure ratios and proves more efficient than centrifugal-flow designs. GE advertises its axial-flow J35 as more powerful at high speed than any other conventional jet engine in the US military inventory, with a significant fuel-burn improvement at full throttle.

The J35 quickly becomes America's most popular turbojet. As the US standoff with the Soviet Union intensifies in the late 1940s, the engine powers several new military aircraft, including the Northrop F-89 Scorpion, the Northrop YB-49A Flying Wing, the Republic F-84 Thunderjet, the Martin XB-48 bomber, and early versions of the Boeing XB-47 Stratojet.

Again, production work eludes GE. The government awards J35 production first to the Chevrolet Motor Division of General Motors and later, to Allison. As a result, the engine is also called the Allison J35, even though it was conceived and designed by GE. J35 production ends in 1955 with 14,000 engines delivered.

✈ Also in 1944...

Rolls-Royce jet power: In England, the Rolls-Royce Welland turbojet, with a centrifugal flow compressor, powers the Gloster Meteor. The Meteor is the first Allied jet aircraft to engage in combat operations in World War II. Rolls-Royce becomes a leading turbojet company and longtime rival to GE in jet engine technology.

1945
Welcome to "Turbo Town"

Lynn the new center: With the war production effort winding down, GE's aviation propulsion work from several sites is consolidated at the newly established GE Aircraft Gas Turbine Division in Lynn.

The reorganization also involves moving the axial-flow compressor design work from the Schenectady Steam Turbine Works to the Lynn plant. Schenectady focuses on turbines for land and sea applications. In the war's final months, the Supercharger Department is eventually absorbed into the Aircraft Gas Turbine Division. Over time, a very colorful billboard in Lynn advertises the city as "Turbo Town."

The T31 milestone: The Consolidated Vultee XP-81 experimental aircraft is powered successfully by the GE T31. It is the first American turboprop engine

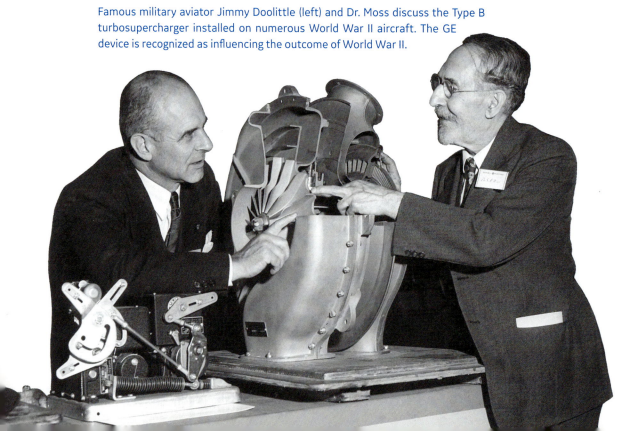

Famous military aviator Jimmy Doolittle (left) and Dr. Moss discuss the Type B turbosupercharger installed on numerous World War II aircraft. The GE device is recognized as influencing the outcome of World War II.

to propel an aircraft. In addition to a turboprop in the aircraft's nose, the XP-81 incorporates a J33 turbojet in the fuselage.

The Army Air Corps calls the XP-81 the world's most powerful jet plane. The T31 turboprop pressurizes the cabin with air siphoned from the axial-flow compressor. At very high altitudes, the turbojet heats the air that flows into the cabin. The turboprop is used at cruise while the turbojet provides bursts of speed.

The "in-between" airplane: In the 1940s, a turboprop-powered airplane is viewed as an "in-between" aircraft: faster than turbosupercharged piston-powered aircraft, but slower than turbojet-powered airplanes. However, turboprop-powered airplanes typically have greater range than turbojet-powered airplanes, but less range than turbosupercharged piston-powered airplanes. It all makes perfect sense.

✈ Also in 1945…

France forms Snecma: At the end of World War II, the government of France nationalizes Gnome & Rhône, an historic aircraft engine company, to create "Société nationale d'études et de construction de moteurs d'aviation," best known under its acronym, Snecma. In addition to Gnome & Rhône, several French design companies are merged under the Snecma umbrella. The historic collaborations between Snecma and GE are still decades away.

Powering a Fireball: The US Navy's Ryan Aeronautical FR-1 "Fireball" is powered by a conventional reciprocating engine to turn the propeller during low-speed flight and by a GE I-16 turbojet for high-altitude operation.

1946
Aviation's most-produced jet engine

Introducing the J47: The end of World War II leads to a predictable drawdown of military mass production and deliveries. At the same time, however, the era of jet power is in full swing. The US government funds development contracts for an array of jet-powered fighter and bomber concepts.

GE's Aircraft Gas Turbine Division seizes the day. On the heels of its breakthrough J35 turbojet, the division successfully proposes to the government an improved axial-flow successor before an aircraft is even defined.

In 1946, with Neil Burgess as project manager, Lynn engineers begin designing the J47 turbojet. The J35-sized, axial-flow military engine incorporates compressor and turbine sections for higher-pressure ratios, as well as lightweight components needed to produce 5,000 pounds of thrust.

This is a bold step forward. Touted as "the all-weather engine," the J47 is the first turbojet with an anti-icing system in which hollow frame struts allow passage of heated air from the compressor. Developed largely by Burgess and Joe Buechel, the anti-icing system is key to meeting demanding missions of fighter jets at high altitude. GE validates the system in a test cell for several months atop Mount Washington in New Hampshire's White Mountains, where winds gust to 140 miles an hour in the bitter cold.

To boost aircraft power at takeoff and for fast acceleration at altitude, the J47 incorporates the first electronically controlled afterburner (using vacuum tubes), a design spearheaded by Ed Woll, a young Lynn engineer who will continue to play a central role in GE's growing jet engine enterprise.

The J47 turbojet with E.S. Thompson, Carl Salmonsen, and project manager Neil Burgess at the Lynn operation. The J47 becomes the world's most produced jet engine.

With the US economy in post-war flux, some GE corporate leaders question the long-term business potential for the new jet propulsion developments. The Lynn team does not want to hear it. However, not even the greatest Lynn optimists could imagine how omnipresent the J47 turbojet will become in US military aviation over the next ten years due to the Korean War and the ongoing "Cold War" standoff with the Soviet Union.

Engineer and project leader Ed Woll leads the design of the J47 afterburner. For decades, he manages several key engine programs in Lynn.

✈ Also in 1946...

Harold D. Kelsey takes charge: A former turbosupercharger manager at GE's plant in Fort Wayne, Indiana, Harold D. Kelsey becomes managing director of the GE Aircraft Gas Turbine Division. While the passage of time has obscured his critical impact in leading the division, Kelsey guides GE's post-war aviation strategy for the next three years by wisely committing the division to exclusively axial-flow designs. He also expands GE's production capability and constructs a large compressor test laboratory in Lynn.

Sanford Moss passing: The beloved Dr. Moss dies in Lynn at age 74, a passing that appears in newspapers nationwide. The 1941 recipient of the prestigious Collier Trophy is praised for turbosupercharger innovations that influence the war's outcome by enabling Allied bombers to operate at high altitudes. During his life, Moss secures forty-six patents. *The Dayton [Ohio] Herald* describes him as "slight of stature and nervous of temperament and dislikes to ride in airplanes himself, except in case of emergency travel."[9]

His fear of flying aside, Moss perseveres and establishes GE's aviation business by pioneering turbosupercharger technology with an undying conviction in the face of disinterest after World War I, both within GE and the government, when high-altitude flying is not deemed a priority.

J33 & J35 milestones: The J33-powered P-80 Shooting Star races across the US and achieves the first transcontinental jet flight. The following year, the Shooting Star sets a world speed record of 629 miles per hour. Meanwhile, a Republic Aviation XP-

84B prototype (later designated the F-84 Thunderjet), powered by the J35, reaches 611 miles per hour.

1948
"Magnificent seven" come to Ohio

GE arrives in Lockland, Ohio: With J47 production underway in Lynn, Harold Kelsey pursues a second assembly line to create more in-house production capacity for the company's new mainstay turbojet.

Encouraged by the US Air Force (USAF), established the year before as a separate military branch within the US Department of Defense, GE selects the former Wright Aeronautical plant in Lockland, Ohio, an hour's drive from Wright-Patterson Air Force Base.

On June 26, GE publicly discloses a lease agreement for the "North Shop." This structure, today's Building 500, is located within the massive complex of mostly empty buildings recently purchased by Electric Auto-Lite Corporation of Toledo, Ohio. Most of the property is owned by the federal government.

Kelsey predicts that up to 2,000 GE employees will be needed in Lockland. He says the operation supports a government policy of dispersing defense assembly and test plants across the US. With the Lockland facilities, GE can triple its engine output for the USAF.[10]

In October, a quiet arrival of GE personnel begins. Seven managers from Lynn take a train together from Boston to Cincinnati's Union Terminal. The intent is for them to become better acquainted on the long ride. The driver awaiting them in Cincinnati is Archie Trabert, father of future tennis star Tony Trabert.[11] The seven managers are Kenneth Houseman, Claude Auger, Paul Nichols, Robert Hinkle, George Simmerman, Everett Foster, and Marty Hemsworth.

On October 18, they formally establish residence in Building 500, initially using cardboard boxes as desks. "We didn't have many lights, so we would walk around in the dark," Hemsworth recalls fifty years later. "But we began to visualize where things would go."[12] Some of the original seven reside briefly in a two-story house near the plant on Springfield Pike in the village of Woodlawn, where card games go well into the night.

However, they quickly form a focused production organization and engine assembly line. The Lynn division transfers about 150 engineers to Lockland.

Hemsworth oversees the creation of fourteen test cells using piston-engine test structures from the Wright Aeronautical days. After equipment and tooling arrives, the Lockland team assembles engines using components from 250 suppliers nationwide. Houseman, the former turbosupercharger production manager in Lynn, becomes GE Lockland's first plant manager.

Eighty-seven skill sets and 8,859 parts are required to complete assembly of the J47 turbojet.

In 1948, GE establishes a second jet engine assembly line at the former Wright Aeronautical plant in Lockland. After the neighboring village of Evendale is incorporated in 1952, the operation is known as the GE Evendale plant.

Stung by massive Wright Aeronautical layoffs at the end of World War II, Cincinnati initially greets GE's new defense operation in the vast Lockland buildings with trepidation. "They worried we would take away their manpower and that we would wreck wage scales, neither of which proved the case," recalls Everett Foster, one of the original seven.[13] In 1948, he and other GE leaders speak to civic groups across the city about GE's long-term intentions for Lockland in order to ease community skepticism.

While GE scales up the Lockland operation, J47 engines delivered from Lynn in 1948 are installed in a North American F-86 Sabre. It sets a world speed record of 670.9 miles per hour on its way to becoming one of the era's most popular jet fighters.

Gerhard Neumann comes to GE: To test compressors for its growing military business, Kelsey initiates construction of a special test facility (Building 29G) in Lynn. Gerhard Neumann, a young German engineer, joins GE in 1948 after being endorsed by Lynn stalwarts Gene Stoeckly, Truly Warner, and Joe Alford.

J47 production in full swing at GE's assembly plant in Lockland.

The energetic Neumann solves equipment and mechanical challenges in the facility, the nation's largest engine test laboratory of its kind. He soon manages Lynn's development test operations.

Though only thirty years old when joining GE, his life already reads like an adventure novel. A Jew raised in Nazi Germany, he earns a degree in mechanical engineering in 1938 and leaves the country with plans to maintain German aircraft engines in China. British officials arrest him in Hong Kong in September 1939 and categorize him as an "enemy alien." To avoid deportation, he joins the Chinese and US cause by becoming a mechanic with the First American Volunteer Group of the Chinese Air Force, better known as the Flying Tigers.

Neumann's wartime heroics include sneaking into Japanese-controlled territory to refurbish a downed Mitsubishi Zero aircraft. It is the first Zero aircraft obtained by the Allies. During 1942-1945, Neumann is a master sergeant and engineering specialist with the Army Air Corps. His work with the Technical Air Intelligence and the Office of Strategic Services (OSS) leads to his being awarded US citizenship in 1946 through a special act of Congress.

In the GE test facility, Neumann observes that compressor stationary stator vanes (which direct air flow in between stages of rotating compressor blades) limit compressor efficiency at various operating modes and contribute to stalls. He proposes a design enabling stator vanes to change angles during flight. Cynical senior colleagues soon learn Neumann is no shrinking violet in defending his technical convictions. In the late 1940s, Neumann leads a development team in creating a "variable stator experimental engine."

Over the next several years, citing Neumann as inventor, GE receives several patents for "variable stator" technology, which becomes a standard feature on jet engines.

1949
A brilliant woman in a man's world

Marion S. Kellogg guides engineering: With jet propulsion in its infancy, developing GE engineering teams to advance the fast-emerging technology is critical. These teams must also collaborate with military counterparts on a plethora of new government-funded programs.

At the Aircraft Gas Turbine Division, Marion S. Kellogg guides future technical leaders. After earning a master's degree in physics from Brown University, she joins the GE engineering laboratory in Schenectady in 1944 but soon gravitates to personnel development. In 1949, she heads technical personnel development and engineering recruitment at Lynn and guides the careers of GE's male-dominated engineering staff.

Over time, Kellogg organizes engineering into separate disciplines such as component design, engine prototype design, and production. By 1951, she heads personnel at the Lockland operation, where the engineering staff grows from ninety-two in 1949 to more than 2,000 by 1955.

Her success drives a career trajectory. In 1958, Kellogg joins the GE corporate staff and oversees employee development for more than a decade. The author of several books on career management, she becomes GE's first female corporate vice president in 1974.

During a long GE career, Kellogg experiences first-hand the challenges facing female technical leaders. Nevertheless, she views the heady years at the dawn of jet propulsion differently. "When I came to GE in 1944, women were very strong in the company because it was the end of World War II," she recalls later. "We had some of the most outstanding women scientists [at GE] in the country.

So strange as it may seem, I never knew there was a problem for women in the corporate world."[14]

First Lockland deliveries: On February 28, the Lockland plant is formally dedicated as the USAF receives two J47 turbojets. More than 150 local dignitaries and military leaders attend a ceremony highlighted by a loud flyover by six USAF fighter jets. The J47 deliveries are touted as two months ahead of schedule.

GE President Charles E. Wilson, while claiming defense contracts are not profitable but serve the public cause, describes the J47 assembly line as "a miracle of our age." He expresses hope that engines from Lockland "never have to be used to repel an enemy"—sentiments expressed only sixteen months before the onset of the bloody Korean War.[15] By late 1949, the combined Lynn and Lockland J47 production collectively reaches 200 engines a month.

Later in the year, the J47 is fitted to power an upgraded, six-engine Boeing XB-47 Stratojet bomber, the world's fastest bomber. In addition, the US Civil Aeronautics Administration approves the J47 for commercial transport planes, though an application is never defined.

A physicist by training, Marion S. Kellogg turns to personnel and develops solid engineering teams at the Lynn and Evendale operations. She recruits hundreds of GE personnel for the J47 program. After being named the first female corporate vice president at GE in 1974, she is profiled in *Business Week* magazine.

✈ Also in 1949...

Cramer W. "Jim" LaPierre at the helm: Former executive of American Machine and Foundry, Cramer W. "Jim" LaPierre becomes vice president and general manager of the Aircraft Gas Turbine Division in 1949.

J35 speed record: The J35 powers early versions of the six-engine Boeing XB-47 Stratojet bomber, which crosses the US in three hours and forty-six minutes. That year, eight J35 engines also power the Northrop YB-49 "Flying Wing" in a flight from California to Washington D.C. at an average speed of 511.2 miles per hour. Northrop revisits the unique YB-49 design decades later with the B-2 stealth bomber.

FAST JETS

J73 introduced: An outgrowth of the J47, GE designs the J73 with 9,000 pounds of thrust and greater weather capability. The J73 produces almost 50 percent more thrust than the J47. It begins operation in 1953, powering North American F-86H fighters for the USAF. Its innovations include variable inlet guide vanes, a two-stage turbine, and a titanium compressor rotor. However, the US military already has several turbojets in a similar thrust class. Only 870 engines are produced.

T31 cancelled: The US government cancels GE's TG-100 (T31) turboprop project and puts more focus on fast-evolving turbojet fighter engines as the "Cold War" with the Soviet Union intensifies. GE turboprop engines resurface several years later to extraordinary success.

1950
J47 power over Korea

Lockland survives and thrives: With defense cutbacks in 1949 under US President Harry S. Truman, GE considers closing the new Lockland operation as the J47 production

For years, GE had its own Chuck Yeager in ace test pilot Roy Pryor (left), pictured with Virgil Weaver, longtime head of GE's flight test operations in California. They are in front of the J47-powered F-86 at Edwards Air Force Base.

48   100 YEARS OF REIMAGINING FLIGHT

outlook dims. However, the USAF favors the plant's proximity to Wright-Patterson and encourages GE to take more J47 component work in-house to centralize production.

Then, seemingly overnight, the Korean War outbreak in June 1950 drives a surging J47 demand, especially for the F-86 Sabre, the war's key American fighter jet. The first swept-wing fighter in the USAF arsenal, the F-86 is fast and maneuverable, bolstered by the J47 afterburner. The jet establishes air superiority in Korea with a 14-to-1 kill ratio in combat with MiG-15 fighters. The USAF's other prominent J47-powered jet in Korea is the high-speed, intimidating Boeing B-47 Stratojet.

In less than two years, Lockland plant employment swells from 1,200 to 8,000 behind an aggressive recruitment program throughout the region. The J47 engineering headquarters moves to Lockland; the engine is now America's most-produced jet engine. For the production ramp, Lockland introduces several manufacturing innovations such as vertical engine assembly to maintain compressor rotor balance and stability.

By the mid-1950s, the J47 powers most frontline US military jets, thirteen applications in all, including the F-86, the B-47, the Convair B-36 Bomber, the North American B-45 Tornado, the Martin B-51 Bomber, and the Northrop YB-49 Flying Wing.

1951

LaPierre: Turbojets will rule the skies

Lockland expands: "The aircraft turbojet industry is still an infant, even though it has grown by leaps and bounds in its very short life," declares C.W. LaPierre in announcing a $40 million expansion at Lockland. "The Lockland plant will be fully utilized, in peace or war, and will be one of the world's truly great jet engine centers."[16]

Through building purchases, leases, and new construction, GE will more than triple the space it occupies in the Lockland complex. GE acquires Building 500, leases several other buildings, and begins construction of Buildings 200 and 501. LaPierre predicts that turbojet engines could surpass even piston engines in powering modern aircraft. "At the rate improvements are being made in aircraft gas turbines, I am convinced that efficiency will be increased within a few years to the point where fuel costs per passenger mile will be comparable or better than is possible with any powerplant now in the air," he says.[17]

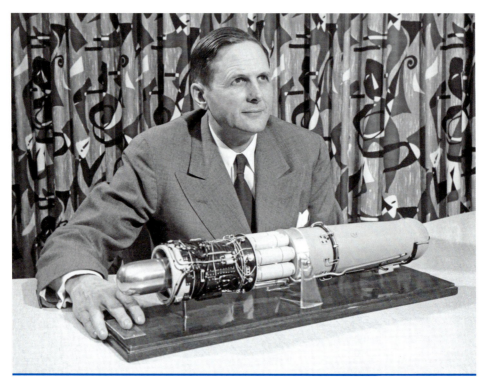

C.W. LaPierre oversees an Evendale expansion in the early 1950s while hiring thousands of workers as the Korean War drives J47 production. The curtains were not his idea.

He says turbojet-powered aircraft are more efficient than piston-powered aircraft at high speed. The challenge is to improve turbojet fuel burn at lower speeds, he says. LaPierre predicts that GE will need both the Lockland and Lynn operations to meet USAF defense needs.

✈ Also in 1951...

Pursuing nuclear propulsion: The US Atomic Energy Commission contracts GE to assess the feasibility of atomic-powered aircraft. Gerhard Neumann works on the program for two years. Under the GE Atomic Products Division, GE establishes the Aircraft Nuclear Propulsion Department in Lockland to research a propulsion system that would combine a traditional turbojet system with a nuclear reactor in the combustion system to provide steady power.

Rutland, Vermont: GE establishes operations near Rutland, transferring twenty-three people from Lynn to manufacture dyes at a former woolen mill in the small town of Ludlow, Vermont. By 1954, the workforce grows to 240. A second site is established in Rutland, which ultimately becomes a significant part of GE's engine airfoils manufacturing network.

Strother Field, Kansas: GE establishes a support and maintenance operation for the J47 at Strother Field in Arkansas City, Kansas. Within several years, the center supports business jets, as well as turboprop and turboshaft engines.

1952
GE's "Mach 2 engine"

Next fighter jet engine: After a weekend badminton match with his wife, a sweaty Gerhard Neumann is called to the office of C.W. LaPierre. He wants Neumann to assemble a team to develop a demonstrator engine using variable-stator compressor technology for a lightweight turbojet capable of propelling future aircraft to Mach 2 speeds.[18] With a new generation of US fighters and bombers under study, LaPierre believes Neumann's technology could better position GE's propulsion leadership.

First, though, GE holds an internal engine development competition. Neumann's single-shaft GOL-1590 engine wins over a dual-shaft engine design in which two shafts operate the forward and aft sections of the compressor separately, with each connected to separate turbine sections. (During this time, a dual-shaft design is introduced with great success on the P&W J57 turbojet.)

The GOL-1590 introduces one of jet propulsion's most forward-looking technological advances with the variable-stator system. Without the system, a compressor with stationary vanes could often draw in more air at certain flight speeds than an engine could accommodate. This extra airflow would be forced forward to produce backpressure on the compressor rotor blades. As a result, the airflow in the compressor would be impeded or stopped, causing the engine to stall.

With the variable-stator system, the stator vanes pivot to regulate airflow within acceptable limits that the engine can accommodate. In other words, the pitch of the stator vanes is automatically controlled to adjust airflow as the engine speed changes. Variable stators also reduce engine weight, because they enable a single-shaft turbojet to produce pressures comparable to dual-shaft engines.

✈ Also in 1952…

Jet Center USA: On the tenth anniversary of the first I-A jet engine tests in Lynn, GE launches an advertising campaign promoting the GE Lockland plant as "Jet

Dr. Chapman Walker (left) and Gerhard Neumann with the GOL-1590 demonstrator, precursor to GE's J79 fighter engine. The GOL-1590 introduces variable-stator compressor technology.

FAST JETS

GE Flight Test Center at Edwards Air Force Base, California, in the early 1950s. Front and center is the J79-powered Lockheed F-104 Starfighter.

Center USA." It highlights the plant's four million square feet of floor space and 8,000 employees. The plant is rededicated to celebrate GE's expansion at the site.

"Lockland provides for rapid expansion to meet national emergencies as well as a foundation for peacetime production," GE declares in *Aviation Week* advertisements. As part of the ceremonies, GE takes an original I-A turbojet out of storage and runs it in a test cell.[19]

The "Evendale plant": Evendale, Ohio, is incorporated as a village outside of the Cincinnati city limits and bordering Lockland in an area that includes GE factory acreage. Over time, the Lockland plant becomes known as the Evendale plant. Everett Foster, one of the original seven GE managers to establish the plant in 1948, helps to write the village's charter.

Power over the California desert: With the dramatic growth of GE-powered USAF aircraft, the company establishes the GE Flight Test Center at Edwards Air Force Base in southern California. Virgil Weaver will run the operation until 1973. Many of GE's future leaders earn their stripes testing military engines in the hot, California sun.

Jack Parker (third from right) heads the GE Committee for Aviation Strategy in 1953. It leads the Lynn engineering team to introduce turboshaft engines for helicopters.

Jackie Cochran breaks a ceiling: Flying a J47-powered F-86 Sabre, Cochran becomes the first woman to break the sound barrier.

Donald (Truly) Warner passing: GE's lead engineer on the I-A engine at the Lynn plant, Warner dies at age fifty-three in nearby Marblehead, Massachusetts.

1953
GE's aviation roadmap

Committee for Aviation Strategy: While J47 production secures for GE's Aircraft Gas Turbine Division a long-term leadership position in US jet propulsion, a new rival has arrived. P&W in East Hartford, Connecticut, establishes a foothold in jet propulsion with its J57 turbojet, which they promote as America's most powerful jet engine.

P&W quickly gains ground. The J57-powered North American F-100 jet surpasses the J73-powered F-86H as a frontline USAF fighter. The J57 also powers the USAF B-52 bomber and KC-135 tanker. Leveraging its position as a leading producer of military piston engines, P&W challenges the young GE aviation enterprise.

Meanwhile, across the ocean, the British government sponsors Rolls-Royce's significant jet propulsion advances. In fact, P&W gains valuable experience in the late 1940s by producing early Rolls-Royce turbojets under license.

Looking over its shoulder, GE must compete more effectively in a fast-evolving turbojet industry with its formidable US and European competitors. The GE division forms the GE Committee for Aviation Strategy, chaired by 35-year-old Jack Steele Parker. Parker joined GE in 1950 in its Aircraft Nuclear Propulsion Department after a successful stint in shipbuilding on the West Coast.

A long-term strategy is established: pursue military and commercial turbojet applications and aggressively market a "Mach 2 turbojet" for military aircraft by building upon the GOL-1590 demonstrator experience. In addition, GE creates the Small Aircraft Engine Division in Lynn to introduce turboshaft engines into the piston-powered helicopter world.

J79 lands the Hustler: GE's strategy soon works to plan. After impressive test runs of the GOL-1590 demonstrator, the USAF designates the GE engine design as the J79 and selects it to power Convair's high-speed B-58 Hustler bomber. The four-engine B-58 fulfills a USAF requirement to deploy a supersonic strategic bomber into its arsenal.

Selected over the much heavier P&W J57, the J79 preserves GE's leading position in producing high-performance turbojets. The sleek J79 is another dramatic step forward: seventeen compressor stages (seven of which are variable-stator stages) and three turbine stages in a small-diameter, lightweight engine, with excellent inlet distortion tolerance, great acceleration, and stall-free performance throughout the flight envelope. In non-technical terms: a fighter pilot's dream. GE assigns Neil Burgess, the innovative J47 leader, to run the new program.

Other aircraft applications will follow, including Lockheed's fast F-104 Starfighter.

✈ Also in 1953...

J47 production: While the J79 is being developed, J47 production continues unabated as the division's financial bread-and-butter. By 1953-1954, production reaches 975 engines per month. In addition to the Lockland and Lynn plants, the engine is produced at Studebaker and Packard auto factories.

High praise for British turbojets: After reviewing British jet engines at the Farnborough Air Show, GE's David Cochran says that British turbojets are more powerful and fuel-efficient than US turbojets. He tells a Wings Club luncheon in New York that US turbojets are more compact with smaller frontal areas. "The British take more pains to cut away every ounce of metal that is not doing any work," Cochran says.[20] He then contends that the US produces more turbojets in one day than British industry produces in a week, adding that GE's turbojets have now accumulated more than one million flight hours in military service.

1954
Thinking small to create something big

T58 turboshaft engine: Jack Parker takes charge of the Small Aircraft Engine Division in Lynn and announces a "baby gas turbine" engine comparable in size to the family automobile engine but six to eight times as powerful. Called the T58 and funded by the US Navy Bureau of Aeronautics for helicopter applications, the program launches the formidable turboshaft franchise in Lynn that continues to this day.

The T58 is an outgrowth of GE's Committee for Aviation Strategy. "One part of the [gas turbine] field that had been really untouched was the small gas turbine business," Parker says. "We thought there was a big void there. We thought that gas turbines of lower power could be very profitably and efficiently employed in a lot of aircraft."[21]

The Lynn team secures Navy funding for an axial-flow turboshaft engine weighing 400 pounds and capable of 800 horsepower. However, after reviewing potential aircraft missions, GE radically redesigns the T58 with an eight-stage compressor, an annular combustor (GE's first in a gas turbine engine), and a single-stage power turbine driving a reduction gear in the back. The gas generator and power turbine are not connected mechanically. At just 250 pounds, the T58 is now designed to produce 1,050 shaft horsepower, which is no small technical feat. GE sells the Navy on the concept.

It is a bold design to match Parker's bold vision: make piston engines in helicopters obsolete. Piston-powered helicopters simply lack the ability to lift a heavy payload. Parker's Lynn team becomes outspoken salespeople for the engine, claiming that gas turbines in a small turboshaft configuration will "make possible a smooth, quiet ride, reducing fatigue for both passengers and crew."[22] GE also

The J79 turbojet, Evendale's popular fighter engine in the 1950s and 1960s, heads to the test cell in 1954.

claims that turboshaft engines will be easier to install and cool, will consume less oil, and will provide twice the power of a piston engine at a comparable weight. The Lynn team will deliver on these promises.

The T58 is also critical in stabilizing the engineering base in Lynn after many key technical people transfer to GE's growing engine site in Evendale, Ohio.

✈ Also in 1954…

Plant designations formalized: The expanding Evendale plant is designated for large engines, and the Lynn plant for small engines. Large engines require the substantial production and testing space available in Evendale.

1955
"Proving Ground" in the Ohio hills

Testing in Peebles, Ohio: In late 1954, GE quietly purchases thousands of acres at the foothills of the Appalachian Mountains in remote Adams County, Ohio, about eighty miles east of Cincinnati. As rumors in the surrounding countryside mount,

GE holds a town meeting in the nearby village of Peebles to deliver the news: the purchase of up to 5,000 acres in an isolated valley surrounded by 500-foot mountain ridges to create an outdoor test facility for top-secret military engines.

With a page-one headline "Pogo Tests in Adams Area!" *The Cincinnati Enquirer* describes it as "one of the most carefully guarded industrial deals ever to take place in this area."[23] GE discloses plans to test military engines for vertical takeoff aircraft (nicknamed "pogo stick planes" at the time) and military engines with thrust reversers. The tests require outdoor sites not confined by walls.

In 1955, GE formally opens "The Proving Ground," as it is known for decades, and runs tests on an outdoor platform with performance data recorded nearby in a former farmhouse. GE tests jet engines, including the J79, as well as rocket engines.

The facility's first manager, Robert D. Knies, describes his duties as "soil conservationist, forester, tobacco farmer, instructor of voluntary fire departments, house wrecker, horse buyer, and game warden."[24] Acres of tobacco grown on the property help GE to finance the site's conservation projects. Area farmers remove abandoned houses on the property in exchange for the lumber. Paths cut into the forestland ensure access by a GE-trained, volunteer fire department. Guards patrol the 5,000 rolling acres on horseback.

By 1959, more test sites are built. A 3,000-foot runway strip is created for landings by private aircraft from Cincinnati. Six ponds with a storage capacity of ten million gallons of water are critical for conducting tests. In the early 1960s, the site is nearly mothballed, though GE wisely maintains ownership of the vast property. In 1966, GE begins testing the all-important TF39 high-bypass turbofan engine at Peebles. Over the next half-century, as GE Aviation grows, the Peebles Test Operation will grow into the largest outdoor jet engine test site in the world.

"Atomic Airplane": The Cold War's atomic energy race between the US and the Soviet Union escalates the funding of exotic US defense projects involving nuclear power. GE begins designing a nuclear propulsion system for the proposed Convair NX-2 bomber. The generically-labeled "Atomic Plane" has a mission to achieve 1,000 hours of continuous flight at high subsonic speed to monitor the vast Soviet empire.

The concept has been studied for years. In the early 1950s, GE engages in nuclear propulsion tests at Idaho Test Station in remote eastern Idaho using modified J47 engines. The results encourage the USAF to define a weapon requirement in

1954–1955 for a long-range, nuclear-powered bomber. GE and P&W are funded to develop competing turbojet propulsion systems paired with a nuclear reactor core. GE teams with Convair; P&W pairs with Lockheed.

German scientist Bruno W. Bruckmann leads the efforts on GE's twin-engine propulsion system, called the X211. He is among many prominent German technologists who immigrate to the US immediately after World War II through the government-sponsored program called "Operation Paper Clip." Other Germans brought to the US to shore up its standoff against the Soviet Union include turbojet inventor Hans von Ohain, rocket pioneer Werner von Braun, and leading GE technologists Walter Brisken and Peter Kappus.

GE designs a forty-one-foot propulsion system (designated the J87), which involves coupling two massive GE turbojets around a separate nuclear reactor that replaces the traditional combustor at cruise flight. Air from the compressors enters bypass doors into the nuclear reactor core. Then, the reactor heats the compressed airflow through a controlled chain reaction before being fed into a conventional turbine section to create a steady thrust flow. At the same time, the compressed air cools the nuclear reactor.

The twin-engine X211 for GE's exotic nuclear propulsion system for the US Department of Defense, 1955.

✈ Also in 1955…

Jack Parker takes over: Jack Parker becomes vice president in charge of the Aircraft Gas Turbine Division. He puts Gerhard Neumann in charge of the division's Jet Engine Department. The formidable Parker-Neumann team establishes GE's presence on several new airplane platforms requiring a wide span of engine thrust.

Parker announces that GE will pursue engine developments ahead of USAF stated requirements. "This is part of the industry's responsibility in the industry/military partnership," he says. "I refer specifically to our program for planning far ahead—five, ten or more years—working out and proving the new principles of propulsion which we believe will be eventually needed."[25] The strategy becomes central to GE's military success in the years ahead.

T58 travails: The turboshaft engine begins tests in Lynn. It's a rough go. The engine faces compressor shortfalls, vibration, and fatigue stress. By June, a compressor with new variable inlet guide vanes for stall margin is introduced. By early 1956, the T58 in ground tests achieves the required military rating of 1,050 shaft horsepower, a remarkable achievement for an engine weighing only 250 pounds. The Lynn team breathes a sign of relief, and government funding continues.

J79 flight tests: The J79's first flight involves placing the engine in the bomb bay of a B-45 Tornado. During flight, the engine is lowered into the air stream, while J47 engines on the wings pull back. That same year, the J79 powers an experimental Douglas XF4D aircraft with GE's test pilot Roy Pryor in the cockpit. He declares "I felt like I had a tiger by the tail!"[26]

1956
Passenger jetliners shrink the world

Commercial jetliner era begins: In the 1950s, the first jet-powered passenger aircraft (generally called "jetliners") begin to populate the skies. From the onset, GE misses a huge opportunity.

The first passenger jetliner out of the gate hails from England. The de Havilland DH 106 Comet begins passenger service in 1952 as the first production jetliner. (As an engineering apprentice at de Havilland, Brian Rowe, future head of GE's aviation business, designs a part for the Comet's engine.) Then, disaster strikes. After three aircraft break up in flight due to metal fatigue, the program is suspended.

The Comet eventually returns to passenger service but never gains market traction, opening the door for two leading US aircraft manufacturers, Boeing and Douglas. Financially bolstered by hefty military contracts, the two industrial giants pursue commercial jet travel.

Both companies have had four-engine jet aircraft under development since the early 1950s for both military and commercial applications. In 1954, the USAF selects Boeing's Model 367-80 for the KC-135 tanker program, from which Boeing develops a commercial variant called the 707. Despite losing the tanker competition, Douglas continues to develop its DC-8 aircraft offering as a commercial jetliner.

The Boeing 707 and Douglas DC-8 jetliners launch in 1956 with great fanfare. Sixteen of the world's largest airlines order either one or both models. Pan American Airways begins 707 overseas flights in 1958, and Delta Air Lines and United Airlines initiate DC-8 flights in 1958. American Airlines introduces 707 domestic flights in 1959. As airlines continue to sign up, the era of jetliner travel is firmly established.

Despite its leadership in military turbojets, GE has no suitable engine for the Boeing and Douglas jetliners. P&W's JT3 dual-shaft turbojet, a commercial variant of the J57 on the B-52 bomber and KC-135, has the inside track on the 707. Douglas also opts for the JT3. Thus, P&W is positioned to become the dominant jetliner engine provider for twenty-five years. In the early 1960s, the Rolls-Royce Conway engine also powers the 707 and DC-8 in limited production runs.

Legendary pilot and eccentric billionaire Howard Hughes is GE's first engine customer for commercial jetliners. Majority owner of TWA, Hughes launches the GE-powered Convair 880. Disputes between Hughes and Convair delay its entry into service. *Rick Kennedy collection.*

GE's jetliner engine: GE enters the jetliner sweepstakes in 1956 with a commercial variant of its J79, the CJ805. In 1956, Convair selects the engine for its new jetliner called the Convair 880 Skylark. GE has a strong relationship with Convair, whose B-58 Hustler is powered by the J79.

While the Skylark is the era's fastest jetliner, its introduction into service experiences a bumpy ride. Billionaire and legendary pilot Howard Hughes, majority owner of TWA, launches the Convair 880 in 1956, but contractual and technical disputes with Hughes delay Skylark service entry until 1960. This extended delay gives Boeing and Douglas valuable time to establish market dominance. To make matters worse for GE, technical problems with the CJ805 are looming on the horizon.

✈ Also in 1956…

J79 on the Starfighter: Lockheed designer Kelly Johnson's F-104 Starfighter makes its first flight with J79 power. Lockheed has secretly selected the engine three years earlier shortly after the engine is launched for the B-58 Hustler. The F-104 meets the USAF requirement for a fast-climbing interceptor by marrying a small airframe with a powerful turbojet. The F-104 is nicknamed "the missile with a man in it" because of its sheer speed, cylindrical fuselage, and small, unswept wings. Also, it proves to be a challenging fighter jet to fly.

J85 for missile decoy: Building on its T58 success, Jack Parker and Ed Woll believe a small turbojet in the 2,500-pound thrust class can also secure multiple applications over time. The Lynn team begins work on the little J85 turbojet, which is first developed in 1956 for the USAF's GAM-72 Green Quail missile decoy for the Boeing B-52.

The strategy is to release the air-launched missile decoy just before the B-52 enters enemy airspace to confuse the defense radar network in differentiating between the larger bomber and the small missile decoy.

The missile decoy is revealed to the pubic in late 1958 after several successful launches. It is just the beginning for GE. The Parker team chases aircraft applications for the efficient J85 engine, which is tested a year later with an afterburner for possible supersonic military jets.

J47 production ends, and J79 begins: The transition from one great fighter turbojet to its successor begins. The J47's unprecedented ten-year production run comes to an end. It is built in Lynn and Evendale, as well as under license by US automotive companies Studebaker and Packard, FIAT in Italy, and Ishikawajima-Harima

Industries in Japan. In total, more than 35,000 J47s are built, the most produced jet engine in aviation history. Meanwhile, the Evendale plant begins J79 deliveries as military aircraft applications expand.

X211 loses application: The US government determines that the WS-125 nuclear-powered aircraft is unfeasible as an operational aircraft. However, GE develops a twin-engine X211 propulsion system in Evendale for three more years. Secret tests continue in Idaho on the propulsion system's nuclear reactor.

1957
Changing the helicopter landscape

T64 wins unusual contract: T58 breakthroughs fuel the US Navy's appetite for more turboshaft power. The Navy awards the Lynn team with a four-year development contract for a larger engine with a higher pressure-ratio compressor in the 2,600-horsepower class.

This government development contract is touted as the first for two types of engines with the same core "hot section" (compressor, combustor, turbine). Without specific applications, the Navy launches T64 turboshaft and turboprop variants for future helicopters, transports, and support aircraft.

With no urgency to integrate the new design into an aircraft, GE views the T64 as a long-term engineering project. The team introduces several unique technologies, including corrosion-resistant and high-temperature coatings, and a

The turboshaft and turboprop versions of the innovative T64 are launched in 1957 with US Navy funding. The engine's operational life extends beyond fifty years.

In 1957, GE designs the J93 turbojet for the unique North American XB-70 Valkyrie, called the "Mach 3 bomber." Only two aircraft are built.

high-pressure ratio, fourteen-stage, axial-flow compressor driven by a two-stage turbine. The titanium compressor resists salt-water corrosion. The T64 is GE's first front-drive, free-turbine engine, which is necessary for easy installation into a helicopter and for future turboprop variants.

By the late 1950s, the T64 demonstrates the highest-pressure ratio of any single-shaft compressor on a turboshaft engine. The powerplant is poised for a long production run in the decades ahead.

J93 takes the heat: Development begins in Evendale on the J93 "Mach 3" turbojet for the North American XB-70 Valkyrie aircraft. The exotic six-engine USAF aircraft is designed as a long-range, high-speed bomber.

In the 30,000-pound thrust class, the J93 has classic GE features: single-shaft compressor with variable stator vanes in the front and back stages to increase airflow during supersonic flight, as well as split casings for the compressor, combustor, and turbine sections to enable easy maintenance access.

Perhaps the biggest advance is in the air-cooled turbine technology involving electrolytically-drilled air-cooling holes in the turbine blades, which becomes a feature in future GE engines. J93 turbine-cooling technology will set the stage for GE's most significant 1960s engine designs, including the TF39 high-bypass turbofan engine.

✈ *Also in 1957…*

X211 testing revealed: Though GE's nuclear propulsion system has no application, the X211 configuration is finalized, and component testing begins on the two massive turbojets without a nuclear reactor attached. In 1957, certain details on the X211 propulsion system are revealed to the public. However, X211 testing is limited to only the two turbojets, and the program ends in 1959.

T58 milestone: Two GE T58 turboshaft engines power the first flight of the Sikorsky HSS-1F, replacing its one piston engine. The HSS-1F becomes the first turboshaft-powered helicopter in the US.

John B. Montgomery takes charge: John Montgomery becomes vice president and general manager of GE's Aircraft Gas Turbine Division (later renamed Flight Propulsion Division). He leads the organization until 1960.

1958
Pioneering the "turbofan" engine

Making turbofans a reality: The concept of "turbofan" engines, which power today's jets, dates back to the 1930s. English engineer Alan Arnold Griffith and jet engine inventor Frank Whittle, who patented a turbofan design before World War II, offered early insights. Yet for decades, the turbofan remains an idea confined to paper.

With the metallurgical and aerodynamic advances of the late 1950s, jet engine titans GE, Rolls-Royce, and P&W turn turbofan concepts into practical applications. 1958 proves to be a landmark year for GE's pioneering work in turbofan technology.

"Turbofan" is derived from "turbine" and "fan." A gas turbine generates energy by burning fuel mixed with compressed air and produces thrust with the resultant high-velocity exhaust gas.

In a turbofan, energy created by a gas turbine also drives a large fan that pulls massive amounts of air into, and around, the gas turbine to push the aircraft forward. The air channeled outside of the engine core surrounds the high-velocity gas exiting the turbine section to improve the engine's efficiency, increase thrust, and reduce noise. In other words, a turbofan is a turbojet with a large fan for additional, more efficient thrust.

The "bypass ratio" of a turbofan is a measure of the amount of air pumped through the fan—and "bypassing" the engine core—and the amount of air passing through the engine core. Turbofans that operate with considerably more "fan-generated" thrust (around the engine core) are called "high-bypass" turbofans. The bypass air of a turbofan lowers fuel consumption while achieving the same thrust as a turbojet.

GE's first turbofan: In 1958, Evendale unveils a unique turbofan with a rear-mounted fan. Directly behind the high-pressure turbine (HPT) is a second turbine section, which uses exhaust gas to power the rear-mounted fan module. The aft-fan module can be attached to a J79 military turbojet or its commercial variant, the CJ805.

GE claims the aft-fan, with a 3:1 bypass ratio (three times as much air passes around the core of the engine as passes through it), increases takeoff thrust of non-afterburning jet engines by 35 percent, while improving fuel efficiency by eight to 12 percent.

GE designs the commercial aft-fan engine, the CJ805-23, for the follow-on Convair 990 jetliner launched by American Airlines in 1958 and designed as the world's fastest jetliner with a .91 Mach cruise speed. The Convair 990 enters service in 1961.

Rolls-Royce lays claim to the first turbofan with its front-fan Conway engine introduced in the late 1950s, although its bypass ratio is well below GE's CJ805-23

Propulsion innovation does not guarantee financial success. GE's CJ805-23 with an aft-mounted fan is arguably the world's first true turbofan. However, it powers only the modest-selling Convair 990.

FAST JETS

engine. In the early 1960s, P&W introduces the JT3D low-bypass, front-fan engine for large commercial jetliners and produces the powerplant in large quantities. P&W has the advantage of a dual-rotor compressor. The front fan is attached to the second rotor in the forward section of the compressor.

Even though GE is a turbofan pioneer, several years will pass before the technology translates into a viable commercial product for the company. In describing the early days of turbofans, perhaps Jack Parker says it best: "GE converted the heathens, and P&W sold all of the Bibles."[27]

✈ Also in 1958…

J79 speeds ahead: In a huge year for the popular J79, West Germany orders 800 Lockheed F-104 Starfighters, followed by orders from Belgium, Italy, Japan, and The Netherlands. Through the aircraft's increased international presence, GE not only grows J79 production but also furthers its experience in creating industrial cooperation and supplier programs with foreign governments.

Speed records keep the J79 in the headlines. A USAF Starfighter reaches a record speed of 1,404 miles per hour, and a world altitude record of 91,249 feet. The jet ultimately becomes the first manned aircraft to exceed 100,000 feet, reaching 103,395 feet, nearly 20 miles high. Meanwhile, the J79-powered B-58 Hustler claims six world speed records for bomber aircraft.

Also in 1958, the J79-powered McDonnell Aircraft F-4 Phantom makes its first flight. Embraced first by the USAF and US Navy, the ubiquitous F-4 will soon become one of the era's most effective attack and fighter jets, with more than 5,000 produced over the next two decades.

Evendale plant investment: GE acquires more portions of the Evendale buildings from Auto-Lite for $15 million. The sale involves fourteen buildings and more than three million square feet of floor space on 135 acres. GE now operates 406 acres at the site.

Blade production breakthroughs: At its airfoil plant at Ludlow, Vermont, GE announces a new manufacturing process for T58 compressor blades and vanes that will reduce costs by 50 percent.

GE Flight Propulsion: GE Aircraft Gas Turbine Division is renamed GE Flight Propulsion Division.

In early 1959, Collier Trophy recipients who contributed to the Lockheed F-104 Starfighter surround US Vice President Richard Nixon. Left to right: USAF pilots Walter Irwin and Howard Johnson, Nixon, GE's Gerhard Neumann and Neil Burgess, and Lockheed's Kelly Johnson. The J79-powered F-104 is the first manned aircraft to exceed 100,000 feet.

1959
The little engine that could

J85 powers Northrop "sister jets": Lynn's small and powerful J85 turbojet experiences a breakout year in 1959 on its way to becoming one of GE's most successful engine production programs.

During the mid-1950s, Northrop selects the J85 for both of its "sister supersonic military jets" under development, the twin-engine N-156F Freedom Fighter, later designated the F-5, and the USAF's twin-engine T-38 Talon, the first supersonic military trainer.

Northrop publicly hails the J85, with the era's highest thrust-to-weight ratio (8:1) for a production jet engine, as making both aircraft possible. The J85 is only eighteen inches in diameter and forty-five inches in length with a two-stage turbine.

The engine is designed to produce 2,950 pounds of non-afterburning thrust. For the Northrop jets, however, the J85 is the first small turbojet to operate with an afterburner, which makes the engine capable of producing up to 5,000 pounds of thrust.

Designed as a low-cost alternative for Allied nations around the world, the F-5 is initially self-funded by Northrop. The aircraft is lighter and smaller than US fighter jets, and designed for short-range missions at high-speeds, and capable of rapid climb rates.

In February of 1959, the US government provides $7 million to Northrop for the F-5, marking the first time the US financially supports the development of a supersonic military jet designated specifically for Allied nations.

Three months later, the T-38 begins flight tests at Edwards Air Force Base, California, with considerable public fanfare. The USAF advertises the T-38 as capable of high-altitude speeds similar to the J79-powered F-104, while enabling instructors to teach pilots the fundamentals of supersonic flying, including takeoff and landing, special nighttime missions, and aerobatics.

Then, in July, the F-5 begins its flight tests. Within three weeks, the F-5 is racing across the desert at Edwards Air Force Base carrying Sidewinder missiles. In all, it is a great summer in the California sun for the little J85 turbojet.

Building upon the high volume of the popular T-38 and F-5, Ed Woll's J85 team in Lynn busily pursues the design of a J85 commercial variant for a new generation of business jets.

✈ Also in 1959...

CT58 certifies: Not to be outdone, GE's other amazing tiny engine, the T58, is the first turboshaft engine certified by the Federal Aviation Administration (FAA) for commercial helicopters. The CT58 soon powers the popular Sikorsky S-61 and S-62 commercial helicopters. The first non-military customers of GE's aviation enterprise up to this point are S-61 and S-62 operators.

Aeroderivative applications: GE begins modifying its successful jet engines for marine and industrial applications. The J79 is configured with a drive shaft and designated the LM1500 for marine and land applications. The T58 is converted to the LM100 for marine and industrial uses, including hydrofoil boats and air cushion vehicles. From modest beginnings, a substantial marine and industrial business will soon emerge.

The Collier Trophy: Gerhard Neumann and Neil Burgess receive the prestigious Collier Trophy for achievements on the J79-powered F-104 Starfighter. The award recognizes the variable-stator design.

1960
The J85 goes commercial

Creating commercial variants: With J85 military applications established, Ed Woll's team pursues corporate jets. The CJ610 variant, a non-afterburning engine, is a J85-derived companion to the 4,000-pound thrust CF700, which has an aft-mounted fan like the larger CJ805-23 turbofan for the Convair 990.

The CJ610 generates more thrust for its size (weighing 335 pounds) than any comparable jet engine in civil aviation. GE advertises that a CJ610 turbojet can be converted to a CF700 turbofan with the addition of the aft-fan module.

CJ805 enters service: The CJ805 begins revenue service on the Convair 880 with TWA and Delta. TWA's Howard Hughes delays the aircraft's service entry, creating a cloud of suspicion, one of several factors forcing him to eventually lose the airline's controlling ownership. Convair 880 and 990 aircraft never gain a foothold, with disastrously small production runs.

✈ Also in 1960...

Leaving on a jet plane: The J79-powered B-58 enters operational service as the first supersonic bomber. The next year, USAF Major Henry Deutschendorf sets six speed records at the controls of the B-58 to win the Distinguished Flying Cross.

His son, Henry Deutschendorf Jr., will become better known in the 1970s as a pop music singer and songwriter under the stage name John Denver. Nine years after his father's record-setting flights of 1961, Denver's song "Leaving on a Jet Plane" is a hit for the folk trio Peter, Paul, and Mary. In 1997, the son dies in an experimental aircraft.

Neil Firestone's brief tenure: Neil Firestone, former production leader at the Evendale plant, serves for one year as vice president and general manager of GE's Flight Propulsion division.

1961
"Herman The German" era begins

Gerhard Neumann lands top job: GE's jet propulsion business will never be the same. A dynamic GE leader and innovator for more than a decade, Gerhard Neumann takes the helm of GE's Flight Propulsion Division as vice president and general manager. After several changes at the top in recent years, leadership at GE's aviation business stabilizes under Neumann, who leads the group until 1978.

Familiar to workers for frequent walks on the shop floor and fiery tent speeches in the Evendale parking lot, Neumann's "FEEL INSECURE" sign behind his office desk speaks to his driven nature. While giving a technical pitch to Neumann, GE engineers typically find him sitting on the edge of his seat a few feet away, leaning forward with his eyes intensely focused.

Neumann becomes a student of organizational management. He establishes the position of "engine project manager" and invests it with the authority to direct and coordinate both engineering and manufacturing efforts to ensure an engine's performance objectives are met.

Neumann benefits from Jack Parker's support as vice chairman, who oversees GE's aviation efforts from GE's corporate headquarters. Strengthened by a long history together, the two leaders commit to chasing the growing commercial jetliner industry. It takes several years and an unwavering focus on an integrated technology roadmap, but GE is about to emerge as both a commercial and military jet engine powerhouse.

Gerhard Neumann is famous for fiery tent gatherings with salaried workers in the Evendale parking lot. "The faithful would gather in the evening to hear the word and be saved," Brian Rowe (Neumann's successor) recalls years later with a big smile.

✈ Also in 1961...

CJ805 milestones: Powering the Convair 990, the CJ805-23 with its aft-mounted fan is touted by GE as America's first "turbofan" engine to enter airline service. Meanwhile, a TWA Convair 880, powered by the CJ805-3, flies from San Francisco to Chicago in two hours and fifty-seven minutes. Average speed was almost 650 miles per hour. Despite limited market success, the Convair 880 and 990 are among the fastest jetliners ever.

Atomic plane canceled: With the X211 nuclear propulsion program canceled, GE is funded for a single turbojet to be paired with a nuclear reactor. Called the XJN140E, the turbojet without the nuclear reactor is tested in Evendale. Finally, US President John Kennedy terminates the nuclear aircraft program. Looking back many years later, GE engineering giant Marty Hemsworth concludes the program "had a lot of thermodynamic technology, but no design you could put on an airplane. It died a merciful death."[28]

X370 demonstrator: Challenged by the USAF to develop a turbojet to power an aircraft at Mach 3.5, a GE team led by John Blanton ground tests the X370 demonstrator. It includes advanced materials and metalworking technologies, including electrochemical machining, laser drilling, and cooling techniques.

LM1500: GE Evendale further penetrates the marine propulsion market with the formal launch of the HS Denison hydrofoil, powered by GE's LM1500 gas turbine, a J79 derivative.

CT58 gets around town: Reminiscent of futuristic cartoon series "The Jetsons" of the same era, the CT58-powered Sikorsky S-61 helicopter garners national media attention by hopping around busy Los Angeles with taxi passenger service, mail, and express deliveries.

J79 speed record: The F-4 "Phantom II" becomes the fastest jet by reaching 1,606.342 miles per hour. Flying at about 45,000 feet, it exceeds Mach 2.5.

The USAF challenges GE to develop a turbojet to power an aircraft at Mach 3.5. Evendale's John Blanton leads the engineering team that designs the X370 demonstrator in the early 1960s. Its advanced materials and cooling technologies influence future generations of GE engines.

FAST JETS

T64 flights: The first flights of the T64 turboprop are achieved on a de Havilland DHC-4. The engine is also selected for the Vough-Hiller-Ryan XC-142 tilt-wing aircraft. GE's original objective is unfolding: establish the T64 on helicopters, short-takeoff-and-landing (STOL) aircraft, and vertical-lift vehicles. The T64 is on its way to becoming the era's most produced turboshaft/turboprop engine.

CJ610 certifies: The FAA certifies the CJ610 for business aircraft. Project manager Jim Krebs secures a launch order with Aero Commander's Jet Commander business jet.

1962
Engine building block for the future

The GE1 demonstrator: By the early 1960s, the skies grow cloudy over GE's Flight Propulsion Division. The CJ805 program is losing more and more money every week, the atomic program is cancelled, J93 production outlook is bleak, and the venerable J79 now lacks the legs to satisfy the demanding requirements of future aircraft platforms.

Meanwhile, archrival P&W's dual-shaft compressor turbojets not only power most of the Western World's jetliners, but also gain ground on military aircraft, including the new Lockheed C-141 transport.

GE must establish a technology roadmap to protect its jet propulsion franchise. Parker and Neumann focus it around the GE1 "building block" demonstrator engine program. The GE1 incorporates a scaled compressor with variable stator vanes, an innovative annular combustor, turbine-cooling technologies, and advanced materials developed through government R&D programs. The program bolsters GE's jet engine portfolio and greatly enhances its ability to compete for future commercial jetliners.

The GE1 expands in several directions. It is the antecedent of the GE4 engine for the US supersonic transport later in the decade, as well as the GE1/6 demonstrator engine. This technology building block for future high-bypass turbofan engines features the core "hot section" technology for a new generation of GE military and commercial engines.

The "building block" approach proves masterful. It creates core technology that GE applies to several commercial and military requirements throughout the decade. "With such an efficient core design as the GE1, we could add a fan or an afterburner or a thrust-vectoring device to satisfy any number of future applications," writes Brian Rowe.[29]

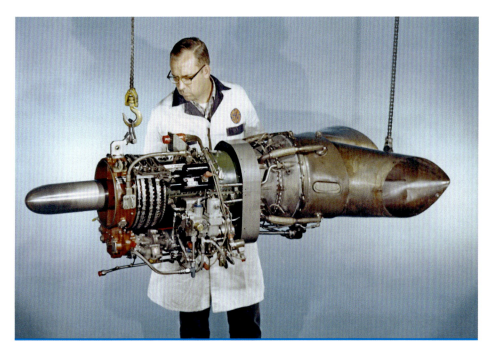

GE establishes the Marine & Industrial (M&I) Division in 1962. The successful practice of converting aviation engines into aeroderivative products for ships and ground applications continues to this day. GE's first M&I product is the LM100 (photo), derived from the T58 engine.

GE's corporate commitment to the GE1 generates tremendous enthusiasm within Evendale's technical community. Several propulsion leaders help to create a technology roadmap for the GE1, including Peter Kappus, Fred MacFee, Jim Worsham, and Rowe, the division's future leader. (Worsham later leads Douglas Aircraft and revitalizes McDonnell Douglas.)

✈ Also in 1962...

CJ805 chapter ends: While the GE1 creates an exciting future, GE must contend with painful issues in the present. The Convair 990 enters service as the last CJ805-23 engines are delivered. All technical achievements aside, a difficult era is coming to an end. Turbine durability issues dearly cost GE and the airlines. GE invests heavily to restore performance and improve field support.

These investments help win customer credibility and pay large dividends later. "Our service [on the CJ805] became a major influence in what sold our CF6 engine later," writes Jack Parker.[30] In the end, 102 Convair jetliners and 408 installed CJ805 engines are delivered. Convair exits the jetliner business. However, GE will be back.

Marine & Industrial Products: In Evendale, Gerhard Neumann establishes the Marine & Industrial Products Division with an initial staff of twenty-five people as GE converts its advanced gas turbines for aviation into aeroderivative products for ships and ground applications. In making the announcement, GE discloses a major project with Cincinnati Gas & Electric Company in which 10 LM1500 gas turbines will be packaged with an electric generator to provide the area with reserve power.

J79 speed records keep coming: The B-58 Hustler claims three transcontinental records at average speeds greater than 1,000 miles per hour. The Mach 2 bomber flies from Los Angeles to New York City in two hours, one minute, and thirty-nine seconds.

Building rocket cases: The Evendale plant wins follow-on contracts from Thiokol Chemical Corporation to produce first-stage rocket motor cases for USAF Minuteman intercontinental ballistic missiles. The cases contain the missile's solid propellant fuel.

Supersonic research begins: The Evendale team reveals an FAA contract to launch a propulsion study for America's supersonic transport (SST), which is being pursued by the US government in partnership with private industry. The study involves research into compressor aerodynamics, combustion temperatures, turbine-cooling systems, materials, and exhaust augmentation systems.

T58 speed record: A T58-powered Sikorsky SH-3A sets a helicopter speed record by exceeding 200 miles per hour.

1963
Birth of the cool: The Lear Jet

CJ610 for Lear Jet: In an era when most people have never stepped in an airplane, self-taught inventor and aviation pioneer William (Bill) Lear captures the public's imagination by launching the small Lear Jet (Model 23) executive airplane.

This aircraft symbolizes American "jetsetter" affluence and swashbuckling innovation. When singer Frank Sinatra purchases his Lear Jet a year later, the sleek plane also attains an ultra "cool" image. Promoted in marketing literature as the "500-mile an hour executive jet," the Lear Jet can carry seven passengers and 300 pounds of luggage. It is among the first luxury aircraft to be mass-produced and targeted at business executives.

Lear derives certain aerodynamic features for his business jet from a Swiss fighter jet prototype. Adding to the jet's swagger are its two GE CJ610 turbojets, derived from the J85 for the popular Northrop F-5 fighter. Lear establishes aircraft production in Wichita, Kansas.

Flight tests in 1963 are followed by the first Lear Jet customer delivery ceremony in 1964 at Lunken Airport in Cincinnati, Ohio, to Chemical and Industrial Corporation.

By the mid-1960s, several high-profile corporations operate Lear Jet fleets and enthuse about the flexibility and convenience they create for the business elite. "Some of our executive salaries are equivalent to $50 and $60 an hour," Dale Leis, assistant president of Rexall Drug and Chemical Company, tells *Aviation Week*. "We don't want them wasting their time in terminals waiting for connections."[31]

The stylish Lear Jet, powered by the GE CJ610 turbojet, helps to define the expression "jetsetter."

The Lear Jet will set numerous speed records for business jets. In 1966, a weary Bill Lear and his crew end a three-day, 23,286-mile journey and the first officially-sanctioned, round-the-world flight for a business jet. The total trip, originating and ending in Wichita, Kansas, is completed in sixty-five hours and forty minutes, including seventeen stops, each averaging less than an hour.

Amid the pizazz created by the flashy jet, Bill Lear is soon in over his head financially. In 1967, he sells his cash-starved company, but the aircraft bearing his name will continue successfully in production for decades.

✈ *Also in 1963...*

CF700 for the Falcon: The CJ610's turbofan sister, the CF700, is launched on the Dassault Falcon 20, the European luxury business jet. A year later, the CF700 becomes the first turbofan to power business jets.

In the 1960s and 1970s, CJ610 and CF700 engines power most of the era's business jets. Neumann's 1961 forecast that GE will sell 2,000 business jet engines comes to pass.

In the late 1970s, GE abandons business jets, citing a lack of return on the investment. Jack Parker explains: "It takes just as much engineering and support to build an engine that produces a very modest amount of thrust as it does to build a big engine and support it. I figured that we have not the engineering manpower to do both."[32]

J93 key to SST strategy: The year before, GE discloses its research contract to prepare for America's supersonic transport (SST). Now, Neumann tells reporters that GE's engine design will be based on a higher-thrust J93 engine, possibly with an aft-mounted fan.

P&W turbofans: P&W introduces the JT3D low-bypass turbofan for large jetliners, as well as a smaller JT8D turbofan for the Boeing 727 and 737-100/200, and the Douglas DC-9. While GE concentrates on more exotic supersonic projects like the XB-70 and SST, P&W makes huge strides with the airlines. Recalling his archrival's early turbofans, Brian Rowe concludes, "P&W should be given credit for producing the first truly reliable commercial engines for these early jetliners."[33]

Jackie Cochran sets more records: Hailed as America's "First Lady of the Sky," Jackie Cochran sets two women's world speed marks with a J79-powered F-104 Starfighter.

1964
Heading straight up with lift fans

GE/Ryan vertical takeoff aircraft: In the 1950s and early 1960s, the US military funds several experimental aircraft with vertical and short-takeoff-and-landing (V/STOL) capability. Having pioneered early turbofan designs, GE is in the thick of lift-fan propulsion for V/STOL aircraft. The efforts forge the way for high-bypass turbofans.

GE's journey begins in 1957 when the US Army funds a study headed by engineer Peter Kappus to develop lift-fan propulsion concepts for V/STOL aircraft. Within three years, GE tests a lift-fan propulsion system and shares ideas for aircraft designs with the Army. Ryan Aeronautical Corporation is simultaneously creating V/STOL aircraft designs.

In an unusual arrangement, GE is lead contractor and Ryan the subcontractor for the Army XV-5A Vertifan flight research vehicle. It is a low-wing aircraft with two J85 engines on top of the fuselage, a six-foot lift fan imbedded in each wing, and a small fan in the nose. All three of the lift fans are powered by ducted-engine exhaust gas for vertical takeoff and landing. The engines supply conventional thrust for horizontal flight. GE's lift-fan propulsion system is designated the X353-5. Art Adamson is project leader.

By 1964, flight tests are underway, and GE's lift-fan propulsion concept is demonstrated. Its success is short-lived. In 1965, one aircraft crashes during a public demonstration, killing a Ryan test pilot when he accidently transitions the aircraft prematurely from conventional power to the hover mode. The next year, a second aircraft crashes. That aircraft is rebuilt and used for NASA testing until 1971.

In the end, no US V/STOL military aircraft are deployed in the 20th century. One view is that they are too susceptible to ground attack. Nonetheless, the British-developed Hawker-Siddeley Harrier V/STOL aircraft is deployed by the US Marines.

GE develops a lift-fan propulsion system for the Ryan vertical takeoff aircraft. While it does not lead to a production program, GE advances the design of complex large fans.

While the GE/Ryan XV-5A fails to enter production, the technology plays a huge role in GE's mid-1960s resurgence. GE will test a six-foot lift fan turned at 90 degrees and powered by a J79 engine, forging the way for a dramatic entry into high-bypass turbofan technology in 1965 with the TF39 engine.

"We demonstrated that we could move huge amounts of air with lift fans," writes Brian Rowe, who leaves England and the de Havilland Company in 1957 to join GE and work on the lift-fan propulsion design team. "When we turned them ninety degrees, we had marvelously efficient cruise fans."[34]

✈ Also in 1964…

CH-53 introduction: The T64 powers the first flight of the Sikorsky YCH-53A, the prototype of the CH-53A Sea Stallion, the Western world's largest transport helicopter. The T64 soon anchors Lynn's turboshaft franchise and powers numerous helicopters, most notably the CH-53 family for heavy-lift applications. That same year in England, Bristol Siddeley Engines signs a licensing agreement to produce T64 engines.

J93 powers the XB-70: The USAF's mammoth and sleek XB-70 bomber, powered by six J93 turbojet engines, makes its first flight.

CF700 certifies: The CF700 becomes the first small turbofan to be certified by the FAA, powering the Dassault Falcon. ✈

1965-

1986

Chasing Jetliners

1965–1986

- ✈ The first passenger jetliners for a growing airline industry put GE jet engines in unfamiliar airspace—on the outside looking in. Commercial aviation blossoms without America's original jet pioneer.

- ✈ GE will turn the tables, however. While forming an enduring alliance with French engine maker Snecma (today called Safran Aircraft Engines), GE parlays its formidable military technologies into a family of innovative turbofans for the fast-growing, commercial jetliner industry.

- ✈ GE's rise to preeminence in commercial aviation combines technology innovation, including the first high-bypass turbofans, with first-rate product support and service.

- ✈ The GE surge also extends to the military arena. GE recovers from significant setbacks in the early 1970s to power an armada of attack helicopters, fighters, bombers, and transports during the 1980s military buildup.

1965

It is hard to overestimate the TF39's importance to GE's aviation business. Selected for the USAF C-5 Galaxy, the Evendale-developed engine is the world's first high-bypass turbofan. TF39 technologies enable GE to re-enter the booming airline industry with a vengeance in the late 1960s.

1986

1965
GE changes jet propulsion forever

TF39 turbofan launch: In 1963, after GE successfully ground tests a large fan attached to the front of a J79 engine, Gerhard Neumann strolls into the Washington, D.C. office of USAF Major General Marvin Demler, head of USAF Research & Technology. Neumann unrolls a cross-section drawing of a high-bypass turbofan capable of twice the thrust of current engines. He claims that the new design will revolutionize air transportation.[1]

At the time, the USAF is launching an engine and airframe competition for a massive military transport capable of carrying up to 700 troops into battle, called the CX-HLS (Experimental Cargo/Heavy Logistics System). US airframers Boeing, Lockheed, and Douglas compete for the program with their largest airplane concepts.

Competing against P&W for the engines, GE's sporty design builds on the large-fan concept presented to Demler. GE's offering, the TF39, draws heavily from technology in the GE1 demonstrator. The TF39 has the largest front fan (ninety-seven inches in diameter) in jet propulsion, along with unprecedented compressor efficiencies and turbine temperatures required to turn it.

In 1965, Lockheed wins the aircraft competition to produce what is designated the C-5A Galaxy, then the world's largest airplane. In a turning point for GE and jet propulsion, the USAF selects the TF39 to power the airplane. The military contract is GE's largest ever: $460 million. GE wins in dramatic fashion with the high-bypass turbofan design, which follows years of innovative research and development. It is arguably the most important jet engine in GE history.

The 41,000-pound-thrust TF39 consolidates GE's best technologies to date: J79 and J85 experience, X353-5 lift-fan and CJ805 aft-fan innovations, air-cooled turbine blade technologies, and engine core advances from the GE1/6 demonstrator. With an 8:1 bypass ratio achieved by the massive front fan, the TF39 is a major leap in design, offering record thrust and fuel efficiency.[2] GE declares the TF39 will operate 25 percent more efficiently than all current turbofans, a claim supported in flight tests.

Thus, a new aviation era begins when high-bypass turbofans can power enormous aircraft for very long distances.

In addition to sheer size, the TF39 fan is unique in design. Half of the inlet airflow is compressed by a single-stage outer panel with inlet guide vanes, and the inner half of the fan has two stages without inlet guide vanes.

The engine's hot section is no less innovative. A two-stage high-pressure turbine (HPT) drives a variable-stator compressor with a 16:1 pressure ratio. The six-stage, low-pressure turbine (LPT) powers the fan. The result: an unprecedented 8:1 front-fan bypass ratio, a 25:1 overall pressure ratio, and turbine temperatures at over 2,300 degrees Fahrenheit. The TF39 introduces new high-temperature alloys and an improved system for providing a cooling film of air over the HPT blades. This air shields the blades from temperatures that exceed their melting point.

Don Berkey leads the TF39 program, reporting to Marty Hemsworth, one of the original seven to establish GE at Lockland's plant in 1948. Engineering stalwarts Jim Krebs and Dave Shaw are significant contributors. Over six years, GE produces 464 TF39 engines for the C-5.

The TF39 win over P&W's lower-bypass JTF14E turbofan sets the stage for a showdown between the two engine titans in the commercial jetliner arena. Months after the August 1965 selection, GE announces plans to create a CTF39 commercial variant to pursue future Douglas, Lockheed, and Boeing jetliners.

✈ Also in 1965...

J93 speed: A J93-powered XB-70 bomber achieves Mach 3, three times the speed of sound, after being airborne sixty-two minutes at altitudes beyond 70,000 feet. It is the first time an aircraft of this size and weight travels so high and fast. The J93 turbine-cooling innovations are critical to the TF39.

1966
GE's secret "stealth" propulsion

Making jets invisible: GE's aviation heritage includes small, handpicked teams secretly creating technology that bolster US military air power, and, in the end, favorably influence the outcome of a war.

Turbosuperchargers boosting piston-powered B-17s during World War II are an example. In the mid-1960s, an Evendale team begins collaborating with the USAF on "stealth" propulsion integral to a new generation of military aircraft.

Stealth propulsion technology grows out of a response to military aircraft vulnerability created by advanced radar detection and "heat-seeking" missiles. For example, US Sidewinder missiles in the 1950s demonstrate the ability to track the infrared (IR) emissions of jet engine exhaust systems.

The IR signature, comprised of wavelengths of electromagnetic radiation, is detectable through temperature and emissivity, and by an object's size and shape. The US military logically pursues ways to reduce IR signatures and radar detection of its aircraft. The focus intensifies in the mid-1960s during the Vietnam War.

During this time, the USAF is funding GE demonstrator engines for future bomber and fighter aircraft. The effort also involves exhaust nozzle designs and other technologies for IR suppression. In 1966, GE Evendale creates the "IR Suppression Unit" within its advanced technology organization. The following year, Glenn Varney begins a long tenure as manager. The group becomes fully funded

GE's massive GE4 turbojet, at more than twenty-five feet in length, for America's supersonic transport (SST). GE is selected for the SST with great fanfare in late 1966. The program is canceled five years later, causing thousands of job losses at Evendale.

within two years by outside contracts covering such technologies as coatings for IR suppression, radar-absorbing materials, and IR analytical computer models.[3]

In 1968, the team collaborates with Rockwell on stealth technology to reduce detection of an engine hot section for an aircraft design that evolves into the B-1 Lancer, a high-speed bomber. Stealth technology is part of GE's winning engine offering, the F101 turbofan. The B-1 has specifications for IR suppression and radar cross-section reduction.[4]

In the mid-1970s, Varney's team supports the Lockheed F-117 "stealth fighter" with its engine nozzle installation and vertical stabilizer configuration. For Northrop's B-2 "stealth bomber," the GE team contributes to the design of the exhaust system for the aircraft's GE F118 engines.

For decades, the small GE group works secretly in tandem with the propulsion labs at Wright-Patterson Air Force Base to advance the science of IR suppression and radar cross-section reduction. Perhaps the most public display of this stealth propulsion occurs in 1991. At the onset of the "Desert Storm" operation in Iraq, USAF F-117 stealth fighters fly undetected over the capital city of Baghdad and destroy Iraq's command and control centers, leaving the country without an air defense system.

"With these technologies, you work in secrecy, but you save lives," says Varney, who is recognized within the military stealth community for leading a pioneering GE research team into the 1990s.[5]

GE wins SST: With supersonic military aircraft racing across the skies, supersonic passenger jets are the next logical step. In 1962, the French and British governments assemble a joint technical team to develop a supersonic passenger jet called the Concorde. The Soviet Union announces plans for its own supersonic transport, the Tupolev Tu-144.

In the US, aircraft manufacturers pursue government-sponsored supersonic aircraft studies. During a full-blown competition by the mid-1960s, Boeing's design calls for "variable geometry" wings that are straight at takeoff and then move closer to the fuselage at higher speeds. For engines, Boeing works closely with GE based on its experience with large, supersonic turbojets like the J93.

After a thirty-month competition, the US government selects the GE4 engine and the Boeing 2707 airframe for America's supersonic transport (SST). Public fanfare greets the announcement on New Year's Day of 1967, as newspapers nationwide call the program America's largest airplane project ever.[6]

The Boeing four-engine 2707 is initially proposed to carry 350 people at 1,800 miles per hour. Boeing forecasts the aircraft's entry into service by the 1970s and a 700 aircraft production run by 1990. GE forecasts $4 billion to $7 billion in jet propulsion business over the next twenty years with hundreds of employees to be hired at Evendale.[7]

The first large commercial jet engine with an afterburner, the massive GE4, at more than twenty-five feet in length, draws upon J93 aerodynamics, high-temperature materials, and intricate cooling schemes. GE designs the engine for thrust levels beyond 60,000 pounds. The GE4 will be optimized to operate at Mach 2.7 cruise speeds at 60,000 to 70,000 feet. GE says the afterburner will be used mostly for transonic accelerations at altitudes from 40,000 to 60,000 feet.

With the highly publicized TF39 and GE4 wins, GE advertises with bravado in area newspapers and trade publications for young engineers to establish their careers with GE in Greater Cincinnati.

However, SST trouble soon looms. By mid-1968, Boeing pushes out the aircraft service entry to the 1980s. Some Congressional leaders loudly object to such high levels of government funding for a private commercial enterprise and question the aircraft's economic and environmental viability.

✈ Also in 1966...

GE passes on Boeing 747: Building on its design experience from the C-5 competition, Boeing unveils an innovative, four-engine 747 intercontinental jetliner and invites GE to compete for the engines. Gerhard Neumann faces a tough decision: With the enormous C-5 and SST development commitments, does GE have the resources to develop yet another new jet engine in a timely matter?[8]

Boeing declines GE Vice Chairman Jack Parker's request to extend the 747-development schedule to enable GE's participation. Boeing selects P&W's JT9D, a commercial variant of P&W's losing bid for the C-5A. With a 5:1 fan bypass ratio, the JT9D is the first high-bypass turbofan to power a jetliner, but will eventually face major development challenges. In the next decade, GE will succeed in powering subsequent 747 models.

XB-70 crash: On September 26, the second XB-70 prototype, powered by the J93, crashes after a midair collision with an F-104 following a GE promotional photo shoot of five GE-powered USAF jets flying in formation.

After photos are taken from a Lear Jet, the five planes (XB-70, F-4, F-5, T-38, F-104) begin to break formation at which point the F-104, piloted by Joseph Walker, strikes the XB-70. XB-70 co-pilot Major Carl Cross and Walker are killed in the crash. (Walker previously set speed records piloting X-15 aircraft.)

XB-70 funding has been declining for years, and the accident leaves one aircraft left in the program. It flies three more years primarily for NASA research, and then goes on display at the Wright-Patterson Air Force Museum near Dayton, Ohio.

CF700 for NASA: GE receives a NASA contract for CF700 engines to power the Lunar Landing Training Vehicle. That same year, the CF700-powered Falcon establishes a speed record over a recognized course for the distance between Newfoundland and Lisbon. The airplane covers 2,250 miles at an average speed of 485 miles per hour.

Hooksett, New Hampshire: GE opens a new plant in Hooksett, New Hampshire, to produce airfoils for military engines. The Hooksett operation is closely affiliated with the GE aviation component plant in Rutland, Vermont.

1967

GE tackles helicopter challenge

GE12 turboshaft engine: During the Vietnam War, US military helicopters assume major roles both as combat vehicles and as troop transports in hostile environments. Gerhard Neumann witnesses these missions firsthand after he receives approval to go to Vietnam and interview Army technicians maintaining GE engines in combat zones.[9]

The Vietnam experience drives a US military requirement for two-engine helicopters with greater capability, including better range and speed, as well as easier engine maintenance in harsh conditions. Building upon the T58 and T64 experience, the Lynn team pursues an advanced turboshaft to meet the new requirements. With US government seed money, design studies commence on the GE12 demonstrator, forerunner to GE's T700.

The GE12 design is revolutionary, introducing the first axial-centrifugal (impeller) compressor. The first stages are axial with compressed air moving parallel to the engine centerline to the centrifugal stage, where the impeller spins the compressed air from the center toward the outside. Lynn veterans from GE's early centrifugal engines join the GE12 team.[10]

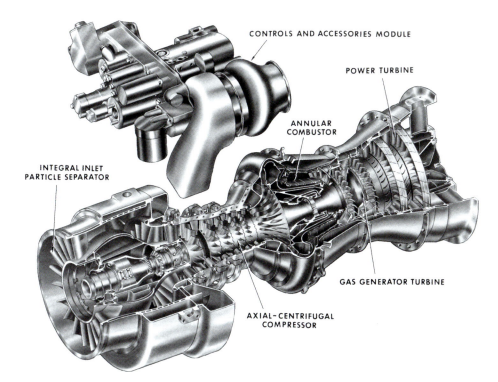

The T700 turboshaft traces its roots to the GE12 demonstrator developed in 1967. Its compressor marries axial and centrifugal stages, a revolutionary concept. The "keep it simple" GE12 philosophy continues today with Lynn's turboshaft designs.

For four years, Lynn engineers refine the GE12, incorporating "blisk" technology where compressor blades and discs are machined from a single forging. Reducing components is a key Army objective. A new inlet particle separation module is integrated, which operates not only during takeoff but also throughout the entire flight.

The GE12 has 80 percent fewer compressor airfoils than the T58, with higher compression capability, and 20 to 30 percent better specific fuel consumption. The GE12 is 40 percent lighter than current production turboshaft engines.

✈ Also in 1967...

Commercial Engine Projects: With the SST engine win and the TF39 tests achieving excellent core efficiencies and record thrust for a turbofan, Gerhard Neumann creates the Commercial Engine Projects operation with Ed Hood as general manager. The division oversees the CJ610 and CF700 engines, the GE4, and a new commercial CF6 turbofan (originally designated the CTF39) derived from the TF39. Brian Rowe leads the new CF6 program.

CF6 unveiled: GE reveals an initial CF6 design in the 34,000-pound thrust class with plans for a three-step growth over six years, including a CF6-6 variant set at 40,000 pounds of thrust. GE claims a conservative design that sacrifices advantages in weight, length, and drag for increased operational life, reliability, and maintainability.[11]

GE plans to commit to 12,000 hours and 8,000 flights of compressor and turbine life. With a modified TF39 core, the CF6 is designed with an eighty-six-inch front fan (eleven inches less than the TF39) to improve noise performance over current turbofan engines.

TF39 flies: The TF39 is flight tested in a modified B-52 at GE's Flight Test Center at Edwards Air Force Base, California. Not only the military customer, but the airline industry as well watches TF39 performance with keen interest.

GE4 sets record: The GE4 becomes the world's most powerful turbojet by producing 69,900 pounds of thrust during ground tests in Peebles, Ohio. No one has ever seen a jet engine so large. The SST program leads to the 1967 construction of Evendale's dual-cell altitude test facility. The unique test facility is used to this day.

GE engines in forty nations: At the Paris Air Show, GE announces that its engines now power commercial and military aircraft in forty countries. Also, several manufacturers in Europe and Asia produce GE engines under license.

1968
GE's bold return to the airline industry

CF6-6 on DC-10: By the mid-1960s, the US experiences an air travel boom with passenger traffic expanding almost twenty percent a year.[12] In 1966, Boeing launches its game-changing 747 with Pan American Airways. The huge aircraft, powered by P&W, is capable of carrying over 400 passengers in luxury over vast oceans. The aircraft inspires other large jetliner designs, which create a much-needed opening for GE.

The incredible 747 economics, including its huge seating capacity for international routes, spurs an industry demand for jetliners with more than 200 seats for domestic routes. Through the hard-fought C-5 Galaxy competition, Douglas, Boeing, and Lockheed all enhance their design capabilities and are up for the challenge. Larger turbofans on the drawing board, inspired by the TF39, will provide the thrust and fuel efficiency.

American Airlines proposes a medium-range aircraft to carry 250 passengers and 5,000 pounds of freight from Chicago to Los Angeles. Following American's

GE returns to the airline industry with the CF6-6 turbofan powering the Douglas Aircraft DC-10, one of the era's most popular jetliners. The photo is from the 1970 unveiling ceremony.

lead, other airlines seek a 250-passenger aircraft for domestic routes. They want the economics that a large, twin-engine airplane can bring.

Yet no engine maker can meet the thrust demands. With its CF6, GE heavily lobbies aircraft manufacturers to pursue three-engine jetliners for long-range flights. Douglas Aircraft pursues the DC-10; Lockheed offers the L-1011 design. Both are three-engine airplanes.

"We went to American Airlines and United, the biggest North American carriers, and KLM in Europe and asked them to give us a chance on the DC-10," writes Brian Rowe, head of the CF6 program. "We had a good engine design (CF6-6), and we promised to give them first-class product support."[13]

The L-1011 launches with Rolls-Royce, whose engine development struggles lead it to bankruptcy three years later. Meanwhile, P&W has its hands full with financial outlays to meet 747 thrust requirements.

For GE to re-enter the airline industry, it is the DC-10 or bust. Adding to the drama, Douglas by 1967 faces financial woes, and McDonnell Corporation takes over the company, creating McDonnell Douglas. The merger ensures financial stability for the DC-10 project and improves GE's chances, building on the strong relationship formed on McDonnell's F-4.

In a landmark win for GE, United Airlines launches the CF6-6 on the new 252-passenger DC-10 in June of 1968. American Airlines, an original advocate for the aircraft, follows suit. The CF6-6 marks GE's return to the airline industry after a painful exit a few years earlier.

This is a hard-fought win. GE's propulsion brand is high-performance military fighter engines and helicopter engines, while P&W powers more than 80 percent of the Western world's jetliners. As part of a large GE conglomerate best known for household products, the jet engine division faces an image problem as an Northwest Airlines executive tells GE leadership in 1968, "Whenever I want a light bulb, I'll pick GE. For engines, I'll stick with P&W."[14]

Nevertheless, TF39 performance on the C-5 is undeniable. It is crucial in selling the commercial variant. In addition, GE re-enters the airline industry during a prosperous era. At the time, analysts are predicting a tripling in airline passenger traffic over the next decade, and McDonnell Douglas touts its new DC-10 family as the future backbone of airline commercial fleets.

GE executive Ed Hood accurately forecasts that the CF6 could ultimately have a bigger economic impact on Greater Cincinnati than the J79, Evendale's production mainstay for more than a decade.[15]

Amid this jubilation, GE's embarrassing CJ805 experience is on everyone's minds and cannot be repeated. While Neumann wants the CF6 design to be as close as possible to the TF39, Rowe instructs his team to redesign the CF6-6 compressor shaft for the higher utilization on airline jetliners. The front fan is simplified with a lower bypass ratio. Through improved mechanical design, materials, and turbine-cooling technology (a GE hallmark), the CF6-6 operates at higher temperatures and brings a new level of efficiency to large turbofans while producing 40,000 pounds of thrust.

Hood and Rowe hit the road and lead the tireless CF6 marketing campaign with airlines worldwide. Hood's role in gaining GE's foothold in commercial aviation helps him rise to GE vice chairman.

✈ Also in 1968...

TF34 launch with US Navy: In what will prove to be one of GE's most successful engine campaigns in Lynn, the Navy selects the TF34 turbofan engine for the Navy

S-3A Viking antisubmarine aircraft. The TF34 engine is a compact, rugged design with a compressor derived from the T64 and a fan and low-pressure system scaled from the TF39 and the GE1 demonstrator.

To increase durability, the combustor is made of a nickel-based alloy with a liner machined from a forging instead of a sheet-metal fabrication. The TF34 is the first GE engine with a forged combustor liner, designed to support the S-3A mission of covering great distances at high speeds. After the initial flights in 1972, the aircraft enters service in 1974.

The TF34 launch is yet another example of a GE engine with far-reaching ramifications. Decades later, it becomes the foundation for a family of prominent commercial turbofan engines well into the 21st century.

C-5 takes to the sky: The C-5A makes its maiden flight. TF39 test hours on the ground exceed 7,000 hours by the first flight.

GE Aircraft Engine Group: The GE Flight Propulsion Division is renamed the GE Aircraft Engine Group.

1969
Powering the first Airbus jetliner

CF6 family grows: Following the critical CF6-6 launch, 1969 is transformative for GE's commercial engine operations when a CF6-50 growth derivative establishes a global presence on two new jetliners.

For European airlines, McDonnell Douglas offers the CF6-50 on the stretch DC-10-30. At the Paris Air Show in June, Gerhard Neumann, Ed Hood, and Brian Rowe raise their champagne glasses in the GE chalet after securing a block of engine orders for the DC-10-30 through the KSSU consortium of KLM, Swissair, Scandinavian Airlines, and UTA.

Then they score another European coup. The new Airbus Industrie of Western Europe selects the CF6-50 for its twin-engine A300, the first passenger

Respected British engineer Brian H. Rowe manages the CF6 program during the formative years from 1967 to 1972. He later runs GE's aviation business.

jetliner from the aircraft design and manufacturing consortium formed by the governments of France, West Germany, Spain, and the United Kingdom.

To win in jobs-sensitive Europe, GE is highly creative. Hood establishes a revenue-sharing arrangement whereby engine makers MTU of Germany and Snecma of France produce CF6-50 engine parts valued at 25 percent of total engine production costs. The agreement extends to CF6-50s for Airbus A300s and DC-10s sold in Europe. Moreover, GE offers free engines for the A300 flight tests.

The CF6-50, which begins testing later that year, firmly establishes GE in the 50,000-pound thrust class for commercial jet propulsion. To manage higher turbine inlet temperatures and thrust, GE's Art Adamson designs the CF6-50 with a front fan based on the CF6-6 design but with a higher speed capability. Three fan booster stages are added behind the front fan, while two stages are removed from the compressor to boost airflow.[16]

✈ Also in 1969…

GE/Snecma relationship: GE establishes day-to-day working relations with Snecma, the government-owned military engine maker in France. While Snecma supplies CF6-50 components, the French government plans its own bold step into commercial jet propulsion.

J97 for unmanned vehicles: In the late 1960s, the USAF creates a requirement for a high-altitude, long-range unmanned aircraft for photo-reconnaissance and surveillance. The J97 turbojet, derived from the GE1 demonstrator, powers the Ryan drone aircraft.

In 1969, Northrop selects the J97 design with an afterburner for a successor to its popular J85-powered F-5. Northrop designs the P-530 and seeks international customers and partners for a low-cost, short-range fighter jet. The aircraft and engine combination is never launched, but the Northrop-GE journey for a new lightweight fighter jet continues.

GE15 and Northrop: GE begins to develop the GE15 for lightweight fighters. Another outgrowth of the GE1 building block, the GE15 is a dual-shaft, low-bypass turbofan with an efficient compressor and simple mechanical structure in the 14,000-pound thrust class. The GE15 will evolve into the J101 engine powering the Northrop YF-17 fighter for US and international markets. Stay tuned: The Northrop-GE partnership in pursuit of a lightweight fighter gets more interesting.

Last J93 flight: The last test flight of the J93-powered XB-70 is on February 4. The aircraft flies to the Wright-Patterson Air Force Base Museum and is placed on permanent display. Only two XB-70 aircraft are produced. The first aircraft logged eighty-three flights; the second forty-six flights.

LM2500: The LM2500 marine gas turbine, derived from the TF39, is installed in the GTS William M. Callahan cargo transport. This is the first application for an engine that would power hundreds of military and civil vessels worldwide. With an original design team led by Walter Brisken, the LM2500 will experience a highly successful entry into service, and will remain in production for decades as the propulsion backbone for US Navy ships.

1970
Core values: GE F101 engine

Critical military engine decisions: Overwhelming US air superiority during the Korean War is not fully replicated during air campaigns over Vietnam during the 1960s. US fighters and bombers still dominate the skies, but North Vietnamese pilots in Soviet-made MiG interceptors, teamed with ground personnel operating Soviet-made anti-aircraft artillery and surface-to-air missiles, destroy thousands of US planes.

In 1967, the Soviet Union introduces a high-speed MiG-25 interceptor, which some military analysts fear will outperform the J79-powered F-4 Phantom, the era's primary high-speed US military fighter jet.[17]

Future US aircraft must adapt. In the late 1960s, the US military specifies a new generation of fighter jets with air-to-air superiority and greater maneuverability. In 1969, the USAF selects the twin-engine McDonnell Douglas F-15 Eagle, an air-to-air fighter, while the Navy launches the twin-engine Grumman F-14 Tomcat for carrier deployment.

The USAF also pursues a new bomber under the Advanced Manned Strategic Aircraft (AMSA) program capable of the Mach 2 speed of the J79-powered B-58 Hustler, but with greater payload and capability. In 1970, Rockwell's four-engine B-1 Lancer wins the AMSA aircraft selection.

With these new military aircraft established, 1970 is a critical year in determining future jet propulsion for US fighters and bombers.

The first major decisions go against GE. The USAF selects P&W's F100 engine for the F-15, and the Navy selects P&W's F401 engine for the F-14 (though the plane is ultimately powered by P&W TF30s). At the time, the perception is that P&W better understands engine and aircraft inlet compatibility through the experience of managing inlet distortion on the high-speed SR-71 spy plane and other fighter jets.[18] Weeks before the USAF decision, GE's engine experi-

Early 1970s GE advertisement for the F101 engine.

ences a compressor failure in the test cell, though its impact on the decision is not clear.

These initial selections also put P&W in the pole position for the USAF's upcoming "Light-Weight Fighter" aircraft. These defeats are a bitter pill to swallow for GE, which has successfully powered most American fighter jets since the late 1940s.

Not all is lost, however. Three months after the F-15 and F-14 engine selections, the USAF selects GE's F101 engine for the AMSA (B-1) bomber. Following the XB-70 bomber cancellation, the F101 win is critical to GE's future.

The dual-shaft F101, GE's first afterburning turbofan, builds upon the GE1 and GE9 demonstrators, along with metallurgical advances from the X370 demonstrator. The F101 is the twentieth version of the GE1 to reach hardware stage. In the 30,000-pound thrust class, the F101 will be twice as powerful as the J79 with 25 percent better fuel efficiency.

After years of F101 development and testing, US President Jimmy Carter cancels the B-1 bomber in 1977. Nevertheless, F101 development and refinement stays funded into the next decade. (President Ronald Reagan reinstates the B-1 program in 1981.)

In the 1970s, the F101's importance extends beyond the B-1. Its highly efficient and compact core (with two bearings versus three) pairs an efficient nine-stage compressor with a highly-loaded, single-stage HPT. It becomes the engine core for future military engines (F110 family and F118) and commercial engines (CFM56 family) across many popular aircraft platforms.

✈ Also in 1970...

On Snecma's menu: At a dinner in Boston, Massachusetts, Snecma leaders propose to surprised GE leaders the idea of jointly developing a commercial jet engine. Snecma has approached GE after unfruitful talks with Rolls-Royce and P&W, which only offers Snecma participation on a new JT8D variant instead of pursuing the French joint-development concept. "You could have bowled us over with a feather," recalls Ed Woll, GE's head of propulsion engineering.[19]

The proposal follows a decade of Snecma technical progress and growth. In the early 1960s, Snecma assembles P&W's popular JT8D engine under license. Snecma also teams with Bristol Siddeley of England on the Olympus engine for the Concorde supersonic jetliner. In 1968, Snecma acquires the French aerospace company

Hispano-Suiza, and a year later, pursues a commercial engine study designated the M56. By 1970, Snecma has become a significant revenue-sharing participant on the CF6-50 as well.

1971
Beginning of a beautiful friendship

GE and Snecma strike a deal: While pursuing formative discussions between Snecma and GE, new Snecma President René Ravaud forges a strong friendship with GE's Gerhard Neumann.

They agree to co-develop the "10-tonne engine," a turbofan in the 20,000-pound thrust class to challenge P&W's dominance on single-aisle jetliners. Timing is fortuitous. Snecma's M56 design concept meshes well with GE's GE13 turbofan concept under study using the F101 core.

Ravaud is a veteran aerospace engineer and French Resistance hero who lost his right arm during the bombing of Brest harbor in 1944. He becomes a kindred spirit to Neumann, an ace airplane mechanic with America's "Flying Tigers" in China during World War II. "He and I clicked from the very first moment we met," Neumann recalls. "GE was formally selected to be France's engine partner."[20]

Snecma and GE have a strong ally in French President Georges Pompidou. High on his industrial agenda for France is world-class jet propulsion capability. Snecma is attracted to GE's technical prowess as well as the opportunity to co-create a new engine using GE's F101 core. Pompidou proves a powerful advocate for the partnership over several challenging years.

While Neumann and Ravaud are tough business operators, they enjoy warm moments of friendship over the years. One night, Neumann cables to Ravaud that an engine deal must be won "even if it costs us an arm and a leg." Neumann soon panics and tries to retrieve the note, but it is too late. He receives Ravaud's response the next morning: "It is better to lose one's arm than one's head."[21]

Shocking GE4 cancellation: Just as GE gains momentum on several commercial engine programs, the US Congress in March kills the American Supersonic Transport (SST). Proponents warn that the Soviet Union and Europe will vault ahead with their SST projects; opponents challenge the SST runaway costs and development delays, in addition to the practicality of supersonic travel.

Snecma President René Ravaud (left) and GE's Gerhard Neumann. The World War II veterans, one French and one German, lead the quest to co-develop a turbofan in the 20,000-pound thrust class.

US Senator William Proxmire of Wisconsin, a leading Capitol Hill dissenter, distributes champagne in plastic cups after the Senate terminates the program with a 51-46 roll call. GE promptly announces 1,500 layoffs in Greater Cincinnati, a loss equivalent to $14 million annually for the local economy.[22]

In May, a Congressional delegation moves to restart the SST, but Boeing and GE demand reimbursement of termination costs from the original program before proceeding. GE's position is that the government should finance 100 percent of a new project, as opposed to 90 percent for the original one.[23] The Boeing and GE positions add to the fading SST support on Capitol Hill. The massive GE4 engine becomes a museum piece in Evendale.

The back-to-back cancellations of the XB-70 and SST programs create great anxiety across GE Aircraft Engines. As history continues to show, business fortunes in aviation can change overnight. In 1971, GE's aviation plants will collectively eliminate 7,000 workers, dropping overall employment from 27,000 to 20,000 workers.[24] "We had a damn good engine for the SST, and I was always unhappy that we didn't have the opportunity to use it," writes GE Vice Chairman Jack Parker.[25]

✈ Also in 1971...

Rolls-Royce bankruptcy: GE is not the only engine maker experiencing turbulence. Rolls-Royce goes bankrupt and ends up in government receivership. This move is necessary to complete the RB211 engine for the L-1011. Costs soar from failures of the Hyfil carbon-fiber composite fan blades. The RB211 will enter service with titanium fan blades.

The Rolls-Royce luxury car and the gas turbine engine division become separate companies. Rolls-Royce Ltd., the gas turbine division, is privatized in 1987. (In the early 1990s, when the GE90 turbofan launches with carbon-fiber composite front fan blades, GE faces some skepticism lingering from the Rolls-Royce experience.)

CF6-6 progress: A CF6-6-powered American Airlines DC-10-10 enters revenue service. GE's dark clouds during this era have some silver linings. At the same time, CF6-50 production commences in Evendale. Despite layoffs within its workforce, GE's jet engine business is staging a dramatic comeback in the commercial jetliner arena.

Neumann honored: Gerhard Neumann is awarded the Chevalier of the Legion of Honor, France's highest civilian honor, for leading GE aerospace collaborations in France.

1972
Turboshaft engine for the ages

T700 turboshaft launched: It is a landmark, long-awaited contract for the GE Lynn team. After engaging in years of technology development and refinement, the team wins a US Army contract award to launch a production version of its GE12 turboshaft engine. It is designated the T700-GE-700, the first model of what becomes the wildly popular engine family. T700 production is positioned to span several decades.

The T700 refines the GE12's radical axial-centrifugal compressor and several unique maintainability and design features. The Army notes that only ten tools in its maintenance toolbox can do most T700 maintenance. In initial ground tests in 1973, the engine demonstrates more than 1,500 horsepower.[26]

In 1974, the Army formalizes the selection of the T700 to power both the UT-TAS (Utility Tactical Transport Aircraft System), designated the Sikorsky UH-60A Black Hawk, and the AAH (Advanced Attack Helicopter), designated the AH-64 Apache. Naval versions are also introduced.

T700 shop-visit rates eventually resemble those of commercial jet engines, a new paradigm for turboshaft engines. In the late 1960s and early 1970s, some of Lynn's best engineering minds are involved in establishing the T700 program: Ed Woll, Bob Turnbull, Fred Garry, Jim Krebs, Pete Chipouras, and Bill Crawford.

In the mid-1970s, GE predicts that T700 turboshaft and turboprop production could reach 5,000 engines, a gross underestimation. The T700 becomes the highest-volume military turboshaft engine ever, powering most intermediate-sized helicopters for the US military and its allies. The first growth T700 programs are the T700-GE-401 in 1978 and the T700-GE-701 in 1980. More powerful variants follow. Thousands of CT7 turboprop variants for commercial aircraft are delivered as well.

F404 genesis: After GE mostly self-funds its GE15-inspired J101 fighter engine, the USAF awards a key $10 million contract in 1972 to further define the J101 design for smaller fighter jets, including Northrop 's YF-17 prototype. Jack Parker and Gerhard Neumann wisely view the J101 as filling a thrust void in the US military portfolio between GE's J85 and P&W's F100.

The J101's scaled core is based on F101/GE1 lineage. GE calls the J101 a "continuous bleed turbojet" (or "leaky turbojet"), because continuous flow of air from the fan cools the afterburner and nozzle downstream. This design feature enables the engine to operate at higher temperatures and pressures, but with less installed drag than a more traditional turbofan. The combustor is based on the CF6 design. Film-cooling technology in the afterburner enables GE to increase turbine inlet temperatures.

In 1972, General Dynamics and Northrop receive USAF contracts to create fighter prototypes for the "Light-Weight Fighter" (LWF) competition. It is critically important to GE and Northrop, whose P-600 design evolves into the J101-powered

In 1972, the proposed engine collaboration between GE and Snecma is in jeopardy when the White House rejects GE's export license application.

YF-17 prototype. Northrop and GE team against General Dynamics and P&W with their single-engine, F100-powered YF-16 prototype.

✈ *Also in 1972…*

USAF TF34 launch: The USAF selects the TF34 for the A-10 Thunderbolt (nicknamed "The Warthog"), a close-air support aircraft. The A-10 mission requires the TF34 to reach takeoff power about seven times per flight. Engineering improvements and component efficiencies to meet aggressive mission profiles position a TF34 commercial variant decades later to successfully power regional jets. In 1972, the TF34 also powers its first S-3A flight for the US Navy.

Headwind for GE and Snecma: Proposed GE and Snecma collaboration appears dead on arrival when the US government rejects GE's export license application of the F101 engine core for its joint development with Snecma.

US Treasury Secretary George Shultz claims that the export license would hand critical, US-funded technology to a foreign government several years before the F101 engine can enter service on the B-1 bomber.[27] GE and Snecma leadership is undaunted. Their representatives continue talks within the halls of the Congress, Pentagon, and White House.

CF6-50 pursues 747: Boeing certifies the CF6-50 as an option to power the 747. In the same year, the USAF selects the CF6-50 as the engine for the Airborne Command Post E-4A Nightwatch, a military 747 variant.

1973

Franco-American engine heats up in Iceland

President Nixon signs on: At a trade summit in Iceland between US President Richard Nixon and French President Georges Pompidou, President Nixon grants an export license for the GE F101 engine core. The stroke of Nixon's pen clears the way for GE and Snecma to jointly develop the CFM56 turbofan in the 20,000-pound thrust class.

To gain approval, GE ensures that the US government receives royalty payments of $20,000 for each CFM56 sold over several years. In 1973, the US government says that it has spent $300 million on F101 development.

GE argues that spreading F101 development across military and commercial aircraft will ultimately save the US government $180 million.[28] GE also guarantees

US President Richard Nixon (left) and French President Georges Pompidou at the 1973 trade summit in Iceland. Nixon grants an export license for the F101 core to further the collaboration between GE and Snecma.

safeguards to protect the classified technology. GE's government representatives work tirelessly for weeks on the agreement.

Pompidou is a catalyst for the Iceland thaw. From the beginning, he insists that the F101 export license issue be included on the summit agenda. Even the year before, Pompidou writes Nixon a letter (leaked to reporters) to seek his cooperation on the stalled F101 export license. Pompidou uses the F101 issue to express broader concerns over trade relations between the countries.[29]

By all accounts, Nixon is indifferent to the engine's potential economic benefits to the US when he signs the export license approval. "He couldn't have cared less about this," recalls Jack Hope, a consultant to President Nixon's White House Office of Science and Technology.[30]

Publicly, Snecma proposes a 180-seat Dassault-Breguet Mercure jetliner as a leading candidate for the new CFM56 engine.

✈ Also in 1973...

NASA's QCSEE program: The Quiet Clean Short-haul Experimental Engine (QCSEE) program begins. The program, cost-shared with NASA, is devoted to reducing noise and pollution without compromising performance. A key engine feature is a variable-geometry front fan, also called a geared fan system. QCSEE testing concludes in 1978.

Variable-cycle concept: GE engages in the Joint Technology Demonstrator Engine (JTDE) program funded by the USAF and Navy. GE mechanically varies a J101 engine cycle during operation to demonstrate the benefits of a turbofan at subsonic speeds and a turbojet at supersonic speeds.

GE powers Federal Express: Fred Smith's two-year-old Federal Express (later named FedEx) begins overnight operations in 1973 with fourteen CF700-powered Falcon 20 jets that connect twenty-five US cities. At Brian Rowe's eulogy in 2007, Smith cites Rowe's key role in providing attractive financial terms for the young company's initial aircraft. "Without Brian, there isn't the FedEx of today," Smith says.[31] FedEx remains a loyal GE customer for decades.

A300 rollout: With great fanfare, Airbus Industrie rolls out its first twin-aisle and twin-engine A300, in Toulouse, France, powered by CF6-50 engines.

1974
CFM International is born

A unique partnership: After years of negotiations, strategic planning, and seemingly insuperable government hurdles, CFM International, a 50/50 joint company between Snecma and GE, is formally established. Testing promptly begins that same year on its new CFM56-2 turbofan.

The joint company is created as a single entity charged with developing and selling the CFM56 engine family. Revenues are split equally; profits are held separately within each parent company's operations. The novel approach proves enduring.

Snecma is charged with designing and producing the front fan and low-pressure system. GE owns the engine "core" hot section, comprised of the high-pressure compressor (HPC), combustor, and HPT. Final engine assembly is split evenly. Snecma delivers fans and LPT systems to GE for final assembly; GE delivers cores to Snecma for final assembly.

To market and support the CFM56, GE and Snecma divide the world geographically. The CFM president will be a Snecma leader with the headquarters in Paris. (After the CFM56-2 is launched, CFM headquarters is moved to GE's aviation headquarters in Evendale.)

The "CF" in CFM is derived from GE's use of the letters to designate "commercial turbofan." The "M" is from M56, Snecma's original designation for the new engine.

"Just about every major Western airframe manufacturer is now committed to major studies of application for this engine," says Jean Sollier, president of CFM International, upon announcing the new company.[32] While CFM is born from years of undying belief in the partnership, the CFM56 engine launch will soon require an equally large act of faith.

✈ Also in 1974...

F101 flights: The USAF flight tests begin for the F101-powered B-1 bomber.

T700 flights: The Army flight tests begin for the T700-powered UH-60 Black Hawk. The helicopter enters service in 1979.

With CFM International formally established in 1974, Snecma and GE waste no time in pursuing the CFM56-2 engine development program.

1975
Lynn's ubiquitous fighter engine

US Navy births F404: It is another significant year in the long-raging battle between GE and P&W to power fighter jets. As most analysts anticipate, the USAF selects the P&W F100-powered, single-engine YF-16 from General Dynamics over the GE J101-powered YF-17 from Northrop and McDonnell Douglas for the "Light-Weight Fighter" program. The US government envisions the winning aircraft in both USAF and Navy fleets.

However, a twist in the story has far-reaching benefits for GE. The Navy has reservations about deploying the YF-16 (later designated the F-16) for carrier service with its single engine and narrow landing gear. Instead, the Navy selects the twin-engine YF-17 prototype.

Its J101 engine, modified for higher thrust, evolves into the F404. The YF-17, redesigned for carrier requirements, becomes the F/A-18 Hornet, with McDonnell Douglas now the lead contractor and Northrop the prime subcontractor.

GE's focus on affordability pays huge dividends. In 1974, defense officials conclude that two J101s cost less than one F100 powering the F-16. The F404 development builds on the J101 core, featuring a larger fan (for increased airflow) and larger nozzle. The increased airflow boosts F404 thrust to 16,000 pounds to make the F/A-18 more maneuverable.[33]

J101 project leader Burt Riemer commits to 30 percent lower maintenance costs for the F404-powered F/A-18 compared to the J79-powered F-4s. The F404 will have 40 percent fewer parts and half the weight of the J79 while generating similar thrust. One of the most successful fighter engine/aircraft combinations in military aviation history is underway.

✈ Also in 1975…

CF6-50 lands 747: In another milestone for GE's growing commercial business, Lufthansa and KLM launch the CF6-50 on the Boeing 747-200, the second version of the world's largest and most popular twin-aisle jetliner. Three years earlier, GE sends a CF6 engine mockup to Boeing to quietly evaluate installation on the aircraft. Lufthansa's satisfaction with the CF6-50 engines powering its DC-10-30s helps to pave the way for GE on the 747-200. GE's multi-year effort to power the 747 breaks P&W JT9D exclusivity.

Soon, P&W, GE, and Rolls-Royce engines are all available on the 747. A three-company high-thrust engine battle ensues across Boeing, Airbus, and McDonnell Douglas long-range aircraft for several decades.

NASA's Energy Efficient Engine: The NASA-funded Energy Efficient Engine program is established. Both GE and P&W participate to improve the fuel efficiency of large commercial turbofan engines by 12 percent over current production models. Marty Hemsworth leads GE's effort in designing a ten-stage, 23:1 pressure ratio compressor demonstrator. Several years later, the design becomes the basis for the GE90 compressor.

The NASA focus on fuel efficiency reflects shifting priorities within a maturing jet propulsion industry. For several decades, commercial propulsion technology advances are focused almost entirely on generating thrust to increase aircraft size. With the oil embargoes of the 1970s, the focus swings toward developing fuel-efficient machines for both commercial and military applications. In addition to its obvious economic benefits, greater fuel efficiency enhances aircraft range.

Fit for a king: Rock'n'roll king Elvis Presley buys a CJ805-powered Convair 880 and names it "The Lisa Marie" after his daughter. For years, the aircraft and one of the GE CJ805 engines are displayed at Graceland, Elvis's home, in Memphis, Tennessee.

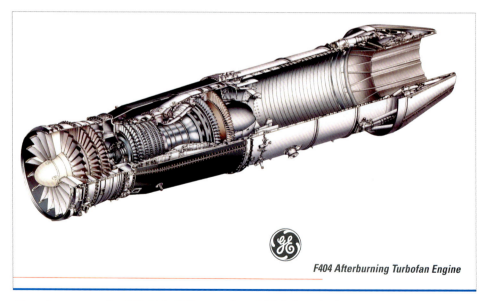

A brochure promoting GE's F404 fighter engine, which is launched by the US Navy in 1975 for the F/A-18 Hornet. The result of a decade of technical refinement, the F404 becomes one of GE's most successful military engine programs.

LM5000 testing: Testing begins on the LM5000 industrial gas turbine, derived from the CF6-50 engine.

T700 flights: First flights of the T700-powered AH-64 Apache attack helicopter are underway.

1978
CF6 engines score the big twins

CF6 family grows: As turbofans get more powerful, Airbus and Boeing introduce competing large twin-engine jetliners, the A310 and 767, respectively, capable of medium-to-long-range passenger flights. The competition between these similar jetliners creates another turbofan showdown between GE and P&W.

In July 1978, Boeing launches the 767 with a thirty-aircraft order from United Airlines, which will deploy some of the planes on transcontinental flights. The engine selection reverberates across the Evendale executive offices because United orders the P&W JT9D over a CF6-50 variant. "Joe Sutter [767 chief engineer] wanted a new engine from us," writes Brian Rowe, GE's commercial engine leader at the time.[34]

The GE engineering team responds with the new CF6-80A in the 50,000-pound thrust class. This engine retains CF6-50 compressor and turbine aerodynamics, but introduces a new support structure for the compressor and turbine rotors to reduce weight and complexity.

Stakes are substantial going into the next 767 campaign involving Delta Air Lines and American Airlines, already a key CF6 customer. Touted "the

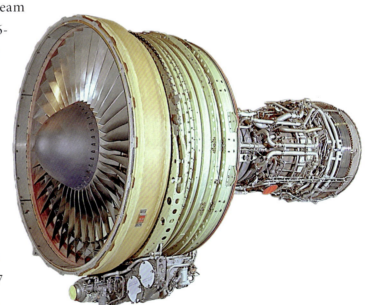

After losing the first Boeing 767 engine competition, GE introduces the CF6-80A in 1978 and wins hefty 767 and Airbus A310 engine orders. The -80A precedes GE's popular CF6-80C2 turbofan.

largest single sales day in Boeing history," Boeing in November sells fifty 767s (thirty for American and twenty for Delta, plus options); the CF6-80A scores all of the 100 installed engines.[35]

The victory is heralded as a significant comeback for GE in the fast-emerging medium-range large jetliner segment. Working to GE's advantage is American's satisfaction with its CF6-powered DC-10s. GE commits to upgrading early-model CF6s at American as part of the agreement.

With both US engine makers launched on the 767, GE and P&W square off on the new twin-engine A310. Swissair selects P&W for its A310s in late 1978, but, early the next year, GE is selected by Lufthansa and KLM Royal Dutch Airlines to power thirty-five aircraft. Eventually, the Rolls-Royce RB211 is also available for the 767 and A310, and another three-way engine battle emerges for large commercial jetliners.

Highly reliable in service, the CF6-80A has a modest production run. However, the engine establishes GE on two strategically important aircraft and is the technical foundation for the most popular CF6 engine of all, the CF6-80C2, aviation's leading high-thrust engine of the 1980s.

✈ Also in 1978…

Boeing 757 launch without GE: In addition to the 767, Boeing also launches the mid-range 757. Rolls-Royce wins the first order for the jetliner with its RB211 engine, and P&W follows with the first win of its PW2037 engine in 1980. GE offers the CF6-32, a 36,500-pound thrust CF6-6 derivative, but eventually abandons the program due to limited GE and customer interest.

Fred MacFee Jr. takes top job: Fred O. MacFee Jr. becomes vice president and group president of the GE Aircraft Engine Group after Gerhard Neumann steps down due to health reasons. For two years, Neumann works as a corporate vice president supporting Vice Chairman Jack Parker at GE headquarters. MacFee heads GE Aircraft Engine Group for one year.

F404 first delivery: The US Navy takes delivery of the first F404-powered F/A-18. The aircraft, an integral part of the Navy fleet for decades, also becomes a successful export aircraft.

T700 first delivery: GE delivers the first T700 to the US Army to power Sikorsky Black Hawk helicopters. This advanced turboshaft soon becomes the world's most popular helicopter engine family for civil and military aircraft.

CFM launches the CFM56-2 for a large DC-8 re-engining program in 1979, just weeks before GE and Snecma plan to suspend the joint development effort.

LM5000 first delivery: The LM5000 industrial gas turbine, derived from the CF6-50 engine, is delivered to its first customer for an electric power generation installation.

GE Aircraft Engine Business Group: A word is added to the name. The GE Aircraft Engine Group is renamed the GE Aircraft Engine Business Group.

1979

Launch saves CFM International

Critical CFM56-2 selection: Several frustrating years follow CFM's formation as the parent companies try to launch its CFM56-2 engine. A study with Boeing on a 707 re-engining program, which predates CFM's formation, is only one effort that goes nowhere. In Europe, CFM pursues studies with Dassault, including one concept jointly proposed with McDonnell Douglas. The projects stall; an airline customer never materializes.

The CFM56-2 is first flight-tested in 1977 on the Sud Aviation Caravelle SE210, the same year US President Jimmy Carter cancels the F101-powered B-1. With the CFM56-2 core derived from the F101, some GE leaders worry that the joint company will never be economically viable without a parallel military program.

By early 1979, patience within GE and Snecma leadership wears thin after having collectively sunk more than $500 million into the joint program. GE Chairman Reginald Jones calls the lack of a CFM56 launch a "personal embarrassment" and tells Gerhard Neumann to make finding a customer his top priority. "I cannot possibly conceive my having to go to the French and tell them that we can't find a home for our joint venture," Neumann writes to Vice Chairman Jack Parker in January 1979.[36]

Chuck Chadwell, a future GE vice president, vividly recalls the Evendale mood within the CFM56 project in early 1979. "I was told to get ready to pack up all of the files and put them into storage," he says. "We thought the whole CFM56 program was over."[37]

However, more stringent noise regulations being evaluated by the FAA on older jetliners like the DC-8 and 707 bolster the CFM56-2 prospects. Boeing and CFM initiate a CFM56-2/707 flight test program in early 1979. At the same time, a program takes shape to re-engine a large fleet of DC-8 jetliners owned by US operators United Air Lines, Flying Tiger Line, and Delta Air Lines.

Freight carrier Flying Tiger Line prefers the more expensive CFM56-2 to a competing offer from P&W for a re-fanned JT8D because of the engine's fuel

United Airlines board member and former astronaut Neil Armstrong endorses the CFM56-2 engine for the DC-8 re-engining program while heading the board's propulsion evaluation team.

efficiency, lower noise, and durability. United and Delta, however, are attracted to the JT8D's commonality with their large P&W engine fleets. In the end, United, with the largest DC-8 fleet of the three operators, will determine CFM's fate.

Former US astronaut and Cincinnati-area resident Neil Armstrong plays a key role in supporting the CFM56-2. He heads United's propulsion evaluation team as a board member and recommends the CFM56-2 over the JT8D derivative favored by many within the airline's engineering team. (Former GE executive Dick Smith, an architect of CFM, reveals Armstrong's critical involvement in the engine launch after the astronaut's death in 2012.)[38]

Finally, CFM launches the CFM56-2 turbofan in March 1979. United, Flying Tiger Line, and Delta, which collectively own the world's largest fleet of four-engine DC-8s, agree to replace the fleet's original P&W JT3Ds with the CFM56-2. CFM nails down the order only weeks before the engine program is slated for suspension. The first engine contract is signed by United to re-engine twenty-nine DC-8s, followed by thirteen for Delta and eighteen for Flying Tiger Line. The re-engined fleet is called the "DC-8 Super 70" series.

With CFM56-2 customers secured, CFM focuses on re-engining the Boeing 707. It results in a game-changing military program the following year.

CHASING JETLINERS 113

Brian H. Rowe era begins: The affable engineer Brian Rowe assumes leadership of GE Aircraft Engine Business Group in 1979, a position that he holds until 1993. After emigrating from England to the US to join GE, he earns his engineering and management stripes on several key programs, including the lift-fan engine, the GE1 demonstrator, and the CF6, for which he serves as program manager from 1967 to 1972, the year he takes over GE's commercial engine division.

It is not lost on Neumann that two Europeans successfully lead GE's aviation business for decades. "Why, one must ask himself, did these two damned foreigners [Neumann and Rowe], amongst the thousands of Americans already aboard the Aircraft Engine Group, get these key jobs?" Neumann writes in his autobiography. "Both of us had the advantage of years of tough apprenticeships before being admitted to engineering schools; both of us were hard-boiled and practical."[39]

Rowe transfers GE's jet engine headquarters from Lynn to Evendale. With a heavy technology focus on engine reliability and customer support, Rowe will lead GE's aviation business during the extraordinary 1980s and leave a lasting impact on the company.

Like Jack Parker, Rowe is a physically imposing figure. He is notoriously outspoken at times but possesses a gentle nature and wit, as well as an infectious smile. Through his technical convictions, he will inspire loyalty from his leadership team while changing the course of jet propulsion.

✈ Also in 1979...

F101 DFE preps for P&W battle: Aware of significant technical issues and USAF frustrations with P&W's F100 engines powering F-16s and F-15s, GE self-funds the F101 Derivative Fighter Engine program, which features a new front fan, an F101 core, and an afterburner derived from the F404. Then, the USAF provides additional seed money for the F101 DFE, setting the stage for "The Great Engine War" between GE and P&W to power fighter jets in the 1980s and beyond.

P&W claims the USAF investment in the F101 DFE is too expensive and illogical. However, those claims fall on deaf ears at the Department of Defense.[40] Successful F101 DFE flight tests on the USAF F-16 in 1980 are followed by similarly stellar flight tests with the engine on the Navy F-14. GE is eager to restore its fighter jet preeminence of the 1950s and 1960s.

CT7 and CF34 breakthroughs: Two of Lynn's stalwart military engines programs, the T700 and TF34, make headway with commercial variants. First, GE designers introduce T700 advanced technology into CT7 commercial turboprop/turboshaft derivatives. A year later, the CT7 turboshaft engine enters service on a Bell 214ST helicopter, the first commercial application for the new GE turboshaft engine.

The TF34's commercial variant, the CF34, is selected in 1979 for the Canadair Challenger 610 business jet. This application marks GE's return to business jets, a market segment GE fostered in the early 1960s. The CF34 is a welcome addition to Lynn's portfolio as its earlier business jet engines, the CJ610 and CF700, have lost ground to new engines from Garrett and P&W.

J79 production ends: J79 production ends, concluding a twenty-five-year program during which nearly 17,000 engines were produced for several historic fighter jets. Powered by the J79, the F-4 Phantom, the B-58 Hustler, the F-104 Starfighter, and the RA-4C jets establish forty-four world speed, altitude, and time-to-climb records.

1980
Refueling tanker fuels CFM

USAF launches F108: The CFM56-2 launch for the Douglas DC-8s re-engining program keeps CFM in business, but long-term economic viability is not really achieved until 1980. The USAF selects the CFM56-2 (designated the F108) to re-engine its massive fleet of four-engine KC-135 refueling tankers. In tandem, the French Air Force commits to re-engine its KC-135 tankers.

Now, CFM is here to stay as the agreement assures a steady engine production run for decades. Twice in two years, the upstart but innovative CFM56-2 defeats the established P&W JT8D in head-to-head competitions.

The USAF KC-135R re-engining program, launched in 1980 with the CFM56-2, is critical to CFM International's long-term viability.

In its public announcement, the USAF cites the F108's lower life-cycle costs, reduced noise, and better supportability. Replacing original P&W J57s, the F108 engines power the tanker's first flights in 1982 and immediately provide far greater takeoff performance, range, and refueling payload.

Securing a Boeing aircraft is a long time coming for CFM. Since the early 1970s, Boeing and CFM have studied a CFM/707 re-engining program for commercial customers. Yet, the tanker program first fosters a strong relationship between the two companies. The first KC-135R (the re-engined aircraft's designation) rolls out in 1982 almost a year ahead of schedule. With the increased payload made possible by the F108, two KC-135Rs equal the fuel transfer capability of three KC-135As.

Through annual engine procurements, the USAF becomes CFM's largest single customer with more than 2,000 F108 engines delivered. Over the next several years, other F108-powered 707 military applications follow, including the E-6A and the E-3A Airborne Warning and Control System (AWACS) aircraft.

✈ Also in 1980...

CT7 for regional airliner: Saab Aircraft selects the commercial turboprop derivative of the T700, the CT7, for its new Saab 340 regional aircraft. The Saab 340 enters service in 1984 and evolves into a highly successful franchise.

1981
A victory changes the competitive landscape

CFM56-3 for Boeing 737: Given the extremely long-cycle nature of the jet propulsion industry, not all landmark events are viewed that way when they happen. A "classic" example is when Boeing selects a CFM56 variant for a new family of single-aisle Boeing 737s, designated the -300, -400, and -500. This best-selling jetliner family will be dubbed the 737 "Classic" series—and for good reason.

Sold first to USAir and Southwest Airlines, the 737 "Classic" breaks P&W's engine lock on single-aisle jetliners and brings CFM's high-bypass turbofan technology to this prolific aircraft segment with the CFM56-3 model. P&W unsuccessfully offers the JT8D-200 engine, a lower-bypass derivative. (In 1980, the P&W PW2000 is launched on Boeing's new 757, which diverts company attention from the 737.)

While the CFM56-3 is one the most important engine launches in CFM and GE history, GE corporate leaders, including new Chairman Jack Welch and Vice

Chairman Ed Hood, initially view the program with skepticism.[41] After all, previous P&W-powered 737-100 and -200 models sold modestly. With so much investment already made with CFM, will the CFM56-3 modifications required for a new 737 series be worth the expense?

Clearly, CFM56-3 installation on the new 737 requires creativity. The front fan, based on the CF6-80A, must be reduced to meet the 737's tight wing clearance. For more accessible flight-line maintenance, the two engines are mounted low to the ground in front of the wing with an oval-shaped nacelle. The accessory gearbox is mounted on the side of the fan casing. Like the CFM56-2, however, the CFM56-3 maintains the efficient, single-stage HPT design for lower maintenance costs.

Brian Rowe claims that hundreds of new 737s will be sold and convinces his GE bosses. Consistent with sales of the earlier 737s, orders for the new jetliner family are modest during the first three years. However, airline deregulation instituted by US President Jimmy Carter in 1978 fuels the expansion of domestic airline operators, such as Southwest Airlines, which aggressively order the new 737s with fuel-efficient, reliable CFM56-3 engines. The GE/CFM competitive position in commercial aviation changes forever.

For more than twenty years, the 737 family is the world's best-selling commercial jetliner. When the last 737 "Classic" is delivered in the year 2000, almost 4,000 CFM56-3 engines have been produced—five times Rowe's original forecast.

✈ Also in 1981...

F101 revived: US President Ronald Reagan restarts the F101-powered B-1 bomber program, with entry into service in the late 1980s. Furthermore, reopening the F101 production line for the B-1 makes the F101 DFE program more cost-effective for the USAF as it seeks a competing engine for F-16 and F-15 fleets. The last engines for the B-1 bomber are produced in Evendale in 1987.

CJ610/CF700 production ends: The final CJ610 and CF700 engines are delivered in 1981. Since the early 1960s, more than 2,000 CJ610 and almost 1,200 CF700 engines are delivered.

While these engines power the lion share of 1960s business jets, GE determines in the early 1970s that business jets do not produce a suitable return on investment. By 1981, however, the mood has changed, and the CF34 is preparing to power Canadair's Challenger 601 business jet.

One decision alters jet propulsion's competitive landscape. Boeing selects the CFM56-3 turbofan over a P&W engine in 1981 for the 737 "Classic" series, which includes this USAir 737-300. It sets the stage for CFM's amazing success in powering single-aisle jetliners.

In secrecy, GE begins testing the F118 engine for the USAF B-2 stealth bomber developed by Northrop in 1982.

Singapore services: GE Aviation Services Operation opens in Singapore reflecting the global acceptance for GE commercial engines and GE's recognition of a growing installed engine base in airline service.

F404 for stealth plane: In secrecy, the non-afterburning F404 powers the first flight of the F-117A stealth fighter for the USAF.

1982
New CFM showdown brews in Europe

Airbus A320 emerges: As CFM busily develops the CFM56-3 engine for its Boeing 737 selection, a competing single-aisle jetliner takes shape in Europe. CFM is soon engaged in another high-stakes engine battle.

At the 1981 Paris Air Show, Airbus Industrie announces a new A320 jetliner for 130-to-150 passengers, throwing down the gauntlet for a head-on battle against the McDonnell Douglas DC-9 and the new Boeing 737.

With a wider fuselage than the Boeing 737, the A320 features a pioneering digital fly-by-wire control system and other electrical and material innovations. Building on the momentum of its A300 and A310 jetliners, Airbus establishes a goal to capture 30 percent of single-aisle jetliners with its A320. The company eventually exceeds its original goal by a wide margin.

In 1982, CFM proposes to Airbus an engine based on the CFM56-2, called the CFM56-4. Rolls-Royce and P&W aggressively offer new engine designs with bold fuel-efficiency claims. Airbus rejects the CFM56-4 variant, demanding a new engine design tailored for the A320.

✈ Also in 1982...

CFM56-2 flying: The CFM56-2 enters service on the DC-8 Super 70 series. CFM is now demonstrating the engine's advantages while also offering even more advanced designs.

F118 behind the curtain: Secret testing begins for the non-afterburning F118 engine, based on the F101 and F110 engines, for the USAF B-2 "Spirit" stealth bomber to be built by Northrop. The B-2 is unveiled in 1988.

CT7 enters service: The CT7 turboprop engine, derived from the T700, enters passenger service. Within ten years, the CT7 will power about 300 turboprop airplanes, including the Saab 340 and the CASA CN-235 aircraft.

1983
CFM's new competitor

GE rivals form IAE: After pursuing competing engine concepts for the new Airbus A320, Rolls-Royce and P&W make peace and join forces with other engine makers to combat the rapid progress of CFM.

International Aero Engines (IAE) is formed as a consortium of P&W (USA), MTU (Germany), Rolls-Royce (UK), Fiat (Italy), and Japan Aero Corporation (Japan) with the objective of developing a new engine family for 150-seat, single-aisle aircraft.

The USAF F-117 stealth fighter, developed by Lockheed and powered by F404 engines, enters its third year of secret flight tests in 1983. The jet is not revealed to the public for another five years.

The ownership was split between P&W (30 percent), Rolls-Royce (30 percent), Japan Aero Corporation (19.9 percent), MTU (12.1 percent), and Fiat (8 percent). The consortium launches the V2500 engine with an initial certification at 23,000 pounds of thrust and deliveries committed for 1988. The new engine is based on technology advances in P&W's PW2037 and PW4000 engines, coupled with the RJ500 engine jointly developed by Rolls-Royce and Japan Aero Corporation.

With the new V2500 design and IAE's claims of superior fuel efficiency, CFM has "no choice but to bite the bullet, get out our checkbooks, and develop a third CFM56 model," writes Brian Rowe.[42] On the heels of the CFM56-3 investment, the parent companies dig in further and initiate development of the CFM56-5 for the A320.

✈ Also in 1983...

GE27 demonstrator launch: The GE Lynn team participates in the Army's "Modern Technology Demonstrator Engine" (MTDE) program with the GE27 demonstrator. Led by Dick Hickock, the team pursues the most modern 5,000-shaft-horsepower turboshaft engine possible, building upon T700 experience.

The full engine runs an axial-centrifugal compressor, featuring an impressive 22:1 pressure ratio. Using single-crystal blades, the HPT operates in the 2,400- to 2,500-degree Fahrenheit temperature range. GE envisions a GE27-based family of turboshaft, turboprop, and turbofan engines.

However, winning applications proves challenging. While the GE27 is not selected for a prime application, the engine core becomes the basis for the CFE738 commercial turbofan later launched by CFE Company, a 50/50 joint company of GE and Garrett.

Then, twenty-five years later, the GE27 is the foundation for the GE38-1B (later designated the T408) selected for the US Army's Sikorsky CH-53K King Stallion. This significant win places GE in a new turboshaft power class for the 21st century.

The exotic UDF engine: In response to rising fuel prices, GE's radical Unducted Fan (UDF) engine design for single-aisle aircraft is revealed. Design drawings of the aft-mounted, unducted fan are released to GE manufacturing to produce initial prototypes. Art Adamson leads the design team on one of the era's most discussed jet engines. The production version is designated the GE36.

F110 takes shape: GE F101 DFE fighter engine is designated the F110 and receives a $112.5 million development contract from the USAF and Navy. A rematch with P&W in the high stakes competition for fighter jets is about to unfold.

CFM56-3 flights: The CFM56-3 begins flight tests on a Boeing 707.

TF39 revival: The USAF orders upgraded TF39s for fifty C-5B Galaxy aircraft. The last TF39 engines are delivered in 1988.

CF34 powers business jets: The CF34-powered Canadair Challenger 601 business jet enters service.

1984
The "Great Engine War"

The arrival of the F110: In February, the anticipated "Great Engine War" unfolds. The first annual US Department of Defense procurement pits the new GE F110 fighter engine head-to-head against P&W's established F100 fighter engine to power USAF F-15s and F-16s.

Even to industry insiders, results from round one are stunning. GE's F110 will power 120 F-16C/D fighter jets, while P&W only wins forty of the aircraft. GE's win is huge, since the F100 has powered every F-16 since the fighter was introduced in the mid-1970s. P&W retains the sole-engine supplier position on USAF F-15s.

GE's Brian Rowe anxiously stays up half the night before the selection watching "I Love Lucy" TV reruns to kill time. In the morning, he learns the GE share is twice as large as he expected. "I was expecting around 30 percent [of the F-16 engines]—get our finger in there and start pushing," he says.[43]

The Hartford Courant, P&W's hometown newspaper in Connecticut, splashes a huge page-one Associated Press photo of a jubilant Rowe learning the news. A framed copy of the edition soon hangs in his second-floor, southwest corner office in Building 501 in Evendale.

Several factors contribute to the GE F110 victory, including the engine's simple mechanical design, unrestricted throttle performance, and demonstrated durability. In addition to praising the engine during flight tests, the USAF is impressed with GE's lower engine support costs, superior spare parts procurement strategy involving competitive sourcing of components, and better warranties.[44]

With the F101 core (compressor, combustor, HPT) established across large military and commercial engine fleets, GE now can more aggressively compete

GE's F110 fighter jet engine is procured for the single-engine F-16C/D fighter jet in dramatic fashion in 1984. An F110 engine sales spree ensues.

on financial terms against the P&W F100.

The GE F110 win also creates a chain reaction. Days later, the US Navy announces that it will replace TF30 engines on the twin-engine F-14 with GE F110-GE-400 engines. Re-engined F-14s are designated F-14A Plus, and new production aircraft with the F110 are called F-14Ds. In May, Israel orders seventy-five GE-powered F-16s, and Turkey follows with 173 GE-powered F-16s.

GE-powered F-16s enter service in 1987. Ultimately, the F110-GE-100 (28,000 pounds of thrust), and its successor, the F110-GE-129 (29,000 pounds of thrust), are best sellers on F-16s worldwide. Many nations, particularly in the Middle East, commit to GE-powered F-16 fleets.

Over the years, the F110 program includes a roll call of GE innovators and strong leaders: George Ward, Jim Krebs, Ed Spear, Brian Brimelow, Russ Sparks, Corbett Caudill, Tom Maxwell, Tom Brisken, Paul Sims, Dan McCormick, Hank Brands, Freeman James, and Dick Anderson, just to name a few.

For this large fraternity of important GE contributors, the F110 engine itself and the extraordinary comeback of GE's fighter engine business remain sources of pride and satisfaction throughout their careers.

CFM56-5 launch on Airbus A320: CFM secures the first engine order for the Airbus A320. Airbus launches the jetliner, with Air France, powered by the new CFM56-5.

CFM invests in substantial engine improvements. The CFM56-5 adopts the CFM56-2 fan size, while adding more efficient fan blades, and an advanced three-stage, fan booster stage, and new LPT. It is the first CFM engine with a full-authority digital electronic control system (FADEC). The CFM56-5 core will take advantage of GE's recent development work on the CF6-80C2 and NASA technology programs.

While the competing V2500 engine claims better fuel efficiency, the CFM56-5's simple, rugged architecture (including the single-stage HPT) proves highly reliable and maintainable on the popular A320. CFM56-5 flight tests on GE's 707 testbed aircraft begin in 1986, and the first flight of the A320 follows in 1987.[45]

The CFM56-5 ultimately wins more engine orders over the next three decades than the V2500. However, both engine programs enjoy an order windfall from the A320 sales success.

✈ Also in 1984...

CF6-80C2 sells like hotcakes: GE tests the high-thrust CF6-80C2 engine in sync with the introduction of several new large jetliners from Airbus, Boeing, and McDonnell-Douglas.

With a production configuration in the 55,000 to 60,000-pound thrust class, the CF6-80C2 incorporates a larger front fan than its predecessors, along with compressor technology from the NASA Energy Efficient Engine program. Both developments contribute to a 13.5 percent specific fuel consumption (SFC) improvement over the CF6-50 engine.

The best-selling CF6 model, the -80C2 becomes the workhorse for large jetliners for the rest of the century and beyond. The engine enters service on the Airbus A300-600 of Thai International Airlines in 1985. Airbus introduces the A300-600 as a response to the new Boeing 767. (CF6-80A engines power early 767s.) Airbus delays the A300-600 introduction to await the efficient CF6-80C2 engine.

The CF6-80C2 soon powers Boeing 767 and 747 families, Airbus A300 families, and the McDonnell Douglas MD-11. It is also selected to power US Air Force One (747).

CFM56-3 enters service: The CFM56-3-powered Boeing 737-300 enters service with Southwest Airlines on December 17, the 81st anniversary of the first flight of the Wright Brothers at Kitty Hawk, North Carolina. A 737 buying spree soon follows. By the late 1980s, the CFM56-3 for the Boeing 737 and the CFM56-5 for the Airbus A320 boast backlogs climbing into the thousands of engines.

T58/CT58 production ends: Production ends after twenty-eight years and more than 6,000 deliveries of GE's first-generation turboshaft/turboprop engine. Jack Parker's original goal in the 1950s of replacing piston engines on helicopters with turboshaft engines is fully realized.

Assessing the T58 legacy, Frank Pickering, GE's vice president of engineering, concludes: "The T58 technical breakthrough was taking an axial-flow compressor and building a successful, efficient compressor in that size—not only from a design standpoint, but learning how to manufacture it, and in a repeatable kind of way."[46]

CT7 variant in service: The CT7-5A-powered Saab 340 enters passenger service.

1985
Military engines roll down the line

The Reagan build-up: The United States military buildup initiated by US President Jimmy Carter in the late 1970s greatly expands under President Ronald Reagan in the early 1980s. By the year 1985, military aircraft and engine production is in full swing. The Evendale and Lynn assembly plants, along with GE's worldwide engine component network, work around the clock to meet aggressive delivery demands.

In 1985 alone, Evendale production begins on the F110-GE-400 (Grumman F-14B/D) for the US Navy, the F110-GE-100 (General Dynamics F-16C/D) for the USAF and international customers, the F118-GE-100 (Northrop B-2) for the USAF, and the TF39 (Lockheed C-5B) for the USAF. Rockwell delivers the first B-1 bomber, powered by the F101, to the USAF.

Employment in Evendale exceeds 15,000 and reaches almost 20,000 by 1987. Eventually, some employees have to be bused into the Evendale complex due to the lack of available parking inside and outside the gates. In Lynn, F404 and T700 production ramp-ups are also well underway.

✈ Also in 1985...

CFM in China: China's first CFM56-powered 737s enter service with Air China Southwest and China Eastern Yunnan. GE and Snecma secure a presence in what will become the largest civil aviation market. Within twenty years, more than 400 GE and CFM-powered passenger jets operate in China.

TEI in Turkey: To support a growing fleet of F110 jet engines in Turkey, Turkish Aerospace Industries and GE create the Tusas Engine Industries (TEI) joint venture with a factory in Eskisehir, Turkey. The facility assembles and tests F110s for Turkish Air Force F-16s. Over time, TEI produces military and commercial components for GE.

Brian H. Rowe honored: Brian H. Rowe is awarded the Chevalier of the Legion of Honor, France's highest civilian honor.

Left to right: Art Adamson, Ed Hood, and Brian Rowe in front of the UDF (Unducted Fan) engine on the Boeing 727 test aircraft. GE's ultra-high-bypass turbofan is the talk of the aviation industry.

1986
The revolutionary UDF engine

UDF fuel efficiency record: Unveiled the year before to a fascinated audience in the exhibit hall at the Paris Air Show, GE's UDF (Unducted Fan) proof-of-concept engine completes ground tests in 1986 and achieves 24,000 pounds of thrust. GE establishes a record for SFC by a turbofan engine.

GE targets the UDF to power a Boeing 7J7 twin-engine jetliner under study. Boeing flies the engine on a Boeing 727-100 testbed aircraft, giving GE the distinction of flying the first "ultra-high-bypass turbofan." Boeing begins marketing the engine/aircraft combination to customers. GE also builds a UDF engine for a McDonnell Douglas MD-80 aircraft to fly the next year.

The UDF's unique design includes counter-rotating, variable-pitch, unducted fan blades driven without a gearbox. The blades are made of carbon-fiber composite material both to reduce weight and ensure engine survival if one of the large fan blades releases. GE anticipates fuel savings of 40 to 70 percent over conventional turbofan engines. The engine's core is derived from the F404.

✈ Also in 1986...

GE-Rolls-Royce fallout: In 1984, Rolls-Royce agrees to assemble twenty-five percent of the CF6-80C2, while GE will assemble the same percentage of the Rolls-Royce RB211-535 for the Boeing 757, on which GE does not have an engine.

In forming the co-production accord, Brian Rowe envisions GE and Rolls-Royce co-marketing the CF6-80C2 and collaborating on future higher-thrust engines. Rowe and Rolls-Royce Chairman Sir William Duncan create the deal, but Duncan dies in November 1984, and his company loses interest in the arrangement.

Two years later, the deal unravels after Rolls-Royce begins to compete against the very CF6-80C2 it is assembling. Rowe publicly unleashes his frustration at the 1986 Farnborough Air Show. "I guess I reacted a little like a wronged lover," he writes.[47] Rolls-Royce is privatized (having fallen under receivership in the 1970s) and develops a three-spool "Trent" engine family, which is formally rolled out in 1988.

CFE738 created: GE and Garrett Engine Division of AlliedSignal (now part of Honeywell) form a 50/50 joint company to produce the CFE738 for the Dassault Falcon 2000 business jet. GE is responsible for the core, derived from the GE27 demonstrator, and Garrett for the fan and low-pressure system. Full-scale development begins in 1988. GE and Garrett fill a mutual engine-thrust gap in their portfolios. The Falcon is the engine's only application.

LM1600 launch: GE launches the LM1600 industrial gas turbine, a F404 aeroderivative, with an order from Ingersoll Rand for a compressor repowering application at the Pacific Gas Transmission Company pipeline in Oregon. Two years later, the LM1600 is selected for a Katana high-speed yacht.

Lynn turboshaft powerhouse: The Lynn plant sets a milestone in turboshaft engine production, shipping more than 15,000 T58, T64, and T700 engines over a stretch of more than thirty years. ✈

1987-

100 YEARS OF REIMAGINING FLIGHT

2006

Big Fans

1987–2006

✈ GE is in an enviable but unfamiliar place as leader in both civil and military jet propulsion. However, as history has proven many times, the aviation climate can quickly change.

✈ After runaway 1980s growth, GE embarks on a radical new turbofan design (GE90) just as both military and civil aviation plummets. GE's aviation employment is cut in half by 1996.

✈ Global events create two decades of aviation turbulence, including the Soviet Union collapse, Operation Desert Storm, oil price shocks, and 9/11 terrorists attacks. Over the same period, GE faces technology challenges, military setbacks, and leadership changes. And yet, GE's aviation business emerges stronger than ever.

✈ Innovative turbofans with huge composite fan blades change airline travel. Building on extraordinary engine reliability, CFM International extends its leadership, while GE powers the golden era of regional jetliners. New strategies evolve for maintaining airline engines as low-cost carriers proliferate.

✈ GE's military engines prove wildly resilient, including a commanding presence and performance in Operation Desert Storm.

✈ GE enters the new century not only an industrial leader, but with its historical culture, values, and vision firmly in place.

1987

The popularity of CF6 turbofans on twin-aisle Airbus, Boeing, and McDonnell Douglas jetliners is driven by reliability, durability, fuel efficiency, and strong product support.

1987
New leaders in jetliner power

Commercial engine leadership: Less than twenty years after GE re-enters the airline industry, the growing CF6 and CFM56 turbofan families are firmly established as both best sellers and leading performers on several popular jetliners.

Since 1968, turbofan selections have favored GE and CFM on a rising wave of new jetliners from regional jets to large twin-aisle jetliners. The die is cast. GE and CFM are positioned for decades to secure more than half of the engine orders for jetliners with 100 or more passengers.

In 1987, GE and CFM commercial turbofan shipments surpass P&W, while GE and CFM secure more than 63 percent of the airlines' multi-year orders during the year. Harry Gray, former head of United Technologies, succinctly describes the situation that year to *The Wall Street Journal:* "GE has been eating Pratt's lunch."[1] However, the storied engine battle between GE, P&W, and Rolls-Royce will continue well into the next century.

As thousands of GE and CFM56 engines power jetliners worldwide, GE's responsive field support organization under Lee Kapor, longtime head of commercial engines, deepens airline relationships. "Capturing the lion's share of the market doesn't just happen," he says. "They [airlines] continue to have confidence that we can consistently meet our commitments. And they have full confidence in our product support."[2]

A340 launches CFM56-5C: After nine airlines order the new long-range Airbus A340 with the IAE "Super-Fan" engine, IAE suspends the program in 1987, citing LPT issues. "Airbus was convinced that a gear-driven Super-Fan engine by IAE would give them what they wanted," Brian Rowe writes. "We did not want to go anywhere near a gear-driven fan design, because gearboxes had always proven to be a weak link in any mechanical system."[3]

Then, Airbus turns to CFM for a propulsion solution. An agreement to power the four-engine A340 with the CFM56-5C is tied to a commitment to launch the GE CF6-80E1 engine on the new twin-engine, Airbus A330 jetliner. The CFM56-5C is derived from the CFM56-5A engine for the A320, with a larger front fan and additional stages to the fan booster and LPT for the aircraft's higher thrust requirement.

✈ Also in 1987...

UDF engine makes progress: The revolutionary UDF engine progresses as the aviation world watches with great interest. After flying on a 727 flying testbed, Boeing selects the engine for a new 7J7 aircraft under study for the 150-seat market. In addition, the McDonnell Douglas MD-80, equipped with one UDF engine, makes its first flight. The engine garners headlines worldwide, as an aircraft launch appears imminent.

CF6-50 durability: Operating like it is just another day in the office, a CF6-50 completes 20,394 hours of operation without a shop visit on a McDonnell Douglas DC-10-30 aircraft for Canadian Airlines International. Such levels of unprecedented reliability across the CF6 engine family help to firmly establish the CF6 family as leaders for large jetliners.

LM500 launched: A TF34 aeroderivative, the LM500 launches on the Royal Danish Navy fast-patrol boats. Two years later, the LM500 is established in the commercial sector on hydrofoil boats.

CF6-80C2 on MD-11: Several airlines launch the CF6-802 engine on the three-engine McDonnell Douglas MD-11, successor to the venerable DC-10.

Same business, different name: GE Aircraft Engine Business Group is renamed GE Aircraft Engines.

1988

Powering the regional jet revolution

CF34-3 for new jet: After launching the successful CF34-powered Canadair Challenger business jet, Canadian aircraft manufacturer Bombardier steps into the uncharted frontier of regional jetliners. GE powers the ride.

Bombardier, which acquired Canadair in 1986, begins a design study in 1987 of a fifty-passenger stretch version of its successful Challenger, believing the range and speed of such a passenger jet in the regional airline space could forever alter route structures worldwide.

The MD-80 test aircraft with the UDF engine on the left side flies from California to the 1988 Farnborough Air Show near London. It is the unique engine's last hurrah.

In 1988, while Bombardier seeks fifty firm aircraft orders to launch the program, the Canadian airframer also reaches financial terms with GE for the CF34-3 turbofan to power the Canadair Regional Jet (CRJ). It is another example of a GE deal with business implications beyond what can be imagined at the time.

During 1988, Canadair forecasts a market for 1,000 regional jets by 1999, a rosy outlook based on projected industry growth and airline deregulation in Europe. With its CRJ better defined, Canadair believes its 1,700-mile range and 530-mile-per-hour speed will enable airlines to establish attractive long thin routes that bypass larger airport hubs.[4]

History supports this argument. Since the late 1970s, US airline deregulation has fueled many new direct routes between smaller cities, as well as "feeder routes," on which turboprop-powered regional aircraft in smaller cities feed passengers into the large-city "hub" airports of major airlines. The business environment appears ripe to replace turboprop-powered aircraft with jet planes on the same routes.

In addition, growing pilot wages by the 1990s lead several large US carriers to subcontract flights to smaller regional airlines with lower pilot wages. "Scope clauses" negotiated by the pilot unions at larger airlines allow for these reduced crew costs for the smaller regional jets. Falling fuel prices by the early 1990s, combined with the greater range of jet power, begin to make regional jets more attractive than turboprop aircraft.

Bombardier launches the CF34-3A1-powered CRJ in 1989, though broad airline acceptance is still many years away. Nevertheless, capitalizing on years of TF34 military and CF34 corporate jet experience, the high CF34-3 reliability on the CRJ influences early sales.

✈ Also in 1988...

GE ETOPS advantage: For many years, the FAA and the International Civil Aviation Organization (ICAO) limit twin-engine jetliners to sixty minutes of flying time away from the nearest airport in the event of an emergency diversion.

In 1985, the FAA and ICAO adopt new standards for Extended Twin Operations (ETOPS) increasing a single-engine diversion from the nearest airport to 120 minutes. To achieve ETOPS status, the engine/aircraft combination must meet stringent reliability rates, including exceedingly rare in-flight engine shutdown events, as well as strict maintenance and operation practices.

In 1988, the standard increases to 180 minutes for single-engine flying time to the nearest airport. Jet engine reliability pushes the agencies to set new ETOPS standards, which, in turn, expand international routes.

For GE, the new ETOPS standards bolster CF6-80A and CF6-80C2 sales, because they are initially the only turbofans to receive 180-minute ETOPS approval for the Boeing 767 and 138-minute ETOPS approval for the Airbus A300 and A310.

UDF's last hurrah at Farnborough: In the most popular flight demonstration at the Farnborough Air Show near London, a UDF engine mounted on the left side of a McDonnell Douglas MD-80 test aircraft flies several times and garners a global audience.

The aircraft also completes a fifteen-thousand-mile round-trip flight from Edwards Air Force Base, California, to Farnborough, and back. During flights, the engine demonstrates a 25 percent improvement in fuel consumption over the much-older P&W engine on the opposite side.

Despite the excitement and banner headliners, the UDF engine is already doomed. Fuel prices stabilize, and Boeing backs out of the 7J7 aircraft in 1987, leaving an MD-91/92 as the lone potential application. There are no takers.

As sales for CFM56-powered 737s and A320s soar, even GE begins to question the UDF engine program. "When the CFM56 took off, we thought, 'What the hell?' All we'd be doing is killing our own business," Brian Rowe says.[5] He is lukewarm on the MD-91/92 concept, believing the UDF requires a new jetliner designed around the engine to maximize its attributes. The UDF engine ends up on display at the Smithsonian Air & Space Museum in Washington, D.C.

J85 production ends: Production ends for the J85 and its variants, with more than 12,000 engines delivered over four decades. The J85-powered F-5 becomes the standard air defense aircraft for more than twenty-five nations in the 1960s and 1970s. Even though production ends, upgraded J85s will power USAF T-38 Talon trainers well into the 21st century.

RM12 for Sweden: An upgraded F404 for Sweden's JAS 39 Gripen single-engine fighter, designated the RM12 engine, begins flight tests.

CFM56-5A enters service: The CFM56-5A enters revenue service on the Airbus A320 with Air France.

1989
The high-thrust workhorse

CF6 scores amazing order: American Airlines agrees to the single largest engine purchase agreement from an airline in GE history. American will purchase up to 200 GE CF6-80C2 and CF6-80E1 engines through 1995 for twin-aisle jetliners yet to be ordered. The deal is expected to generate more than $2 billion for GE over the agreement's life.

The unusual deal covers CF6 pricing structures tied to agreed-upon volume levels. It doesn't specify which jetliners American orders. CF6 engines already power various large jetliners for the airline. Orchestrated by GE sales leaders Ed Bavaria and Frank Byrd, the agreement further cements the CF6-80C2's place as the era's bestseller for twin-aisle jetliners.

The win also impacts GE's growing installed base of high-thrust engines in airline service, and influences the company's services strategy in the following decade.

✈ Also in 1989...
F118 flies: GE delivers F118 engines to the USAF for flight tests on the radar-eluding B-2 stealth bomber. GE reveals details on the F118: the engine shares the F101

The USAF B-2 stealth bomber, developed by Northrop and powered by four F118 engines, begins flight tests in 1989.

engine core and the same fan case and fan duct as the F110. Due to this commonality, the F110 and F118 will cost the same for the USAF. The F118 front fan increases airflow by six percent over the F110.

F110-GE-129 production: Production begins on the F110-GE-129 Improved Performance Engine (IPE) rated at 29,000 pounds of thrust for F-16C/D fighter jets.

CFM56-5 for A321: Airbus launches the A321, a stretch version of the A320 single-aisle jetliner, with the CFM56-5 engine.

1990
Brian Rowe's bold vision

Unveiling the GE90: Commercial aviation in the 1980s gives rise to the era of large twin-engine jetliners such as the Airbus A330 and Boeing 767. In addition, driven by reliable high-thrust turbofans, new ETOPS regulations enable airlines to create direct international routes that are flown more efficiently with these aircraft.

Rowe believes twin-engine jetliners will continue to fly longer distances over water, carry more passengers, and demand more engine thrust than ever before. Boeing supports his view at the Paris Air Show in June 1989, forecasting that higher-thrust turbofans will power a new generation of more capable, twin-engine jetliners.

At the show, Boeing also reveals studies for its 767X aircraft (later designated the 777) to fill a gap in its product family between its medium-to-long range 767 and the very-long-range, four-engine 747. Boeing establishes "working together" airline teams that offer hundreds of suggestions for a 325-seat airplane aimed at greatly improved economics.

GE considers developing a CF6-80C2 derivative for the 777, but concludes that it cannot efficiently exceed 75,000 pounds of thrust. This shortfall exposes a potential weakness in GE's portfolio, a view not lost on financial analysts. "The CF6-80C2 is limited in thrust because of its smaller core," says analyst David Gardner of Nomura Securities of Japan in late 1989. "As we go into the 1990s, GE could have a big problem."[6]

Rowe and his team make a bold move. Betting that future twin-engine jetliners will need turbofans generating more than 100,000 pounds of thrust, they move daringly to position the company's turbofan strategy for the 1990s and beyond.

Two weeks into 1990, Rowe hosts a satellite broadcast from the basement of Building 100 in Evendale to announce the GE90, the largest and most powerful turbofan in aviation history. The prime application is the 777 and other future jetliners.

The GE90 is the company's first new centerline turbofan design in twenty-five years (since the TF39) and its first civil engine not derived from a military engine design. Starting with a "clean sheet of paper," GE can optimize the engine cycle for both better SFC and future thrust growth. "The GE90 will be the engine that will lead the way into the 21st century," Rowe tells a worldwide audience.[7]

Record thrust levels with lower noise, emissions, and fuel consumption requires many innovations. Drawing from the UDF composite fan blade technology, the GE90 adopts carbon-fiber composite fan blades. Because the GE90's front fan is so large at 123 inches (a diameter comparable

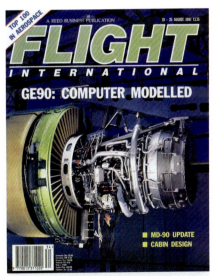

The GE90 becomes larger than life. GE must overcome technical and business hurdles before the GE90 proves itself and changes the course of jet propulsion.

to the Boeing 727 fuselage), titanium blades and a metal fan containment system would cause a massive weight penalty. Composite blades significantly reduce overall engine weight.

Similarly, large bird ingestion tests, required for engine certification, would be problematic with titanium blades of this size. GE has already successfully demonstrated bird-strike tolerance with birds up to eight pounds using the UDF composite blades. The GE90 capitalizes on this track record.

The composite material is comprised of carbon fiber in a resin matrix formed into thin sheets. These sheets of composite material are layered over one another to form the blade, then heated and pressurized to merge the resin and lock the fibers into place. This advanced composite technology builds upon decades of GE research.

The huge fan system requires a super high-energy engine core to turn it. The GE90 compressor is a scaled version of the GE/NASA Energy Efficient Engine (E3) developed earlier. The GE90 is designed with the highest fan bypass ratio in commercial aviation (9:1), combined with an overall pressure ratio exceeding 40:1, resulting in the greatest propulsive efficiency of its day.

Rowe explains the GE90 in simple terms: The slow-turning front fan creates enormous thrust with significantly reduced noise, while the fast-turning HPC provides better fuel efficiency and lower emissions. In other words, the engine core works hard so the fan doesn't have to.

GE90 program leader Ron Welsch and engineering leader Ambrose Hauser recruit some of GE's best young talent for the exciting GE90 design, including David Joyce (future GE Aviation president and CEO), who leads the design team for the control system.

Rolls-Royce and P&W quickly enter the 777 competition, and a brutal three-way engine battle ensues. GE's two competitors opt for more conservative growth derivatives of the Rolls-Royce Trent and PW4000 engines.

While the GE90 creates tremendous industry buzz, its future success faces huge challenges from the outset. For one, Airbus remains committed to four-engine aircraft like the A340, and McDonnell Douglas, which fails to launch another twin-aisle jetliner after the MD-11, merges with Boeing later in the decade. The GE90 will power only the 777.

The initial 777-200 model for intercontinental flights requires no more than 75,000 pounds of thrust, leaving the GE90 heavier and more expensive than the competing engines. As many analysts predict, Boeing moves slowly in growing the 777 in order to avoid competing directly with its popular four-engine 747.

The GE90's unique composite fan blades concern some airlines. The 777 will be the first commercial jetliner able to achieve FAA ETOPS certification at service entry, an important selling point for the aircraft. However, this objective requires stringent requirements especially tough for a new baseline engine.

As key revenue-sharing participants on the GE90, Snecma, FiatAvio, and Volvo Aero will join GE to confront the tough years ahead.

✈ Also in 1990...

Paradigm revenues shift: GE Aircraft Engines produces revenues of $7.5 billion in 1990: 50 percent commercial engines and services, 45 percent military engines and services, and five percent marine and industrial. For decades, military engines have accounted for most of the company's revenues and profits. From 1990 onward, GE's growing commercial engines and services portfolio will be the largest share of revenues and income, reflecting a new era in the company's history.

Going forward, a significant contributor to this revenue shift is the 1991 collapse of the Soviet Union, terminating the global Cold War standoff. Years of hefty US defense procurement end, forcing painful moves within GE Aircraft Engines operations, despite the fact that the GE and CFM base of engines in service is growing fast.

GE and P&W revisit SST concepts: While the longtime engine rivals battle head-to-head to power the 777, GE and P&W jointly conduct a feasibility study to produce a Mach 1.5 to Mach 3.5 long-range civil transport. The GE/P&W team focuses first on both advanced propulsion materials for a new combustor and exhaust concepts to tackle emissions and noise.

Enthusiasm for supersonic jetliners is in the air. In Europe, Rolls-Royce and Snecma, joint producers of the Olympus engine for the Concorde, pursue a similar study. With airline traffic growing dramatically in the Pacific region, the aerospace industry believes that demand exists for high-speed jetliners.

The next year, NASA awards the GE/P&W team a $177 million research contract over nine years to develop advanced, high-temperature composite materials for variable-geometry engine designs. Engine certification is forecasted for 2005, with a 2010 aircraft service entry.[8]

Within three years, however, the project is dismantled. In additional to technical risk, the dramatic commercial aviation recession of the early 1990s, exacerbated by the 1991 Gulf War, kills all enthusiasm for the program.

CF6-80E1 thrust: The CF6-80E1 for the Airbus A330 attains a thrust level of 73,000 pounds during ground tests. The engine has a ninety-six-inch front fan, an advanced fan booster from Snecma, new single-crystal airfoils in the LPT, and advanced engine core materials.

F110-GE-129 deliveries: F110-GE-129 Increased Performance Engines (IPE), rated at 29,000 pounds of thrust, are delivered to the USAF to power F-16 aircraft in a field-service evaluation.

1991
GE military engines: ecstasy & agony

GE powers Desert Storm: In January, GE military engines are the propulsion backbone for one of the largest military air campaigns in world history.

During the five weeks of Operation Desert Storm, the US-led response to Iraq's invasion of Kuwait, about 80 percent of all US and Allied military aircraft in the conflict are GE powered—more than 5,000 engines in all. The air campaign, orchestrated by USAF Lt. General Chuck Horner, involves 2,000 US and Allied attack aircraft (1,800 from the US) flying more than 100,000 sorties.

GE-powered aircraft, encompassing more than forty years of jet propulsion innovation, include F-16s, F-18s, F-4s, Black Hawk and Apache helicopters, and numerous military transports. The F404-powered F-117 stealth fighters, which destroy Baghdad's command and control centers, inspire headlines across the US. In addition, the TF34-powered A-10 "Warthog" aircraft fleet destroys 1,000 Iraqi tanks and 2,000 vehicles.

For veterans of GE's military engine business, the fleet performance is particularly satisfying. "For years, engine reliability was a huge concern for the US military," says Bob Turnbull, head of GE's military division, in 1991. "The amazing performance of the fleet in Operation Desert Storm was almost treated like a given. That shows the tremendous progress we made."[9]

While the Gulf War provides a dramatic display of GE technology, the conflict also creates a chain reaction leading to a major aviation recession. Fuel prices skyrocket during the war, passenger travel declines, and numerous airlines face bankruptcy. Add the defense procurement declines created by the collapse of the Soviet Union, and the aviation industry radically retrenches.

Painful YF120 decision: Only two months after Operation Desert Storm, GE's military engine operation faces a stunning defeat with far-reaching impact. After a five-year competition, the USAF selects the P&W YF119 engine over GE's YF120 variable-cycle engine for the Advanced Tactical Fighter, soon designated the F-22. Air Force Secretary Donald Rice states that P&W underbid GE, adding that the Lockheed aircraft and P&W engine combination "offer better capability at lower cost."[10]

That assessment is hard for GE's leadership to swallow. GE spent $200 million of its own money, involving more than 1,000 engineers and technicians, to develop the YF120 variable-cycle design, recognized within the US Department of Defense as a remarkable propulsion achievement.

The engine's unique bypass doors near the front fan enable the engine to operate as a more fuel-efficient, low-bypass turbofan at subsonic speeds and as a hotrod turbojet at supersonic speeds. During USAF flight test evaluations, the YF120-powered Northrop ATF prototype's top speeds are classified— and remain so to this day.

Days before the ATF engine decision, government insiders and aerospace analysts are betting against GE. A dramatic multi-year drawdown of the US defense budget is underway. P&W's public campaign in the final weeks of the competition raises the issue of "US industrial base," suggesting the possibility that a GE selection will leave only one viable US military engine supplier in the future. Perhaps GE's dominant engine presence in Desert Storm is now working against the company.

Some analysts are not subtle about the industrial base issue. "We hope that the Air Force realizes that if it picks GE, Pratt could quite well be out of the military business," David Franus, analyst with Forecast International, says three days before the decision.[11] Longtime analyst Nicholas Heymann of County NatWest Securities concludes, "It's a question of how do you keep two guys going."[12]

Even worse for GE, the ATF engine selection better positions the P&W engine for the upcoming multi-service Joint Strike Fighter (JSF) program. At the time, production estimates for the multi-national JSF aircraft range from 3,000 to 5,000 aircraft.

✈ Also in 1991...

GE90 launch in England: Eighteen months after the GE90 development is announced, GE secures a launch customer. British Airways selects the GE90 for the 777-200 in a must win amid a brutal financial battle against P&W and Rolls-Royce. Days later, Brian Rowe celebrates by being photographed sipping tea standing inside the GE90's fan module.

In parallel with the selection, GE acquires the British Airways engine overhaul shop in Nantgarw, Wales. Suddenly, GE is overhauling P&W and Rolls-Royce engines. The Wales operation influences GE to develop a strategy in the 1990s to broaden service offerings on competitor engines. This new dynamic also contributes to years of internal soul-searching on the best approach for GE's fast-growing engine services business.

Improved CFM56-5: Testing of the improved CFM56-5B for A320 jetliners begins. The -5B increases airflow with a new fourth stage in the LPT. The engine core is common to the CFM56-5C on the A340.

McDonnell Douglas and GE move quickly to introduce the F414-powered F/A-18E/F Super Hornet in 1992. The F414 team delivers on a highly successful engine development program.

CF6-80C2 goes presidential: The new US Presidential Air Force One, a CF6-80C2-powered Boeing 747-200, enters operational service with George H. W. Bush as its first Presidential passenger.

Frank Homan honored: GE's longtime CFM56 project manager, Frank Homan, is awarded the Chevalier of the Legion of Honor, France's highest civilian honor.

1992
Powering a super-sized Hornet

New Hornet for F414: As if the F-22 engine decision were not enough for GE, the US Department of Defense in 1991 also cancels the US Navy A-12 carrier-based stealth bomber due to delays and cost overruns. Meanwhile, the aircraft's non-afterburning GE F412 engine in Lynn is near completion and meeting specifications without significant issues.

With the A-12 (developed by McDonnell Douglas and General Dynamics) now out of the picture, McDonnell Douglas and GE move quickly to develop a replacement. After all, the Navy still needs a medium-attack aircraft. The companies define a larger carrier-based F/A-18E/F Super Hornet equipped with a new GE F414 engine, successor to the F404. The powerplant includes an improved engine core from the F412 engine, a bright spot salvaged from the failed A-12 program.

In July 1992, the GE military team breathes easier. The Navy awards a $754 million engineering and manufacturing development contract to GE for the F414, the largest military development contract in Lynn's long history. In the 22,000-pound thrust class, the F414 produces 35 percent more thrust than the F404, even though both engines are nearly the same size. The F414 has one of the highest thrust-to-weight ratios (9:1) of any fighter engine ever created.

The engine also benefits from recent GE investments in the YF120, the F110, and the RM12 fighter engines. The front fan generates a 16 percent increase in airflow over the F404 and incorporates bird-strike tolerance features from the RM12 (for Sweden's Gripen JAS 39) and the F412.

The F412-derived hot section evolves from Lynn's successful GE23A demonstrator engine. The first three stages of the F414's compressor are a blisk design. The control system is derived from the YF120, as well as an afterburner derived from technologies across GE's portfolio of fighter engines.

The F414 program, first led by Dick Ruegg, is hitting all performance and schedule benchmarks right from the onset, a huge boost to GE's military operations. It begins ground tests in 1993, which is two-and-a-half-years before first flight. The Super Hornet proceeds quickly and becomes one of the era's most produced fighter jets.

✈ Also in 1992...

CF34-3 enters regional service: CF34-3A1 engines power the first fifty-passenger Canadair Regional Jet (CRJ100), which enters service with Lufthansa CityLine in Germany. The performance for Lufthansa CityLine is outstanding: no engine-caused flight delays, in-flight shutdowns, or unscheduled removals in more than 2,000 training and revenue flights in the first six months.

Lufthansa raves that the CF34-3's fuel burn is even lower than expected, which reduces annual operating costs per aircraft by $100,000 compared to original cost estimates.[13] Word spreads quickly that the new CRJ operates like a mature jetliner. US airlines will lead a CRJ surge in popularity later in the decade, which ramps CF34 production at a critical time for GE.

CFM56-5C certified: The CFM56-5C2 and CFM56-5C3 are certified for the four-engine Airbus A340 program.

1993
CFM's next engine for new Boeing 737

Boeing launches new CFM56 engine: Since the 1980s, a strong relationship has been forged between Boeing and CFM on the best-selling 737 "Classic" series. It pays huge dividends for CFM when Boeing commits to upgrade the wildly popular jetliner.

In November 1993, Southwest Airlines launches the new CFM56-7 engine for the Boeing "Next-Generation" 737 Series. As the sole engine for a new family of 737s, CFM will extend its leading position on single-aisle jetliners well into the 21st century.

The launch is an emotional boost to GE and Snecma. The aviation recession is driving sharply lower revenues and engine deliveries. Thousands of jobs at both companies are being eliminated. Boeing is no less immune and cuts its overall commercial aircraft production by 35 percent in 1993 alone.

The CFM56-7 for Boeing's "Next-Generation" 737 Series continues the strong relationship between CFM and Boeing. Boeing launches the jetliner in 1993 amid a severe aviation recession. Within a decade, the aircraft family sets sales records.

Nevertheless, Boeing must protect the future of its best-selling jetliner. Competing head-to-head against the innovative Airbus A320, the company commits to developing a faster, longer-range 737 with redesigned wings for greater fuel capacity. Despite the current aviation slump, Boeing projects that thousands of Next-Generation 737s will be sold between 1997 and 2010.[14]

Obviously, this is a difficult time for investing in a new engine development. However, the new CFM56-7 will incorporate technology derived from the recent GE90 and CF34 developments, as well as the CFM56-5B upgrade package for the Airbus A320.

These improvements are needed. The CFM56-7 must significantly improve performance with little change in size from the CFM56-3. CFM commits to Boeing's demand for 15 percent lower maintenance costs and 20 percent longer on-wing life over the CFM56-3. In service, the CFM56-7 is expected to demonstrate eight percent better SFC.

To protect its exclusive position, GE and Snecma roll out an aggressive technology package. Snecma provides a sixty-one-inch front fan with titanium wide-chord blades designed with 3D aero computer modeling and a redesigned LPT.

GE's core is built on component and material improvements from the CFM56-5B/P, along with a new 3D aero-designed booster section. The engine is offered with either GE's single- or double-annular combustor (DAC), developed for the CFM56-5B to address Europe's NOx (nitrous oxide) emission regulations.

GE focuses heavily on building EGT (exhaust gas temperature) margin for lower maintenance and on-wing life. GE introduces N5 single-crystal blades into the HPT after having proven the technology in the F110 fighter engine.

For two years prior to launching the new 737 series, Boeing and CFM work closely on the configuration, focusing heavily on reducing aircraft noise while improving fuel burn and maintenance costs.

✈ Also in 1993...

Gene Murphy heads business: Brian Rowe retires after an extraordinary tenure at the helm of GE Aircraft Engines. Gene Murphy replaces him. He is an attorney, former RCA executive, and ex-head of GE Aerospace, which has been recently sold.

During the aviation recession, Murphy drives dramatic cost cutting. Between 1993 and 1996, GE Aircraft Engines worldwide employment drops from 34,000 to 22,000. Enthusiasm at the corporate headquarters for the aviation business is waning. Nonetheless, determined GE engine program leaders introduce some of the era's most important jet engines and will strongly position the business for the new century.

GE90 record thrust: GE90 ground tests begin at Peebles, Ohio, followed by flights on the GE flying testbed aircraft in Mojave, California. Later in the year, on a test stand at Peebles, the GE90 generates a record thrust of 105,400 pounds.

Durham plant: GE opens its Durham, North Carolina, factory for GE90 assembly. A new generation of manufacturing and shop-floor teaming processes is introduced in Durham, which will influence the entire GE factory network. Over time, additional engine models are assembled in Durham, including the GEnx, the CF34, and the LEAP engines. The Durham plant represents the genesis of a gradual decentralizing of GE's engine supply chain. While manufacturing volume in Evendale and Lynn continues to decline, GE opens a network of smaller, specialized factories across the US and internationally.

CFAN created: GE and Snecma create a 50/50 joint company called CFAN to produce GE90 composite fan blades at a manufacturing site in San Marcos, Texas. (Later, GEnx composite fan blades are produced there.) CFAN furthers the strong collaboration between GE and Snecma, which gains experience through CFAN for its own journey to develop composite technology for the LEAP engine into the next century.

F110 at 1,000: The USAF takes delivery of the 1,000th F110-powered F-16/CD. Over eight years, almost 1,900 F110 engines are delivered to power F-16s for the US military and foreign governments, as well as for US Navy F-14s.

CFM56-5 distance record: The Airbus A340, powered by the CFM56-5C engine, enters service. The aircraft sets a world record for long-distance flight, traveling from Paris, France, to Auckland, New Zealand.

CFM56-5 in service: The CFM56-5B-powered A320 and A321 enter revenue service.

1994
F-16 fighter engine leadership

Great Engine War great for GE: In the 10th and final year of the US Department of Defense's "Great Engine War," the annual engine procurement competition between GE and P&W for the USAF F-16s and F-15s, the GE F110-GE-129 receives 100 percent of the F-16 engines. P&W retains its sole F-15 engine position.

During the ten-year competition, the GE F110 wins 75 percent of the F-16 engines. US procurement of F-16 engines continues for several years in smaller volume, and international F-16 engine competitions stretch on for decades.

The Pentagon praises the "Great Engine War" as a model competitive program that dramatically reduces engine operating costs, improves overall fleet readiness, and saves taxpayers billions of dollars. By the turn of the century, 100 percent of all "combat-coded" F-16s in the active USAF fleets are powered by the F110 engine.

✈ Also in 1994…

F118 for spy plane: The USAF reveals that the U-2 high-altitude "spy plane" will be re-engined with the F118, yet another application for the storied F101 engine core. The re-engined U-2, designated the U-2S, weighs 1,200 pounds less than J75-powered U-2s. The F118 creates better aircraft range and payload, while improving fuel burn by 15 percent. A fleet of thirty-seven U-2S aircraft is re-engined and will remain in service into the next century.

The USAF re-engines a fleet of U-2 "spy planes" with the F118 engine.

Key GE90 tests: GE90 carbon-fiber composite fan blades complete medium bird-strike certification tests at Peebles, Ohio. The results boost GE90 sales efforts. Some airlines express concern about the new technology after the FAA enacts new bird-ingestion testing standards, including special conditions for the GE90 fan blade. The GE90 completes an eight-pound (large) bird test the next year. Industry fears will prove unwarranted. GE90 fan blades perform with extraordinary reliability and durability, including during bird-ingestion events.

In the same year, four separate GE90 engines exceed 100,000 pounds of thrust during ground tests, demonstrating the thrust potential to power future 777 variants.

Growing T700: GE launches the T700/T6E growth program with Alfa Romeo Avio (Italy) and FiatAvio (Italy), along with participation from Hamilton Standard (US) and EGT (UK). Civil and military applications are pursued.

CFM56-3 reliability: The CFM56 family's remarkable reliability and durability make headlines. A CFM56-3 with Germania Flug logs 20,000 flight hours over six years without a shop visit. That same year, six CFM56-3 engines accumulate more than 17,000 flight hours without a shop visit. CFM56 reliability will influence airlines to fly A320 and 737 fleets more aggressively.

Chengdu, China: GE and CFM International establish an engine maintenance training school in Chengdu, China, bolstering their presence in a country where more than 340 GE and CFM56 engines have been delivered or ordered. Other GE/CFM facilities in China soon follow.

CF6-80E1 enters service: The CF6-80E1 enters service on the twin-engine Airbus A330. The fleet logs more than 10,000 initial flight hours without an unscheduled engine shop visit, establishing a reliability rate comparable to the CF6-80C2.

Rolls-Royce acquires Allison: In an aggressive US expansion, Rolls-Royce acquires Allison Engine Company in Indianapolis, Indiana, for $525 million to expand its portfolio of helicopter and large military turboprop engines. Allison and its new owner will soon collaborate with GE on the government-funded "Alternate Engine Program" for the multi-service JSF program.

1995
Regional jets take a growth step

CF34 for bigger regional jets: The fifty-passenger Canadair Regional Jet (CRJ100) makes steady progress in its first two years in service. Six airlines operate fifty aircraft, which are demonstrating the reliability of mature jetliners. By late 1994, Bombardier has the confidence to pursue a larger, seventy-passenger version with even better economics called the CRJ700.

GE has the inside track to supply the turbofan for the new aircraft, after bringing high reliability to the CRJ100 with the CF34-3 engine. Over several weeks of discussions, GE and Bombardier move close to an exclusive engine agreement for the CRJ700. GE offers the growth CF34-8C, which will produce 50 percent more thrust than the CF34-3 while requiring minimal change to the engine nacelle.

Then, the plot thickens. With GE90 program costs straining development budgets at GE Aircraft Engines right in the middle of a severe aviation recession, GE corporate leaders challenge the funding proposal for the CF34-8C program.

Chuck Chadwell, GE's head of commercial engines, has no time to waste. He promptly orders Lloyd Thompson, head of CF34 programs, to camp out at Bombardier headquarters in Montreal, Canada, until a deal is signed between the two companies. "Lloyd was not to come home without a contract in his hands," Chadwell recalls.[15]

The strategy works. In February of 1995, the freshly signed contract with Bombardier legally obliges GE to develop the new CF34-8C, which uses a larger widechord front fan and a new seven-stage compressor derived from the F414 fighter engine to boost the thrust to 13,000 pounds. The 3,000 hours of F414 compressor testing builds confidence in the commercial engine program.

The CF34-8C also adopts the F414's blisk (disc and blades fabricated as a single piece) design for the first three compressor stages. Drawing from CFM56-7 and F110 experience, the HPT blades are made of single-crystal material to better manage the higher operating temperatures. The engine's multi-holed combustor is derived from both the F414 and GE90 engines.

Ishikawajima-Harima Heavy Industries Co. of Japan plays a significant role as the leading revenue-sharing participant.

Bombardier's seventy-passenger CRJ700 powered by the CF34-8C turbofan.

While GE is confident in the new engine, CRJ700 sales still require a leap of faith because the fifty-passenger CRJ has yet to gain momentum with airlines. (The sales proliferation occurs a few years later.) Bombardier is counting on the CRJ700 to fill a market need between the fifty-passenger CRJ and 100-to-120-passenger jetliners from Boeing and Airbus. Bombardier launches the CRJ700 in 1997 with Brit Air, based in Morlaix, France.

Over time, the CF34-8C proves to be a terrific investment for GE. By 2000, 100 CRJ700s are on firm order, mostly with US and European airlines, and hundreds more are on the books as option orders that are firmed up over time.

Additional CF34-powered variants of the CRJ700 are introduced later in the 1990s, and the entire family of CRJs becomes even bigger sellers in the next century. These aircraft far exceed the market outlook back when Thompson was ensconced in Montreal busily closing the engine deal while his boss back in Evendale waited by the phone.

✈ Also in 1995...

GE90 enters service: On February 2, the GE90-powered Boeing 777 makes its maiden flight in Seattle with the new turbofan's "father" watching nervously near the runway. "It was the first 'first flight' of an aircraft powered by a GE engine that I ever witnessed in person and I was hoping I wouldn't jinx it," writes Brian Rowe.[16]

The retired GE executive's anxiety reflects several tough months in which GE90 development faces public setbacks, including a failed bird-strike test (remedied by modified fan platform spacers) and an engine surge during flight tests. Troubling for GE shareholders, the investment community focuses on the nearly $2 billion sunk into the GE90 only to find the large turbofan trailing Rolls-Royce and P&W in overall 777 engine sales.

However, Russ Sparks, a slow-talking, highly-respected engineer managing the GE90 program since late 1992, stabilizes a tumultuous development effort, while ace GE engineer Corbett Caudill (the company's future head of engineering) leads the technical team in addressing various GE90 issues.

Sparks tells *The Wall Street Journal* in mid-1995 that GE has "taken its pain upfront with a new engine that will grow with the [777] program." He compares the GE90 to a "puppy with large ears and feet. We just need to grow into it."[17] His homespun analogy, while drawing a few chuckles in the halls of Evendale, is correct. With the baseline GE90 certified, the team is already testing a growth GE90 variant for higher-thrust 777 requirements.

In December 1995, the GE90 enters service on a British Airways 777-200 after achieving certification at 84,700 pounds of thrust. However, the 180-minute Extended Twin Operations (ETOPS) "out of the box" approval is delayed almost a year.

Meanwhile, GE90 data in 1995 are posted on a new communications tool called the World Wide Web.

Bold services moves: 1995 marks a new era for GE's engine services strategy. The company consolidates its overhaul and component repair operations with the engine spare parts department within commercial engines to form a separate business unit called GE Engine Services.

While servicing CFM56, CF6, CF34, and GE90 turbofans, GE also competes to overhaul P&W JT8 and JT9, and Rolls-Royce RB211 engines. GE spends $150 million in new facilities and technologies while introducing new programs such as Maintenance Cost Per Hour (MCPH), in which customers pay a flat rate for each hour an engine is flown, and GE provides all the maintenance.

The program grows in popularity because it enables airlines to forecast and budget engine operational costs more accurately. Key carriers such as Southwest Airlines, British Airways, KLM, and Continental Airlines are among GE's early MCPH customers.

CF34 smooth introduction: The longer-range Canadair Challenger 604 is introduced with the CF34-3B, which achieves three percent better specific fuel consumption than previous CF34 engines for improved aircraft range and faster climb rates.

The performance improvements are achieved through higher compressor airflow and greater turbine efficiency.

Shut out of JSF: Lockheed, Boeing, and Northrop Grumman, each competing for the multi-service US Joint Strike Fighter (JSF) program, select the P&W F119 engine for JSF integration studies. McDonnell Douglas initially selects GE's F120 engine, but the airframer then teams with Northrop Grumman. Eventually, they design an aircraft configuration using the F119 engine. Lockheed wins the JSF airframe selection. Though GE's engine is locked out of the program, the company's long saga with the JSF is only warming up.

CFM56-5 upgrade: A CFM56-5B/P improvement package is launched for the Airbus A320 as CFM becomes the leading turbofan provider on the popular A320 family.

F414 flies: The F414-powered F/A-18E/F Super Hornet begins a highly successful flight test program.

Around the world: Two USAF B-1Bs, powered by the F101, complete nonstop, around-the-world flights.

CFE738 enters service: The CFE738-powered Falcon 2000 begins passenger service.

1996
The unique engine alliance

GE and P&W partner: A casual conversation between GE and P&W executives at the Singapore Air Show eventually leads the companies to create the "GE P&W Engine Alliance" to jointly develop a high-thrust turbofan for proposed Boeing 747-500X and -600X jetliners being offered to airlines.

Intense rivals since the dawn of US jet power, GE and P&W establish the surprise company to develop a turbofan with well-defined thrust parameters exclusively for four-engine aircraft.

Business realities drive the formation of this team of rivals. Boeing rejects competing offers from GE and P&W to power its 747 stretch variants with GE CF6 and PW4000 turbofans. The airframer wants the improved performance of a new turbofan at the same time GE and P&W wage a costly financial war to power the Boeing 777. "We each know how to make the perfect engine but they are too costly," says P&W President Karl Krapek.[18]

The jointly developed GP7200 engine marries GE90 core technology with a P&W low-pressure system (front fan and LPT) from the PW4000. Final engine assembly is performed at P&W operations in Connecticut. GE's Larry Scott, former CF6 program

The Engine Alliance develops the highly reliable GP7200 large turbofan.

manager, is the new company's first president. Like CFM, the actual joint company has fewer than 25 employees, while the two parent companies provide the resources.

However, the Engine Alliance ("GE P&W" from the name is eventually removed) establishes a single, unified sales team comprised of both parent companies. "It was important to unify sales as one team with good GE people willing to work closely with P&W and vice versa," says Bruce Hughes, who (like US President Grover Cleveland) serves two separate terms as Engine Alliance president. "We parked our competitive differences at the door and got on with it."[19]

✈ Also in 1996...

GE90 records strong first year: After a difficult engine development, the GE90 team hangs tough, and the baseline engine experiences a strong first year in passenger service. During the year, the GE90 experiences no in-flight disruptions and records a dispatch reliability of 99.97 percent. China Southern Airlines flies a GE90-powered Boeing 777 from China to the US—the world's first nonstop, non-refueled transpacific flight of a twinjet aircraft.

The first GE90 growth derivative, the GE90-92B, is certified at 92,000 pounds of thrust with 99 percent of the engine parts common to the original GE90 baseline engine, further demonstrating the engine's growth capability.

JSF Alternate Engine Program: With no formal engine competition held for the JSF program, the US Department of Defense provides seed funding to a team comprised of GE, Allison, and its parent company, Rolls-Royce for the JSF "Alternate Engine Program." The funding enables the three companies to conduct a preliminary study to determine the feasibility of a competing JSF engine based on GE's F120 fighter engine.

Using history as a guide, US lawmakers cite the huge cost and performance benefits from the USAF's "The Great Engine War," which pit GE's F110 against P&W's F100 for F-16s and F-15s. Tom Cooper, head of the GE Aircraft Engines office in Washington, D.C., sells the virtues of competing engines for high-volume fighter jet programs on Capitol Hill, which is based on his personal experience as the former Assistant Secretary of the Air Force during the early days of the original "Great Engine War."

GE acquires CELMA: GE Engine Services continues to expand its global network by acquiring CELMA, an overhaul and repair shop in Petropolis, Brazil, focused on supporting the Brazilian Air Force and overhauling mostly P&W JT8 engines. Over time, the engine mix changes and CELMA becomes a high-volume CFM56 overhaul shop.

F110-GE-129 on the F-15: The F110-GE-129 successfully completes qualification testing on the F-15E for the USAF. However, the engine is still not launched on the twin-engine fighter for several more years.

T700/CT7 production: The T700 and its turboprop derivatives reach 10,000 engines in service, including 1,200 CT7 turboprop engines for the Saab 340. The CT7 powers 540 aircraft worldwide.

CF6 milestone: The CF6 celebrates twenty-five years in service, powering multiple jetliners for 150 airline customers. More than 4,000 engines have been delivered across the CF6 family.

Boeing/McDonnell Douglas merger: The Boeing Company announces plans to buy its long-time rival McDonnell Douglas Corp. for $13.3 billion in stock to create the world's largest integrated aerospace company.

1997
GE's buying spree in engine services

GE Engine Services expands: In a bold consolidation of the civil jet engine maintenance and overhaul industry, GE acquires Greenwich Air Services, the world's largest independent jet engine repair and overhaul company, and UNC, a leading services provider for small engines. Total purchase price: $875 million and one of the largest acquisitions in the 20-year era of GE Chairman Jack Welch.

Jim McNerney leads GE's aviation division during an industry rebound. He fosters an expansion of GE's jet engine portfolio. Later, he heads The Boeing Company.

With United Technologies Corporation (P&W's parent company) making acquisition overtures for Greenwich, GE sweeps in with the winning bid at the same time Greenwich is acquiring UNC, based in Annapolis, Maryland. Greenwich, based in Miami, Florida, has recently acquired the engine overhaul operations of Aviall, another large provider with shops in Texas and Prestwick, Scotland. This mega-acquisition consolidating Greenwich, UNC, and Aviall gives GE Engine Services nine overhaul shops.

That same year, GE Engine Services also creates an overhaul joint venture with Malaysia Airlines (MAS) in Subang, Malaysia, focusing on the growing CFM56 overhaul demand in the Pacific region.

GE's insatiable appetite for acquiring overhaul facilities parallels a dramatic growth in GE and CFM56 engines in airline service, now exceeding 12,000 engines. Also, GE aggressively offers multi-year MCPH contracts to carriers, which are especially attractive to newer airlines established without in-house overhaul capability. GE Engine Services revenues in 1996 reach $2.6 billion, a 44 percent increase over 1995. In 1997, revenues grow to $3.6 billion, a 38 percent increase over 1996.

McNerney era begins: GE executive Jim McNerney becomes president and CEO of GE Aircraft Engines, replacing Gene Murphy. The personable McNerney leads the company during an aviation recovery. A former leader across several GE organizations including aircraft leasing, McNerney declares in introductory remarks to Evendale executives, "It's time to start having fun again."[20] And they eventually will.

Though he lacks an engineering background, McNerney is a motivational leader who recognizes industry opportunities and establishes strong rapport with customers. A popular leader, McNerney also slows the acquisition frenzy of GE Engine Services and drives a services strategy with greater sensitivity to GE's airline customers who are also competitors as engine services providers.

During his five-year tenure leading GE Aircraft Engines, McNerney promotes new engine development programs, most notably the GE90-115B, to great employee enthusiasm. Perhaps the highest compliment paid to him is etched on a brick inside Evendale's Brian H. Rowe Learning Centre. The brick (from an anonymous donor) reads: "Jim McNerney: He Gave Us Back Our Business."

✈ Also in 1997...

Most dependable engines: GE and CFM56 engines demonstrate the industry's best reliability and durability with strong milestones in 1997. A Germania Flug operates a Boeing 737-300 for almost a decade with a CFM56-3 engine accumulating 30,000 flight hours without being taken off the wing—surpassing the record held by a GE CF6 engine at 28,888 flight hours without being removed. CFM56-3 engines are averaging 14,000 hours on wing before the initial shop visit.

GE50 that never was: For a year, GE negotiates with Airbus on a 50,000-pound thrust GE50 turbofan for a stretch A340, designated the A340-500/600. However, GE ultimately backs out of the talks, and the A340-500/600 becomes the first Airbus jetliner not launched by a GE or CFM56 turbofan. A Rolls-Royce Trent turbofan fills the void. In 2011, Airbus suspends A340-500/600 production after 133 aircraft are sold.

CFM56-7 and Southwest: The fast-selling CFM56-7 enters service powering 737 "Next Generation" jetliners for Southwest Airlines. Eventually, the massive Southwest fleet will be exclusively CFM56 powered and exceed 700 737 jetliners.

GE90 gains momentum: The extended-range 777-200ER enters revenue service, and the GE90 becomes the jetliner's most fuel-efficient turbofan. As GE often says at the time: the higher the thrust requirement, the bigger the GE90 advantage for the 777.

Gerhard Neumann passing: An architect of GE's aviation rise, Gerhard Neumann dies at the age of 80. From the variable-stator vane system on the J79 to the creation of CFM International, his contributions make him a central figure in GE's aviation history.

1998
The Engine Alliance pursues the A380

GP7200 for the A380: As GE and P&W seek regulatory approval in the US and Europe for its proposed joint company, the prime aircraft application disappears. Boeing abandons the 747-500X and 747-600X program, claiming a lack of airline enthusiasm for the stretch four-engine aircraft.

GE and P&W consider pulling the plug on the joint engine company. "By 1998, we hit an unexpected lull and enthusiasm dimmed," recalls Bruce Hughes, president of the Engine Alliance.[21] However, Airbus is aggressively promoting a double-decker, four-engine A3XX, the world's largest jetliner with more than 500 seats and a range of 8,000 nautical miles. A freighter version is also under study.

In the end, GE and P&W view the Engine Alliance as a cost-effective response to the proposed Airbus project, soon called the A380. This program is a source of European pride amidst an aerospace consolidation across the continent caused by the civil and military aerospace decline. GE and P&W also see a long-term, strategic value in teaming together on a turbofan development.

The GE90 team wrestles through high-profile issues in the late 1990s.

Perhaps most importantly, without a competing engine, Rolls-Royce's latest Trent turbofan has the A380 engine business all to itself. "We had to ask ourselves, 'What if this aircraft takes off, and we're not on it?' " recalls Chuck Chadwell, head of GE's commercial engines.[22] To further hedge their bets, GE and P&W agree that they can each sell up to 30 percent of their respective ownership in the engine to revenue-sharing participants.

Later in 1998, the Engine Alliance signs a Memorandum of Understanding with Airbus to offer the GP7200 engine, rated at 75,000 pounds of thrust, for the 500-passenger, two-story A380. Some industry insiders call the engine competition an unfair fight with the two US titans teamed against Rolls-Royce. Yet the UK engine maker is a determined competitor with strong, historic ties to the first A380 customers.

✈ Also in 1998...

GE Engine Services "hospital shops": A flurry of joint ventures, acquisitions, and multi-year service packages drives annual GE Engine Services revenues past $5 billion, nearly doubling volume over a two-year period. Also, GE pioneers "front-line" engine support with a growing On-Wing Support Network, first introduced at London's Heathrow Airport. By 1998, GE is pursuing a network of twenty "hospital shops."

Rapid-response GE technicians on call also prove critical to new engine introductions. Over time, the network supports issues with large GE and CFM56 engine populations through field inspections, on-wing modifications, or engine swaps. The network is a selling point in GE and CFM56 sales campaigns.

GE90's mixed signals: GE discloses a $275 million tax write-off after cancelling a GE90 derivative at 102,000 pounds of thrust for a larger Boeing 777. Meanwhile, GE invests in a growth GE90-94B with a redesigned compressor to be certified at 94,000 pounds of thrust for the 777-200ER. These mixed signals lead the industry to question the GE90's long-term future.

Privately, GE Chairman Jack Welch is less subtle. "The GE90 is dead, put a stake in its heart," Welch writes in bold ink to an Evendale executive across an article detailing the GE90-94B compressor in *Aviation Week & Space Technology*.[23] To rub salt into the wound, British Airways, the GE90's launch customer, switches to Rolls-Royce power in ordering additional 777s.

McNerney and his commercial team hold fast. They methodically develop big plans for the GE90. With the GE90, patience and faith are required virtues.

CFM56-7 the fastest seller: The CFM56-7 mounts an extraordinary production run as the "Next Generation" 737 becomes the fastest-selling jetliner family in airline history. Boeing's original forecasts are proving accurate. By 1998, more than fifty carriers order more than 1,000 of the CFM56-7-powered jetliners.

F404/RM12 expansion: The F404 fighter engine family, with 3,600 engines in operation, expands again when South Africa orders twenty-eight JAS 39 Gripen fighter jets from Sweden. The F404 variant designated the RM12 is produced by Volvo Aero Corp. of Sweden and by GE in Lynn.

LM2500 for cruise ships: LM2500+ gas turbines are selected for the world's first gas-turbine-powered cruise ships being built for Royal Caribbean International and Celebrity Cruises.

1999
GE90: The comeback kid

Launching the GE90-115B: In 1998, the GE90 turbofan family is still in third place in a three-engine battle for Boeing 777 orders. By mid-year, GE abandons a development program to take the large turbofan to 102,000 pounds of thrust for future growth 777 variants. Wall Street analysts, looking to poke holes in the high-flying GE financial juggernaut, are calling the GE90 an economic failure. For many industry insiders, including a fair number of GE managers, the world's largest engine is considered at the end of its road.

However, the story behind the curtain is very different. For starters, the GE90's leading fuel efficiency is attracting rave reviews from operators of the extended-range 777-200ER, which entered service in 1997. For the GE90-94B engine variant developed in 1998, GE designs a more capable compressor, which serves as the foundation for much bigger things to come.

In late 1998, GE leaders travel the globe to generate enthusiasm from several major carriers, most notably Air France. They are touting for a new GE90 designed to produce an unheard-of 115,000 pounds of thrust for bigger, longer-range 777s being evaluated by Boeing. At the same time, Boeing balks at GE's initial proposal for an exclusive engine agreement to power these jetliners.

GE is undeterred. Eight months of negotiations and lobbying with Boeing ensues, involving a host of GE leaders, including GE Chairman Jack Welch, GE

The GE90-115B has an outstanding entry into service. Its launch on longer-range Boeing 777 jetliners in 1999 marks a critical moment in GE's history.

Aircraft Engines President Jim McNerney, Vice Presidents Chuck Chadwell and Herb Depp, GE90 general manager Chaker Chahrour, and their ace negotiator Robert Conboy. While this intense activity is underway, P&W and Rolls-Royce are also proposing higher-thrust engines to compete for these longer-range 777 jetliners.

Conboy, GE's head of Aircraft Programs, leads day-to-day negotiations with Boeing in the first half of 1999, supported by veteran GE engineer Wayne Lord. "Trust and transparency between Boeing and GE are critical, because airplanes and engines have different business models for recouping these huge investments, and the final negotiated agreement required it," Conboy recalls.[24]

In a dramatic GE comeback, Boeing selects the GE90-115B turbofan in early July as the exclusive engine for longer-range Boeing 777-300ER and 777-200LR jetliners. At 115,000 pounds of thrust, the GE90-115B will become the "world's most powerful jet engine," surpassing its GE90 predecessors and all competitors. In one fell swoop, the 777's propulsion landscape is transformed.

The stakes for GE Aircraft Engines are huge, and tensions run high in the president's office in Evendale's Building 100. After all, the company's future in high-thrust turbofans has been in the balance, and the winning sole-source bid is financially complex and aggressive. In common aviation parlance, the bid is a "huge bet." Two days before Boeing announces the deal, McNerney turns to Chadwell, his trusted lieutenant, and asks pointedly, "We didn't get snookered, did we?"

With a broad smile and calm assurance, Chadwell, who has a history of selling "big bets" to his bosses, responds, "Jim, it's a good deal. It will make money for Boeing and GE."[25]

Days later, Jack Welch seems to reflect McNerney's anxiety during a press event with Boeing at Rockefeller Center in New York City to announce the GE90-powered 777-300ER and -200LR. "The GE90 is the most money I've ever spent on a new product, so let's hope it all works out," he says in the presence of GE and Boeing leadership.[26]

With a big win in his pocket, Chadwell now must sell the sole-source concept to airlines with 777s powered by non-GE engines. John Roundhill, head of Boeing's new airplane development, concedes that several carriers prefer competitive engine offers. He recruits Chadwell and Chahour to join Boeing leaders on a worldwide airline tour to explain the sole-source rationale.

Chahrour teams up with Lars Andersen, Boeing 777 program manager, in presenting to twenty major carriers, including future 777-300ER customers Singapore Airlines and Cathay Pacific. "The briefings were very technical in order to win credibility for the aircraft and engine combination," Chahrour recalls. "They [airlines] wanted to be able to look us straight in the eyes and feel confident that we would deliver."[27]

Publicly, Roundhill says the 777-300ER and -200LR fill a niche market, and forcasts a conservative 500 orders. GE's financial deal is built upon 750 jetliners being sold, however.[28] In fact, many analysts view the 500-aircraft forecast as too optimistic, because major carriers such as United, American, and Singapore already operate large 777 fleets with P&W and Rolls-Royce engines.

In the end, the naysayers are flat wrong. While GE's competitors boosted the power of their derivative engines in the 1990s, they still required substantial design changes to achieve thrust beyond 100,000 pounds. The GE90-115B is the right solution for the new jetliners. "The GE90-115B is a culmination of our original strategy to build a new centerline engine," says McNerney, adding that the engine "hits the sweet spot" of the original design.[29]

GE90 technical improvements bring greater efficiency at lower risk to longer-range 777s. The fan grows to 128 inches, with composite blades in a more efficient, swept-aero design. The 3D aero-designed GE90-94B compressor is adopted, which eliminates one stage (10 to 9) and adds one booster stage (three to four), a technical solution reminiscent of the 1970s CF6-50 growth step introduced by Art Adamson. This new design increases airflow while managing core temperatures. For the -115B fan mid-shaft, GE uses a new GE1014 steel alloy for higher torque at the same diameter.

McNerney salutes his team for keeping the faith in the GE90 promise while the engine has been anxiously viewed companywide. Among the disciples is Mike Benzakein, head of advanced engineering, who sports "GE90" vanity license plates on his sports car.

Over time, Boeing receives orders for more than double its original forecast of 500 deliveries. The GE90-115B launches in 2000 with a Japan Airlines order for 777-300ERs and then demonstrates a fabulous service entry. The 777-300ER becomes the most profitable long-range jetliner and the most popular 777 by a wide margin.

Despite Welch's early frustration with GE90 setbacks, one of his first calls after the GE90-115B win is to congratulate retired executive Brian Rowe, a gesture Rowe deeply appreciates. He writes: "I felt vindicated that I had made the right choice in the size and configuration of the engine. Good airplanes grow, and they require good engines to grow with them."[30]

The Embraer ERJ-170 jetliner is launched with the CF34-8E turbofan.

Today, one can barely imagine GE's commercial engine portfolio without the GE90-115B. Not only would the engine tally robust sales and airline accolades, but also its architecture and mechanical design would influence every GE and CFM turbofan for the next twenty years, from the popular GEnx and record-selling CFM LEAP to the Passport for corporate jets.

CF34-8/10 for Embraer: At the Paris Air Show, GE's CF34 family secures another regional jet application when Embraer, the Brazilian manufacturer, announces the selection of the CF34-8E for its seventy-passenger ERJ-170 regional jet and the new CF34-10E for its 98-to-108 passenger ERJ-190.

Five years earlier, government-owned Embraer faced bankruptcy. A sale to private investors, along with a $500 million capital infusion, enabled Embraer to launch its smaller regional jets with Rolls-Royce power.[31]

To grow its regional jets to compete with larger Bombardier aircraft, Embraer turns to CF34 technology. The CF34-8E is 87 percent parts-common with the CF34-8C turbofan that powers larger Bombardier's CRJs. For the CF34-8E, GE designs the propulsion system for a new under-wing nacelle installation. CF34-8E testing begins the next year.

In the 18,000-pound thrust class, the CF34-10E incorporates CF34-8E compressor design with a larger booster fan and modified turbine section. Ishikawajima-Harima Heavy Industries of Japan supplies a substantial portion of CF34-8E and -10E content as a revenue-sharing participant. Quickly, GE expands its formidable CF34 franchise with larger regional jets. By the century's end, CF34 engine orders for 70-to-108 passenger jets will exceed 1,300. And, that's just the beginning.

✈ Also in 1999...

Stunning CFM56 production: As the century draws to a close, the last CFM56-3 engines roll off the production line at Evendale for the 737 "Classic" series. In total, about 4,000 have been produced since the mid-1980s. Meanwhile, CFM56-5 and CFM56-7 production continues to ramp upward. CFM produces more than 1,100 CFM56 engines in 1999; total orders and deliveries since the 1979 CFM56 launch now surpass 10,000 engines.

CT7-8 testing: CT7-8 turboshaft engines, co-developed and co-produced by GE and FiatAvio of Italy, begin flight testing on the Sikorsky S-92 helicopter.

2000
The offspring replaces iconic parent

CF6-80C2 for C-5: The brand new century begins with the offspring engine replacing its iconic parent. The USAF selects the CF6-80C2 to re-engine C-5A/B transports as part of the $8 billion C-5 Reliability Enhancement and Re-engining Program. In replacing GE's TF39 turbofan on the C-5A/B, hundreds of CF6-80C2 engines are added to the long-term production schedule over the next two decades.

In the new century, the CF6-80C2 enters its third decade in production, powering a dozen jetliner models, including US Air Force One and the C-5 Galaxy.

The TF39 turbofan, launched in 1965 for the C-5, would propel GE back into the commercial jetliner business by giving birth to the CF6 turbofan. Ultimately, GE will deliver more than 7,000 CF6 turbofans for nearly 200 customers on 12 jetliner models, including US Air Force One and several military applications. Continuous CF6 production extends well beyond forty years.

Entering the new century, the TF39 has two million flight hours on the four-engine C-5 Galaxy, which has done the heavy lifting in every major US military conflict for more than thirty years. At 41,000 pounds of thrust, the TF39 now gives way to a CF6-80C2 certified at 60,000 pounds of thrust.

De-rated to 50,000 pounds of thrust for the C-5 missions, the CF6-80C2 gives the massive transport far greater takeoff and climb capability. Through better fuel burn, lower maintenance, and longer on-wing life, the re-engining program is expected to easily pay for itself over the operational life of the aircraft.

✈ Also in 2000...

CF34 sets new sales records: In the 1990s, GE's CF34 engine family for regional jets secures more than 2,500 engine orders, well beyond original market forecasts. The new century opens, however, with GE's largest regional jet win ever: Delta Connection carriers order CF34 engines to power ninety-four Bombardier CRJs, with options for another 406 CRJs.

Atlantic Southeast Airlines and Comair, both subsidiaries and feeder airlines for Delta, plan to purchase a total of 500 aircraft in a mix of fifty-passenger and seventy-passenger CRJs. By 2000, the range of jet-powered regionals is wildly attractive to major carriers as well as to "feeder" operators, especially in the US. From 1998 to 2002, about 25 percent of all passenger aircraft sold are regional jets.

Big JAL order for GE90: Japan Airlines (JAL) launches the GE90-115B with an order for eight 777-300ERs. This influential order begins a 777-300ER sales bonanza far exceeding industry expectations. By mid-year, five customers sign up for the longer-range 777s. The GE90-115B is certified in 2003.

The JAL launch is gratifying to GE, given the long, roller-coaster history with this important carrier. In the early 1960s, GE's CJ805 struggled with durability issues powering JAL's Convair jetliners. This bad history contributes to JAL's refusal to order GE engines again until its 1988 selection of CF6-80C2-powered 747-400s, which prove a huge operational success.

In the early 1990s, JAL opts for the P&W derivative engine on its early-model 777-200s. By 2000, however, JAL acknowledges the GE90-115B's unique technical attributes for the 777-300ER, as well as GE's excellent CF6-80C2 product support for its fleet of 747-400s.

With the JAL selection, 777 operators with P&W and Rolls-Royce fleets grow more comfortable with the undeniable economics of GE90-powered, longer-range Boeing 777s.

GE90-94B certifies: The GE90-94B is certified for the 777-200ER and begins flight tests. The "one-two punch" of the GE90-94B and GE90-115B assures GE's solid presence on the 777 family of aircraft. GE90 turbofans cover a thrust range extending from 85,000 to 115,000 pounds. The days when the GE90's future was in question now seem far in the past.

Higher thrust F110-GE-132: United Arab Emirates launches the F110-GE-132, rated at 32,000 pounds of thrust, for F-16 Block 60 fighters. A long-chord front fan from the F118 and F414, and a radial afterburner from the F414 engine increase the -132's thrust capability.

2001
GE commits to a shaken industry

9/11 shocks airline industry: The September 11 terrorist attacks, involving four hijacked large jetliners, kill almost 3,000 people and injure 6,000 more across three US states. Two jetliners crash into the Twin Towers of the World Trade Center in New York City, a third jet strikes the Pentagon headquarters in Arlington, Virginia, and a fourth jet, headed for Washington, D.C., crashes in rural Pennsylvania thanks to heroic passenger actions.

Never have jetliners been used as assault weapons for such destruction. In addition to stunning human and property losses, a shaken airline industry will lose an estimated $5 billion over the next two years, including $1.5 billion alone during the four-day airline shutdown following the suicide attacks. Several airlines go bankrupt, and many travel routes disappear.[32] Passenger volume doesn't return to pre-9/11 levels for four years. With more strict security at airports, the airline passenger experience changes forever.

Shock waves immediately rock GE and its Aircraft Engines business. Cincinnati native Jeffrey R. Immelt, who replaces icon Jack Welch as GE chairman and

CEO only four days before 9/11, and David L. Calhoun, head of Aircraft Engines for only nine months, move to protect GE's aviation enterprise amid extraordinary uncertainty.

Within three weeks of the 9/11 attacks, GE forecasts 25 percent lower than expected airline engine deliveries in the coming year. With airlines flying unprofitably and passenger load factors below 50 percent, GE Aircraft Engines moves in October to reduce 4,000 jobs worldwide, approximately 13 percent of the total workforce. "It's a signal that nobody knows the answer," the ever-candid Calhoun tells local reporters.[33]

Leading GE Aircraft Engines for less than a year when the 9/11 attacks occur in 2001, Dave Calhoun steers the company through uncertainty.

However, GE investment in the airline industry never wavers. In the three years leading up the 9/11 events, GE launches the GE90-115B, the GP7200, and several variants of the CF34—a broad turbofan portfolio representing GE's future in commercial aviation. With support from Immelt, GE Aircraft Engines retains R&D budgets in the aggressive $800 million to $900 million range in both 2001 and 2002. Calhoun assures that "nothing [engine development programs] will be canceled."[34]

Bolstered by the R&D funding, GE can move forward with Snecma on its TECH56 demonstrator program to develop technologies for upgrades of current CFM56 engines that will help to lower airline operating costs. In preparing for the greater demands of future jetliners, the TECH56 team, operating on both sides of the Atlantic Ocean, tests a 68-inch front fan, a Twin-Annular Pre-Swirl combustor (TAPS), a new six-stage compressor with contoured airfoils, a new HPT, and an LPT system with 35 percent fewer parts.

Also, the GE commitment to airlines extends directly into their operations. Led by quality leader Kevin McAllister, GE teams are deployed to airlines worldwide and initiate thousands of cost-saving quality and process-improvement programs. In addition, GE establishes payment deferral plans and advances another $5 billion in financing for cash-strapped carriers.

The GE90 composite fan blade is viewed as a work of art, displayed at The Museum of Modern Art in New York City and at The Cincinnati Art Museum.

Immelt, whose father, Joseph Immelt, was a manager for decades at the GE Aircraft Engines plant in Evendale, stands behind the aviation enterprise in the challenging years ahead. "I had an inherent knowledge of the business that I saw through my father's eyes when I was growing up near the [GE] plant," Immelt says. "You win when your customers win. It takes that kind of attitude, and it's embedded in the jet engine culture. The 9/11 experience was one of those moments that showed the true strength of the company."[35]

GE Aircraft Engines weathers the post-9/11 uncertainty by increasing military sales and by servicing the fleet of 14,000 GE and CFM56 engines in airline service. Despite the retirement of older GE-powered jetliners and reduced flight hours by carriers worldwide, more than half of Aircraft Engines' 2001 revenues of $11.3 billion is derived from GE Engine Services.[36]

✈ Also in 2001...

GP7200 secures life-saving launch: After recovering from Boeing's 747-500X and -600X jetliner cancellations, the Engine Alliance survives another near-death experience after losing the initial engine campaigns for the Airbus A380.

Singapore Airlines, Qantas, and Virgin Atlantic collectively sign firm and option orders for sixty-one A380s with Rolls-Royce power. The Engine Alliance finds some solace in Rolls-Royce's long history with Singapore Airlines and Qantas. Nevertheless, the tally still remains: 240 firm and option engines on the books for Rolls-Royce, versus zero for the Engine Alliance, which has now been in operation for five years.

However, in the high-stakes aviation industry, competitive shifts can occur quickly. In May of 2001, the Engine Alliance, led by GE's Lloyd Thompson, secures its long-awaited launch of ten A380s from Air France, a loyal GE and CFM customer. That same year, the Engine Alliance successfully runs both an engine core based on a scaled GE90-115B and a scaled 3D aero-design front fan. With the GP7200 launched, a strong recovery for the Engine Alliance is just around the corner.

Dave Calhoun leads in challenging times: Unlike the Jim McNerney era at GE Aircraft Engines, Calhoun's tenure requires steering the company through a prolonged aviation recession. Despite his non-aviation background, Calhoun is an industry advocate during his four years running the company. He launches the GEnx turbofan on the Boeing 787 and 747-8. He also supports the military team's initiative, led by Russ Sparks and Tom Brisken, to procure large inventories of military spare parts well ahead of customer requirements. The strategy bolsters GE income during the airline recession, while supporting critical military aircraft readiness for US deployments to Iraq and Afghanistan.

J85 lives on: The USAF awards a $601 million contract for hardware kits to upgrade 1,202 J85 engines powering the ageless T-38 Talon supersonic trainer. The upgrade kit, including a redesigned compressor rotor and stator assembly, an improved HPT, and new afterburner liner, is intended to extend the J85 service life to 2040.

CF6 reaches thirty years: The CF6 commercial engine family celebrates thirty years in airline service as the new CF6-80E1A3, rated at 72,000 pounds of thrust, begins flight tests on the Airbus A330-200.

GE90-115B sets record: During ground tests at Peebles, Ohio, the GE90-115B reaches a thrust record of 120,316 pounds.

Honeywell acquisition denied: In a setback to GE's long-term strategy to expand further into the aerospace industry, the European Commission denies GE's proposed acquisition of Honeywell's aerospace operations.

CF34-8 enters service: The CF34-8C-powered CRJ700 Series enters revenue service.

2002
China and Middle East breakthroughs

Middle East success: The Engine Alliance experiences a dramatic sales turnaround in 2002. Emirates of Dubai, the Middle East region's fastest-growing airline, orders thirty-two GP7200-powered Airbus A380s. Shortly afterwards, FedEx follows with an order for ten GP7200-powered A380s. The next year, Emirates orders yet another twenty-three A380s with the GP7200. In short order, the Engine Alliance is here to stay.

Because only a limited number of customers are able to operate jetliners the size of the A380, the Engine Alliance orders from Emirates, the largest A380 operator, become a critical long-term anchor. Within two years of the GP7200's launch in 2001, the Engine Alliance wins 300 engine orders from four customers, including 199 from Emirates.

The Emirates orders in 2002 and 2003 also reflect GE's growing aviation presence in the Middle East, particularly with high-thrust turbofans, during the new century.

Since the 1960s, GE fighter engines have played an important role in the defense of Allies in the Middle East, powering US-exported fighter jets such as the

Emirates is a critical customer for the GP7200 turbofan, which powers the airline's A380 fleet. The early 21st century is marked by GE's growing aviation presence in the Middle East region.

F-4 and F-16. However, GE's commercial inroads with the region's airlines did not begin until the 1980s with CF6-powered and CFM56-powered jetliners. Then sales leader Muhammad Al-Lamadani wins a critical GE90 campaign for early-model 777s with Saudi Arabian Airlines in 1995.

Then, 2002 becomes a breakaway year. Adding to its large GP7200-powered A380 fleet, Emirates acquires or leases 68 GE90-powered 777s over the next three years. By the time Qatar Airways orders GE90-powered 777s in 2006, carriers in the region operate almost 2,000 CFM56, GE, and Engine Alliance engines. Even larger blocks of GE and CFM56 engine orders in the region are still ahead.

Chinese select CF34 engine: In 2002, AVIC I Commercial Aircraft Company (ACAC) of China selects GE's fast-selling CF34-10 to power the new ARJ21 regional jet under development. It is GE's first jet engine for an indigenous Chinese passenger jet.

With 450 GE- and CFM-powered Western-made jetliners operating in China by 2002, GE has maintained strong relationships with the growing Chinese aviation industry since the 1980s. However, the ARJ21 program enables GE to collaborate on the front end of a new Chinese aircraft development.

The CF34 campaign, led by David Joyce, further aligns GE with China's ambitious aviation strategy, which includes becoming a first-tier aviation technology provider. At the time of the ARJ21 engine announcement, another 100 civil airports are slated for construction in China over the next decade.

✈ Also in 2002...

GE acquires Unison: To expand into aviation adjacencies, GE purchases Unison Industries of Jacksonville, Florida, a leading producer of ignition systems, accessories, and sensors. As GE closes the deal, Brad Mottier, an original Unison leader, is named Unison president. In 2005, he will join the GE Aviation leadership team in Evendale. Eventually, he leads GE's re-entry into general and business aviation.

F110 on the F-15: In a classic example of GE tenacity, the Republic of Korea Air Force selects the F110-GE-129 to power forty twin-engine F-15s. Since securing a lead position on single-engine F-16s in the 1980s, GE has continued to pursue F-15 applications. In 1996, the F110 even powers the F-15 in a successful USAF flight-test program. However, as F-15 procurement declines, the USAF cannot rationalize a second-engine support structure for its F-15 fleet.

It takes an international F-15 sale to break the P&W engine lock. After the Korean breakthrough, additional GE F110 orders for F-15s soon follow from Singapore and Saudi Arabia.

Record engine developments: At the Farnborough Air Show near London, GE promotes its huge commitment to commercial aviation during a difficult era. With its GE90-115B, GP7200, CF34-8, and CF34-10 development programs, GE is experiencing the most aggressive refresh of its commercial engine portfolio in decades.

GE90-115B rollout: Boeing rolls out the 777-300ER at Everett, Washington. Alan Mulally, president and CEO of Boeing Commercial Airplanes, says the aircraft meets the company's original vision of growing the 777 into a family of five models.

The future is now: The US Defense Advanced Research Projects Agency (DARPA) and the USAF select the versatile F404 to power Boeing's X-45B Unmanned Combat Air Vehicle (UCAV). The single-engine X-45B is designed to evaluate the feasibility and capability of unmanned combat missions.

CF34 anniversary: The CF34 family celebrates ten years of powering regional jets. More than 5,000 CF34 engines have been delivered, or are on order, for business and regional jet applications.

CF34-8 E enters service: The CF34-8E-powered Embraer ERJ-170 enters revenue service.

2003
One for the record books

You can look it up: The GE90-115B produces 127,900 pounds of thrust on a test stand at GE's test operations in Peebles, Ohio. The feat soon appears in the *Guinness Book of World Records* for the highest thrust ever achieved by a jet engine. That same year, the GE90-115B is certified and begins flight tests on the Boeing 777-300ER.

The GE90-115B earns its way into the *Guinness Book of World Records* by producing 127,900 pounds of thrust in 2003.

CF34 buying spree: The buying spree for regional jets continues. US Airways orders 170 regional jets from Bombardier and Embraer. Three different CF34 models will power the aircraft.

JetBlue Airways orders 100 firm CF34-10E-powered Embraer 190 jets, with options for an additional 100. By 2003, GE has invested more than $1.5 billion in its CF34 regional jet enterprise.

CT7 for the Superhawk: Sikorsky selects the CT7-8C growth turboshaft engine for its H-92 Superhawk. The 2,500-shaft-horsepower engine provides a 25 percent power increase over the CT7-8 and an 85 percent power improvement over the original T700 engine. The greater capability is derived mostly from new HPT and LPT systems.

200 LM2500s: GE delivers the 200th LM2500 aeroderivative engine for the US Navy's DDG-51 Aegis destroyer program. In total, GE has delivered more than 600 LM2500 engines for US Navy applications.

2004
Unveiling the GEnx

GEnx-1B on The Dreamliner: *The Wall Street Journal* bills the competition for the much-anticipated Boeing 787 "the biggest face-off among the three big jet engine makers in more than a decade."[37] The all-electric and composite-structure jetliner, soon called "The Dreamliner," will replace the popular, twin-engine 767. Boeing's engine decision will influence jet propulsion's competitive landscape for decades.

However, the "big three" turbofan titans refuse to enter another costly arrangement like the Boeing 777, where all three invested heavily in new engines, and then duked it out on every airline campaign for almost a decade. As a result, Boeing takes a different approach with The Dreamliner: hold an engine competition upfront and downselect only two competing turbofan suppliers for the aircraft.

At the onset, some GE leaders advocate a new turbofan offering through the Engine Alliance. This approach eliminates the risk of being left off the 787 and allows GE to split with P&W the cost for a new engine development. David Joyce, head of commercial engines, respectfully will have none of it. "My attitude reflected a strong sentiment within the rank and file to develop a GE nameplate engine again," he says.[38]

GE's engine offering, eventually called the GEnx, is based heavily on the company's advanced technology program (the GENX). However, two weeks before submitting the final proposal, Joyce fears the engine design is lacking, especially in fuel efficiency. Joyce, Rick Stanley (head of engineering), and engine program

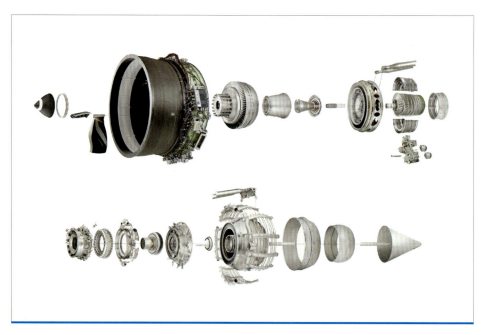

Expanded view of the GEnx, which becomes GE's fastest-selling large turbofan in decades.

leaders revisit the design front-to-back and make aggressive technology commitments, including higher pressure ratios and new technologies such as titanium aluminide LPT blades.

"We emptied into the kitchen sink everything we knew how to do," Joyce recalls. "You can't always control when you introduce new technology. Whether you like it or not, you will face moments like this where you are either in or you aren't."[39]

Joyce's sentiments mirror GE Chairman Jeff Immelt's philosophy. After a business briefing with Evendale leadership on the financial proposal for Boeing, Immelt leans back in his chair and asks the team, "Isn't this really a question of whether we are in this business for the long haul or not? We all know that we have to do this. Or we can spend the next 30 years explaining why we didn't."[40]

Wisely, GE fights for the airplane. On April 6, Boeing downselects GE and Rolls-Royce turbofans. As with any huge competition between the big three jet engine makers, the atmosphere resembles high-stakes poker. George David, head of United Technologies, claims P&W lost solely on financial terms and questions the rationality of the winning bids. However, he fails to recognize P&W's limited experience in developing large turbofans in recent years.

GE's David Calhoun describes a "highly aggressive" winning package that will not turn a profit for at least a decade.[41] It could be worse. Calhoun has already held the line on additional concessions proposed by GE Corporate in the heat of the campaign.

Two trends soon firmly justify GE's bold efforts to win a place on the jetliner. For one, soaring 787 orders in the next three years far exceed market forecasts. Second, GE's engine design serves as an excellent platform for introducing new technologies onto the proven architecture of the GE90.

The new GEnx turbofan is a dramatic advance over the venerable CF6-80C2 engine it replaces: 15 percent better SFC, 35 percent higher exhaust gas temperature margin, 30 percent fewer parts, 30 percent longer wing life, and 30 percent lower noise.

With a 111-inch front fan, the GEnx embodies the beauty of high-bypass engine technology. While better materials and aerodynamic designs continue to reduce the engine core size, greater propulsive efficiency requires a larger front fan. To reduce fan weight, GE introduces both composite fan blades and a composite fan case. Using 3D aero technology, the GEnx fan reduces blade count to eighteen, compared to

The Brian H. Rowe Learning Centre at the Evendale headquarters is established in 2004.

twenty-two on the GE90-115B and thirty-six on the CF6-80C2. With fewer blades and composite materials, the GEnx fan system reduces aircraft weight by 800 pounds.

Boosted by a compressor derived from the GE90-94B, the GEnx has the industry's highest pressure ratio at 23:1. The twin-annular, pre-swirl (TAPS) combustor, with high-energy swirlers near the fuel nozzles, radically reduces emissions. Counter-rotating HPT and LPT blades prove highly efficient. The GEnx is clearly a step forward in technology.

Like the GE90 on the Boeing 777-200 and the GP7200 on the A380, the GEnx is slow out of the sales gate, losing early 787 engine competitions to an aggressive Rolls-Royce. The UK company's Trent 1000 engine wins the launch order for 50 787s from All Nippon Airways (ANA). The initial loss is a cruel blow because ANA's jetliner fleet is 89 percent powered by GE and CFM56 engines. However, Rolls-Royce engine leadership on The Dreamliner is short-lived.

✈ Also in 2004...
GE Honda Aero Engines formed: In the late 1980s, Honda Motor Company of Japan, the largest producer of combustion motors, begins developing a small turbofan engine to power a Honda prototype business jet.

By 2001, Honda and GE officials in Japan discuss a teaming concept to bring the Honda engine to market. David Joyce's trips to China during the ARJ21 competition include low-profile stops in Japan for briefings with Honda senior engineers on the company's small turbofan. In 2003, Honda's HF118 prototype powers "proof-of-concept" flights of the HondaJet in Greensboro, North Carolina. However, the engine is still far from qualifying as a certified turbofan for passenger service.

In 2004, ongoing dialogue between GE and Honda results in the formation of GE Honda Aero Engines, a 50/50 joint company, unveiled at the National Business Aviation Association Show in Las Vegas, Nevada. The plan is for GE and Honda to jointly produce and sell an improved HF118 with a durable design, low emissions, and excellent fuel efficiency.

In the joint company, GE leads certification efforts with the FAA and provides a global support network. Over the next several years, GE's advanced materials and 3D aero designs bolster the engine redesign. Meanwhile, GE marvels at Honda's ability to rapidly prototype design iterations. The combined Honda and GE effort creates one of business aviation's most efficient and durable turbofans. The joint company also furthers the relationship between two industrial titans.

The fabulous GE90-115B service entry: In an exciting year for the GE90 family, the GE90-115B-powered 777-300ER enters revenue service and achieves the most successful service entry for a high-thrust GE engine ever: zero unscheduled engine removals or in-flight shutdowns in the first twelve months of service. In addition to enhancing 777 sales, the GE90 performance also helps to promote the GEnx.

GE90-115B orders accumulate quickly, including a breakthrough win with Singapore Airlines, which orders thirty-one Boeing 777-300ER aircraft. For decades, Singapore Airlines has been a nearly exclusive Rolls-Royce customer for large jetliners. By late 2004, Boeing sells more than 100 777-300ERs to ten customers.

New Learning Centre: The Brian H. Rowe Learning Centre is created at Evendale. During an airline slump, David Calhoun makes a strong statement. The Centre underscores GE's commitment to aviation by providing better training facilities. Facilities manager Frank Woolard places the structure next to the original Wright Aeronautical buildings as the new "front door" to GE's historical aviation complex. Ace engineer Jan Schilling organizes the engine museum.

Fit for a museum: The GE90-115B is literally a work of art. The swept composite fan blade, with its beautiful aerodynamic design, is displayed at the Museum of Modern Art (MoMA) in New York City. Max Farson, who led the original GE90 blade design, charms reporters by saying he is considering a visit to MoMA to see the blade on display for his first-ever visit to "The Big Apple."

F110 upgrade creates role reversal: For decades, military engine technology has fueled commercial engines. Now, GE and the USAF experience the reverse. The efficient CFM56-7 core for the Boeing 737 is incorporated into the F110-GE-129 Service Life Extension Program (SLEP), which undergoes Accelerated Mission Testing. GE targets 800 F110 engines in the USAF inventory for engine upgrades with the new core. The program is launched the next year with an initial ninety-five orders.

T700/CT7 deliveries: Deliveries of the T700/CT7 family reach 13,000 engines. New applications include the upgraded T700-701D, a 2,000-horsepower turboshaft, to power the Sikorsky UH-60M Black Hawk, and the CT7-8 variant for the Sikorsky S-92, the AgustaWestland EH101 and US101, and the NHIndustries NH90.

F404 in Korea: The popular fighter jet engine finds a new home powering the T-50 indigenous trainer for the Republic of Korea.

2005
Memorable year for the big fans

GE90/GEnx order spree: GE's fifteen-year odyssey to establish a new generation of high-thrust turbofans (replacing the best-selling CF6 family) culminates with an airline order spree, placing the GE90-115B and GEnx at the forefront of jet propulsion for large jetliners.

During 2005, GE secures orders and commitments for more than 750 large turbofans: 525 GEnx engines for the Boeing 787 and 747-8, and 240 GE90-115B engines for the Boeing 777-300ER and -200LR. Noted for aviation's first carbon-fiber composite fan technology, the two high-thrust turbofans will join the fleets of several influential carriers, including Japan Airlines (GEnx), Continental Airlines (GEnx), Emirates (GE90), and Cathay Pacific (GE90).

GE's $3 billion investment in large, composite-fan engines since 1990, powered by breakthrough core technologies, comes to full fruition.

The year opens with Boeing's selection of the -2B version of the GEnx (comprising the GEnx-1B core with a smaller 104-inch fan) as the sole-source engine for the new 747-8 being sold as both a passenger jetliner and cargo freighter. Cargolux and Nippon Cargo Airlines launch the freighter version.

In February, the critical GEnx-1B launch is achieved for the 787. After falling

Jeanne Rosario, head of engineering for new engines, closely collaborates with engineering and manufacturing to get the GEnx ready for prime time.

behind Rolls-Royce in initial engine orders for The Dreamliner, the UK tour operator First Choice orders the GEnx-1B for thirteen 787s.

At the time, GE is immersed in a critical 787 campaign with JAL, a highly influential carrier recognized for extensive technical evaluations. During the marathon process, Tom Brisken, GEnx program manager, travels to Japan six times to brief JAL leadership. At the final meeting, JAL's chief engineer asks Brisken a personal question: What are *YOU* most worried about with the new GEnx?

"I reiterated that NOx reduction, lean-burning combustion makes the GEnx the 'greenest' engine in its class, almost a non-contributor to smog around an airport," says Brisken, like a trial lawyer making his closing arguments. "I said it was a risk worth taking, and that I didn't expect problems due to a thorough development program. But it is new technology, and if we developed an issue, we had the best control methodology built into the design and the most experienced team to execute an upgrade."[42]

In May of 2005, the verdict is delivered. JAL selects thirty firm, twenty option GEnx-powered 787s. "From then on, it was 'Katy bar the door,'" Brisken recalls, describing the JAL win as the "linchpin" for affirming GEnx credibility. (The JAL order is announced several months later.) Over the next ten months, more than a dozen airlines commit to GEnx-powered 787s, including four of five Chinese airlines ordering The Dreamliner. The GEnx is established as the lead engine on the 787.

Clearly, the impressive GE90-115B service entry on the Boeing 777-300ER the year before inspires great confidence in both the GE90 and its GEnx successor. Ten additional carriers order the GE90-115B-powered 777 in 2005. At the time, GE's regional sales director Muhammad Al-Lamadani pitches the GEnx to an executive for a Middle East carrier who points out the window toward a GE90-powered Boeing 777 on the runway. "He told me the GEnx isn't flying yet," Al-Lamadani says. "He was watching the GE90 out there on the wing." In essence, one big turbofan is used to evaluate another.[43]

During 2005, several airlines also order the new Airbus twin-engine A350 with the GEnx engine. However, Airbus later changes its A350 family plan and opts to develop three jetliner variants. GE chooses not to develop two separate high-thrust turbofans, which the company believes will be required to accommodate the thrust requirements for all three A350 variants. This decision leaves the A350 family powered solely by Rolls-Royce engines.

Overcoming GEnx challenges: While the order book for 787 jetliners is steadily growing, a myriad of Boeing technical problems and aircraft sourcing challenges will delay the planned 2008 service entry by three years. The 787 delays give GE critical time to resolve GEnx development issues. Initial ground testing reveals engine performance and durability shortfalls. For several years, it is "all hands on deck" for GE's engineering and manufacturing teams.

Jeanne Rosario, vice president of engineering, takes charge of GE's new engine developments in 2005. "The GEnx was a wake-up call," she says. "We had to attack performance, cost, weight, and durability simultaneously."[44] The GEnx combustor and LPT are redesigned, and focused teams from manufacturing and engineering prepare the new GEnx technologies for large-scale production. The extensive redesigns are an expensive and stressful exercise.

Fortunately, the "lessons learned" in developing GE's first new centerline high-thrust turbofan since the GE90 will prove instrumental to the development of the next round of CFM and GE engines. "In the aviation business, you must be so committed to these technologies for a very long time," Immelt says. "A good example is how we stuck with the GEnx until we got it right with everyone pulling together and understanding that we had to get this done."[45]

✈ Also in 2005...

Scott Donnelly takes charge: Scott Donnelly heads GE Aircraft Engines, replacing David Calhoun, who is promoted to corporate vice chairman. Previously, Donnelly led GE's Global Research Center in New York. During his three years as president and CEO, Donnelly expands GE's aviation portfolio to include aircraft systems, and he creates a business and general aviation division.

JSF Development Contract awarded: The US Department of Defense awards the GE Rolls-Royce Fighter Engine Team a $2.4 billion, multi-year development contract for the F136 fighter engine. This decision is influenced by many in the US Congress who vocally advocate the benefits of two competing engines for the high-volume JSF program.

The JSF engine award is the largest military development contract involving GE Aircraft Engines in more than a decade. A new version of the "Great Engine War," pitting GE/Rolls-Royce against P&W, the lead engine supplier on the JSF, is gaining momentum.

CFM readies for the future: At the Paris Air Show, CFM announces the "Leading Edge Aviation Propulsion" (LEAP56) technology initiative to define and prepare technologies for CFM's next-generation engine. The LEAP56 program builds on the TECH56 technology program.

Bill Clapper honored: A longtime CFM and GE executive, Bill Clapper is awarded France's Chevalier of the Legion of Honor. During his tenure as CFM engine program leader, the joint company takes orders for almost 10,000 CFM engines.

Safran formed: In France, Snecma merges with the French security company Sagem to form a new holding company called Safran. Later, the jet engine division of Safran is renamed Safran Aircraft Engines.

GE Aviation: GE Aircraft Engines is renamed GE Aviation by Scott Donnelly to reflect the company's gradual expansion into aviation beyond jet engines.

CF34-10 in service: The CF34-10E-powered Embraer ERJ-190 finally enters revenue service.

2006
Revamped GE Engine Services strategy

Services customization: The number of GE and CFM56 commercial engines in airline service double in ten years and exceeds 20,000 by 2006. To support this extensive fleet, GE Engine Services undergoes a sweeping strategic revamp with a greater focus on providing materials and customized services and establishing a global network of engine overhaul partnerships.

Gone is the 1990s playbook to grow GE-owned overhaul shops while also pursuing work on competitors' engines. The prolonged airline recession after 9/11 creates an industry overcapacity of engine overhaul and repair facilities. GE closes several of its overhaul shops and sells Garrett Aviation Services, a network of nine aircraft and engine overhaul facilities for small aircraft.

GE Engine Services partners with airlines that operate engine overhaul shops and with independent third-party overhaul providers, such as StandardAero, to create a network of providers using GE-licensed overhaul and repair technologies, and GE materials. This "open-network" concept creates more choices for customers while helping to grow GE's materials business. Over several years, GE invests more than $400 million in services technology and engine upgrades to support the new collaborative approach.

In mid-2005, GE Engine Services brands "OnPoint solutions," a menu of customized offerings, including overhaul, on-wing support, new and used-serviceable parts, component repair, upgrades, engine leasing, and engine monitoring and diagnostics. In 2006, the first full year of the "OnPoint" campaign, GE Engine Services revenues surpass $6 billion, doubling the figure of the decade before.

The backlog of multi-year services contracts approaches $40 billion by year's end. "Low-cost carriers want services agreements at the point of a new engine sale," says Brian Ovington, veteran Engine Services marketing leader. "There's a recognition by 2006 that our services model is more than overhaul and services contracts. We are also a materials business, including upgrade kits and used parts, supported by GE-licensed providers along with our own shops."[46] GE also

A GE technician uses water flow technology to refurbish turbine blades.

The HF120 turbofan from GE Honda Aero Engines is launched on the HondaJet in 2006.

rolls out upgrade packages for early-model CFM56, CF6, and GE90 engines at the same time.

By 2006, GE is monitoring more than 10,000 GE and CFM56 engines on-wing in real time to better manage the growing fleet under GE's multi-year service contracts. Engine sensors feed streams of performance and trending data to engineers on the ground at GE's support operation near Cincinnati, Ohio. Airlines recognize the value of real-time monitoring in preventing unscheduled engine shop visits and disruptions, thus improving engine utilization.

However, the journey into data collection through real-time monitoring is still at its infancy. Over the next decade, GE's analytical competency continues to improve in understanding and responding to what the massive reams of engine data are revealing.

HF120 launched on HondaJet: The GE Honda Aero Engines HF120, the redesigned version of the original HF118 prototype, is launched on the HondaJet from Honda Aircraft Company. Aircraft and engine production facilities are established in Greensboro, North Carolina.

The engine showcases several technologies unique to business jets, including an 18.5-inch-diameter, wide-chord front fan, blisk technology in the front fan and booster, a high-performance titanium impeller from Honda, and a turbine system with the most advanced materials from GE's military and commercial engine portfolio.

However, certifying the HF120 on the HondaJet proves to be a learning process, as challenges with the front fan must be overcome. The engine is certified in 2013 and experiences an excellent entry into service beginning in 2015.

✈ Also in 2006…

CFM order record: The CFM 2006 order book sets a company record: 1,640 commercial and military CFM56 engines, surpassing the 1989 record of 1,343 engines. Among the orders are CFM56-7 engines for seventy-nine Southwest Airlines 737-700s.

T700-701K launched: GE and Samsung Techwin agree to develop the T700 turboshaft engine for the Korean Helicopter Program. Then, the Republic of Korea selects the T700-701K to power 245 new indigenous helicopters. The -701K is the first rear-drive variant of the T700.

LMS100 launched: A derivative of the LM6000, the LMS100 enters operation. It produces about 100 megawatts at more than 40 percent efficiency, making it the largest, most efficient aeroderivative gas turbine. ✈

2007-

2018
Wider Horizons

2007–2018

- More than a decade of sustained commercial aviation growth worldwide finds GE Aviation operating on an unprecedented scale. The sheer number of GE and CFM turbofans in airline service far surpasses levels ever experienced before.

- GE aggressively introduces new technologies into its massive engine fleets to improve engine performance and aircraft utilization. From new lightweight and high-temperature materials to additive manufacturing, GE is changing what an engine is made of and how it is made.

- Digital technology, such as in-flight engine diagnostics and data analytics, is redefining how airline fleets are managed day-to-day.

- Staying true to its heritage, GE innovates military jet propulsion with breakthroughs that will influence US and Allied fleets for decades to come.

- As GE opens several new engine factories, the company also moves into aircraft systems and structures, and electrical power and distribution.

- In addition, GE establishes a large presence in Dayton, Ohio, where powered flight all began.

2007

Core computing system for the Boeing 787. The Smiths Aerospace acquisition broadens the GE Aviation product portfolio.

2007
Beyond the jet engine

GE acquires Smiths Aerospace: By 2007, GE Aviation's revenues, income, and engine fleets in service steadily grow with the recovery of the commercial airline industry. However, GE Aviation still desires to expand beyond the enviable jet propulsion franchise, despite the European Commission's denial in 2001 of GE's proposed acquisition of Honeywell's aerospace operations.

The opportunity presents itself with Smiths Aerospace, a UK-based supplier of integrated systems and components for aircraft and components for engines. The company has a rich aviation heritage. Dowty Propellers, one of its best-known brands, began in 1937 in Gloucester, England. The British government selected Smiths' Cheltenham site during World War II to produce aircraft instruments, because the city was out of the range of German bombers striking central London. In 1987, Smiths acquired the US avionics operations of Lear Siegler Holdings Corp. in Grand Rapids, Michigan. Famed US inventor and aviation pioneer Bill Lear first established operations in Grand Rapids in the 1940s.

GE acquires Smiths Aerospace for $4.8 billion and broadens its portfolio into flight management systems, electrical power management, aircraft structures, and aircraft computing systems. In the US, GE acquires avionics operations in Grand Rapids and Clearwater, Florida, and electrical power and distribution operations in Vandalia, Ohio; and Long Island, New York. With operations in the English cities of Cheltenham, Hamble, and Gloucester, the Smiths acquisition strongly establishes GE Aviation in Europe.

The Smiths operations also make GE Aviation an important non-engine supplier on several high-profile aircraft programs, including the Airbus A380 (avionics systems and wing structures), the Boeing 787 (computing systems and flight recorders), the McDonnell Douglas F/A-18E/F (electric generator and flight recorders), the Lockheed Martin F-35 (electrical power management and avionics systems) and the Lockheed Martin F-22 (power distribution and avionics products).

Within a decade of the acquisition, GE will establish a new composite factory for aircraft structures in Hamble, as well as electrical power and distribution research facilities in Cheltenham and in Dayton, Ohio.

Generational turboshaft win: The Lynn team does it again. At the forefront of turboshaft technology since the 1950s, the team assures GE prominence on military helicopters far into the 21st century after Sikorsky Aircraft selects the GE38 (designated the T408) turboshaft for the US Marine Corps' three-engine CH-53K heavy-lift helicopter, which replaces the venerable T64-powered CH-53E. GE wins over bids from P&W Canada and Rolls-Royce.

The T408 is another example of how GE's focused technology efforts can bear fruit decades into the future. The engine's core is based on the GE27 demonstrator first developed in the 1980s and upgraded on the CFE738 turbofan for the Dassault Falcon 2000 and the T407 turboprop for the US Navy P-7 (a program later canceled).

However, the T408 is not your father's GE27 demonstrator. Significant material and design improvements enable higher turbine efficiencies and operating temperatures. "We started with a mature core and incorporated several new technologies, including GEnx turbine blade cooling schemes," says Harry Nahatis, GE's general manager of turboshaft engines.

Through GE's commercial and military R&D investments, "we developed the T408 at half the cost of a new turboshaft engine," Nahatis says.[1] Incorporating an architecture based on the T700, the T408's five-stage axial compressor is coupled with a single-stage centrifugal impeller compressor.

The T408 is similar in size to the T64 but produces 57 percent more power with 63 percent fewer parts. The parts reduction is achieved through a blisk structure and fewer compressor stages. The Full Authority Digital Engine Control (FADEC) automates several control and monitoring functions to reduce parts.

Early in the helicopter engine campaign, GE considers a less-expensive T64 derivative. After all, the Marines initially express interest in turboshaft commonality with its V-22 Osprey, powered by the Rolls-Royce T406, in order to contain costs.

However, Sikorsky is attracted to the T408's unique capability and favorable logistics support. "Our team knew how this aircraft operates in the field and the logistics support required on the ships," says Ed Birtwell, longtime head of turboshaft programs.[2]

Scott Donnelly and Russ Sparks, head of GE's military engines, take a long-range strategic view in aggressively competing for the program. With the T408 at 7,500 shaft horsepower, Sikorsky's selection will put GE in a higher horsepower class, creating future opportunities for military and civil applications. "At the

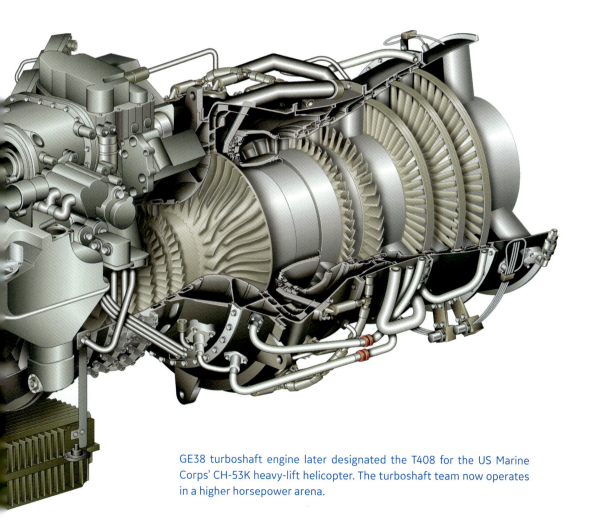

GE38 turboshaft engine later designated the T408 for the US Marine Corps' CH-53K heavy-lift helicopter. The turboshaft team now operates in a higher horsepower arena.

time, Rolls is essentially in that power class by itself," Birtwell says. "Russ and Scott are telling us, 'We've got to win this!'"[3]

In the end, Birtwell and Nahatis attribute the T408 selection to its advanced technology, GE's commitment to lower life-cycle costs, and an aggressive support package. Furthermore, the engine's superior fuel efficiency during a typical Marine mission provides the helicopter with an additional 1,400 pounds of payload.

The T408 is also an immediate success story on the CH-53K, accumulating more than 6,500 hours at the onset without a single unscheduled engine removal. The program will be a significant source of revenue for the Lynn turboshaft operation well beyond 2020 as new applications arise.

✈ Also in 2007...

GE turboprop move in Prague: Reflecting Donnelly's desire to migrate jet engine technology into general aviation, GE acquires Walter Engines in the Czech Republic, producer of the small M601 turboprop. At the time of the acquisition, Walter has seen better days. Of the 37,000 M601s delivered since 1975, only about 1,500 are still flying. The company overhauls M601s, but delivers fewer than ten new engines each year from its antiquated, World War II-vintage factory in Prague.

Everything changes with GE's acquisition. As part of the agreement, GE establishes a new factory, and the former Walter owners demolish the old facility and use the land for luxury condominiums in the historic city. This arrangement makes the Walter assets available at a more attractive price.

Shortly after the acquisition, GE invests in an improved M601 derivative, the H80 H Series, for new and retrofit airplanes. The H80 incorporates new components, advanced materials, and a blisk design in the compressor to significantly improve fuel burn, power, and durability.

Over the next several years, the GE Czech operation establishes a global support network as the GE turboprop engine family in Prague expands. H80 variants are certified through the European Aviation Safety Agency (EASA), an important strategic move for GE Aviation. Walter Engines is GE Aviation's first step in a long-term strategy to enter the small turboprop sector in a big way through its European operations.

CMC commitment: GE Aviation acquires Ceramic Composite Products in Newark, Delaware, from GE Energy. It becomes part of GE Aviation's "lean laboratory" network. At Newark, GE develops processes for mass-producing components made of ceramic matrix composite (CMC) components. Bob McEwan, head of GE Aviation's lean laboratories, describes the process best in his own homespun style: "After you bite into one of grandma's cookies, you ask yourself, 'How can I scale up to make 5,000 of them and have each one taste exactly the same?'"[4]

The Newark acquisition signals GE Aviation's growing commitment to incorporate CMCs into its engines. The acquisition also begins GE Aviation's journey to establish a fully integrated CMC supply chain in the US. The lightweight, heat-resistant CMCs soon appear in GE military and commercial jet engines.

Peebles expansion: To handle rising production and development work, GE Aviation launches a three-year, $90 million expansion at its 7,000-acre Peebles Test Operation in rural Adams County, Ohio. The expansion includes a new engine production building, as well as outdoor and indoor test sites.

GEnx and GE90 fan cases and composite fan blades now ship to Peebles where they are attached to engine propulsors (booster, compressor, combustor, and turbine modules assembled together) delivered from GE's Durham, North Carolina, factory. With deliveries of GE's large turbofans growing from 700 in 2006 to 1,200 by 2009, Scott Donnelly declares at a public celebration in Peebles, "If you think we are busy now, just hold on."[5]

Adaptive Versatile Engine Technology (ADVENT) contract award: GE Aviation receives a USAF Phase I contract award to explore concepts, develop components, and begin preliminary designs of a variable-cycle fighter engine. The contract signals GE's return to variable-cycle technology, which is later called "adaptive-cycle" technology by the USAF, to better reflect the engine design's enhanced capabilities. Rolls-Royce also competes and is awarded a separate ADVENT contract. The five-year ADVENT goals include reducing SFC by 25 percent compared to early 2000 baseline fighter engine designs.

Brian H. Rowe passing: Jet pioneer Brian Rowe dies at age 75. He led GE Aircraft Engines from 1979 to 1993, launching the F110 fighter engine, CF34 regional jet engine, and his signature program, the GE90. Earlier in his career, he directed the CF6 program and was integral to GE's rise in commercial aviation. Perhaps Dick Ostrom, the GE90's indefatigable sales engineering manager, sums up Rowe's legacy best: "Brian was a brilliant maverick whose arguments were based on physics. He had so much credibility. When he spoke, you listened. In our engineering community, he was loved because of who he was."[6]

2008
Game On: CFM "LEAPS" to 2040

The CFM power play: The buzz at July's Farnborough Air Show is dominated by the emerging "engine war" to power the next generation of single-aisle jetliners, the most lucrative commercial aircraft segment in jet propulsion.

For months leading into the show, P&W creates a tsunami of publicity around the development of its geared turbofan. The previous year, P&W launches its geared turbofan on the Bombardier C Series jetliner and the Mitsubishi regional jet. Now P&W is initiating a head-on battle against CFM to power future Airbus and Boeing single-aisle jetliners yet to be defined.

CFM stays quiet no longer. At London's Dorchester Hotel on a Sunday morning before the show, GE and Safran leaders announce three transformative moves: an agreement to extend the CFM joint company to the year 2040, the launch of the LEAP-X engine development program (without an aircraft application), and the establishment of a single CFM engine services company between the two partners to support future CFM engines. This new service entity will unify offerings, resulting in more seamless support to customers.

The two partners extend the 50/50 joint company four years before the original agreement expires. The new agreement ensures engines in the 18,000-to 50,000-pound thrust class are developed under CFM, with GE continuing to provide the engine core "hot section" (compressor, combustor, and HPT) and Safran, the front fan and low-pressure system (LPT and shaft). The new engine project, the LEAP-X, is now full steam ahead.

The 2040 partnership extension evolves from recent negotiations between GE and Safran to correct imbalances in the 50/50 revenue split caused largely by the growing volume of CFM engines. Moreover, Safran is eager to improve the engine services dynamics between the two longtime partners. "Extending to 2040 brought stability and protection to the partnership for a very long time," says CFM executive Bill Clapper, an architect of the 2040 agreement. "We also felt it was a broadside at IAE [International Aero Engines] and improved our competitive position."[7]

A broadside indeed. While the ink dries on CFM documents signed by GE's David Joyce and Safran's Jean-Paul Herteman and Marc Ventre in the downtown London hotel, discord simmers between P&W and Rolls-Royce within the competing IAE consortium. P&W's geared turbofan engine concept is not supported by

CFM International at its finest. In July 2008, Safran's Philippe Petitcolin (far left) and GE's David Joyce (right) caucus with CFM leaders (from left) Eric Bachelet, Bill Clapper, and Olivier Savin just minutes before announcing an extension of the CFM partnership to 2040.

Rolls-Royce, which is independently pursuing a more traditional turbofan design in its separate talks with Airbus and Boeing. P&W and Rolls-Royce are moving in different directions.

The IAE fracture is clearly an undercurrent at the CFM signing. "In talking with customers around the globe, it became so clear that long-term CFM viability is extremely important," says David Joyce, who is named GE Aviation president and CEO two weeks before the show. "The GE and Safran relationship is the strongest it has ever been."[8]

With fuel prices rising, airlines are calling for more efficient single-aisle airplanes, the most utilized aircraft models in the industry. However, Airbus and Boeing, awash in wide-body aircraft developments, publicly say they are awaiting new engine designs with double-digit fuel burn improvement before committing to the next generation of single-aisle aircraft.

CFM launches the LEAP-X engine to pursue a fuel burn reduction up to 16 percent compared to engines on current Airbus A320 and Boeing 737 jetliners, while sharply reducing NOx emissions, carbon emissions, and noise.

The stakes are high to protect CFM's long-standing preeminence. After holding numerous customer symposiums and conducting market surveys to prioritize LEAP performance characteristics, GE and Safran deploy their best technologies to meet aggressive targets that focus primarily on reliability, fuel efficiency, maintenance costs, and on-wing life.

After evaluating eighteen different engine architectures, including a geared fan system, CFM opts for a more traditional architecture to ensure the company's legacy of high reliability on the airline industry's most utilized jetliners. Jan Schilling, GE Aviation's chief engineer, is quick to point out at technical conferences that a geared fan system is inconsistent with several long-held GE and CFM design practices.

However, the LEAP-X is anything but traditional. It includes Safran's three-dimensional, woven resin transfer molding (RTM) composite blade and fan case technology and GE's CMC shrouds in the HPT. GE's advanced compressor, with the industry's highest pressure ratio, draws from years of commercial and military demonstrator engine developments. The fuel nozzle injectors will be ultimately produced using the new additive manufacturing technology, though it is a well-kept secret at the time.

Perhaps the biggest break from CFM56 tradition, and a hard internal decision, is a two-stage HPT. All previous CFM56 models used the single-stage HPT adapted from the original F101 military engine core. The additional HPT stage increases efficiency and supports the longer flights now demanded of single-aisle jetliners. With the second HPT turbine stage, the LEAP core more resembles a scaled GEnx core.

Waging a public war of words with CFM, P&W touts a geared fan that uses a gearbox to enable the front fan and LPT to turn at different speeds. Annoyed but undaunted, the GE and Safran team stays focused. "We've been pretty quiet for the last couple of years, but we've been doing plenty of work in secret," Joyce tells reporters at the Farnborough Air Show. "So be it. Game on."[9]

David Joyce era begins: Scott Donnelly's departure to lead Textron creates an opportunity for David Joyce, the first GE Aviation president and CEO since Brian Rowe to spend his entire career in jet propulsion. He is also the first to spend his entire propulsion career at GE.

He joins GE Aviation in 1980 and is immersed in engine design and development for fifteen years. As with Gerhard Neumann and Brian Rowe, Joyce's apprenticeship in the company's disciplined (and sometimes very outspoken!) engineering culture pays huge dividends as he climbs the ladder, including managing the product support center and large commercial engines, before establishing residence in Building 100's corner executive office.

Jeff Immelt hands Joyce the reins at a critical juncture in the company's history. Within weeks, he teams with GE and Safran leaders to launch the LEAP engine and extend the CFM partnership, along with reorganizing GE Aviation's global network of production and overhaul sites under one organization.

Over the next decade, commercial engine sales soar under Joyce's leadership while GE pursues several new technologies, including CMCs and additive manufacturing. GE moves boldly into electrical power and distribution and digital collaboration, while opening eight new US factories and revitalizing the Evendale headquarters.

David Joyce takes the helm of GE Aviation in 2008 just as the engine selections for several new aircraft programs are up for grabs. Under Joyce, GE experiences more than a decade of phenomenal growth in commercial aviation.

✈ Also in 2008...

eCore goes primetime: GE Aviation launches the new CFM LEAP-X engine as part of a larger GE technology initiative called "eCore," in which the GEnx core hot section, scaled for different engine designs, forms the foundation of a new generation of engines. The first eCore for the LEAP-X runs in 2009. Over time, the eCore program extends to the GE9X and Passport engines, as well as to military and marine and industrial engine applications.

CFM launches TRUEngine™: In a move influenced by input from commercial aircraft appraisers, CFM launches the TRUEngine™ designation to provide for a better evaluation of CFM56 engines redistributed over time into different airline fleets. The program tracks engines by individual serial number. The designation requires that CFM engines be maintained to CFM standards, including overhaul practices, spare parts, and repairs used to service the engine. Over time, the program extends to GE nameplate engines as well.

Batesville, Mississippi: GE Aviation selects Batesville, Mississippi, for a new factory producing carbon-fiber components. Mississippi Governor Haley Barbour encourages GE to locate in the state's northern area where unemployment is high. For the new plant, GE works closely with Mississippi State University to establish carbon-fiber manufacturing processes.

"Unhappy" Emirates pilot: The Engine Alliance GP7200 enters service on Emirates A380s. Despite the engine's excellent performance, an Emirates pilot complains with a smile to Engine Alliance salesman Dennis King about engine noise or actually, the lack thereof. On long flights, the pilot is kept awake during breaks in the A380's crew rest compartment because the four GP7200 engines are too quiet! He relies on engine noise to lure him to sleep.

More F110 orders for F-15s: The Royal Saudi Air Force of Saudi Arabia selects the F110-GE-129 engine to re-engine forty-one F-15 fighter jets. Saudi Arabia becomes the third international customer to power its F-15s with the venerable F110 engine.

Nexcelle venture: GE and Safran form Nexcelle, a 50/50 joint venture company to produce nacelles for single-aisle airliners. The first customer is the COMAC C919.

T700 upgrade: Flight tests begin for the T700-GE-701D, selected in 2005 for the US Army's upgraded UH-60M Black Hawk.

F414 for the Gripen: The Saab Gripen demonstrator aircraft powered by the F414G engine successfully completes its first flight in Sweden.

2009
A LEAP to China

A LEAP launch in China: CFM launches the LEAP-X in the same year that China establishes the Commercial Aircraft Corporation of China (COMAC) to develop larger civil jetliners. The following year, COMAC confirms that its new C919 single-aisle passenger aircraft will be powered by Western-made jet engines.

Because China is the world's largest commercial aviation market, the engine competition for a new indigenous civil jetliner is of utmost strategic importance to CFM. Again, the combined influence of GE and Safran proves formidable as both companies have long relationships and significant investments in China, not to mention a successful twenty-five year CFM56 presence.

Not only does the LEAP engine secure a sole-source engine position on the C919 aircraft in 2009, but COMAC opts for a complete integrated propulsion system with Nexcelle, another GE and Safran partnership, which will provide the nacelle and thrust reverser.

Within ten months, Air China, China Eastern, China Southern, Hainan Airlines, CDB Leasing Company, and GE Capital Aviation Services order a total of 100 C919 aircraft for delivery into the next decade.

The C919 targets a 2016 service entry target, which the jetliner will not meet. However, the target creates a firm development timetable for CFM to assure that LEAP technology will meet anticipated Airbus and Boeing schedules for their new versions of single-aisle jetliners.

✈ Also in 2009...

GEnx at Paris: With the Rolling Stones song "Paint It Black" blaring, the best-selling GEnx engine for the Boeing 787 is unveiled in the Paris Air Show exhibit hall. The banner reads "Black is the New Green," a slogan built on the engine's environmental benefits combined with its black, carbon-fiber fan blades and fan case.

Make that the "GE H80": Thrush Aircraft launches GE's new H80 turboprop engine, an improved derivative of the Walter M601 engine family for a Thrush 510 crop duster. Thrush is a joint venture between Boschung Global AG and Inter Sinex AG of Switzerland, which plans to initially operate the aircraft in Kazakhstan, one of the world's largest producers of grains. Strongly encouraged by Thrush to brand the engine a GE product, the "Walter Aircraft Engines" brand name is removed and replaced with "GE H80."

CMC breakthrough: The GE Rolls-Royce team runs stationary HPT shrouds made of CMCs during F136 engine ground tests. For the first time in jet propulsion, CMC components are run in an engine core.

Upgraded Evendale site: An Ohio job retention tax credit package sparks a revitalization of the Evendale complex. GE commits to investing $100 million of its own money to upgrade the facilities, which is achieved in just three years. During the next decade, GE invests almost $500 million into the historic site, including creating new test facilities, renovating buildings, and demolishing old structures.

ADVENT fighter engine development continues: While GE and Rolls-Royce both continue to lobby for funding to jointly develop a competing JSF engine, the two companies separately pursue new technologies for the next generation of military aircraft.

Thrush Aircraft launches GE's H80 turboprop engine, developed in Prague, Czech Republic, for a new fleet of crop dusters. They initially operate in Kazakhstan, a major grain producer.

GE and Rolls-Royce both win separate USAF Phase II follow-on contracts for the Adaptive Versatile Engine Technology (ADVENT) Program to conduct fan rig testing, several system rig demonstrations, and a full-scale core engine test.

This phase enables GE to focus on USAF next-generation propulsion requirements within a complete adaptive-cycle propulsion system. GE increases its contract cost share to fully fund the turbofan program. GE will demonstrate significant advances in core technology, including CMC materials and the highest overall pressure ratio ever for a GE turbofan. The demonstrator incorporates GE's unique variable-geometry fan design, which provides a cool third-stream flow through the engine for high power extraction and thermal management.

2010
GE electrifies aviation's birthplace

Pursuing electrical power and distribution: Through its growing electrical power facilities in Vandalia, Ohio, and Cheltenham, England, GE Aviation is exposed to the enormous potential of electrical power and distribution.

The question becomes: How does GE Aviation better position itself in this growing industry? After interviewing aircraft manufacturers, the answer is clear: Establish a full systems engineering and modeling capability in-house for your customers. "We had to be able to model, simulate, propose, and demonstrate a full electrical systems architecture," recalls Vic Bonneau, former Smiths executive and GE's first leader for electrical power distribution. "An electrical aero lab is necessary to play in this space. Boeing and Gulfstream were particularly outspoken during our interviews with airframe companies."[10]

GE invites the state of Ohio into the process. On the University of Dayton (UD) campus along the Great Miami River, GE Aviation establishes the Electrical Power Integrated Systems Research & Development Center (EPISCENTER). The center is a short drive from the neighborhood where Orville and Wilbur Wright operated bicycle shops west of downtown Dayton. GE receives financial assistance from state and local governments with UD as the center's landlord.

The center focuses on the various aspects of electrical power systems, including conversion, distribution, and energy storage technologies. In other words, the center will develop the optimum "electrical grid" for aircraft and ground vehicles, including futuristic hybrid electric propulsion systems.

While breaking ground on the Dayton facility in 2011, the company also announces a second electrical power and distribution center in the UK, the Electrical Power Integration Centre (EPIC) at the GE Aviation Bishops Cleeve campus in Cheltenham.

Like the Dayton center, the new Cheltenham site can test complete aircraft electrical systems by exploiting GE's electrical power and distribution modeling and simulation capabilities. Matching UK government support supplements GE's investment in Cheltenham.

The two centers open to brisk business as GE Aviation's electrical power business doubles between 2009 and 2014. The centers play a key role over the next five years in GE's securing several significant commercial and military contracts, including a Boeing award for the electrical load management system, the backup generator, and backup converter for the 777X.

Not anticipated when GE makes the huge commitment to electrical power and distribution is the fast-emerging field of hybrid electric propulsion technology. GE's Global Research Center and the EPISCENTER team on numerous projects for customers worldwide. "No one saw that coming back in 2010," Bonneau says. "Bolstering our testing and modeling

The Passport engine for Bombardier's Global 7000 and Global 8000 jets is GE's largest business jet engine.

capabilities in advance of the hybrid electric propulsion movement will place GE Aviation in a strong position."

Combining the EPISCENTER, GE's electrical power facility in Vandalia, and the Unison engine components factory in Beavercreek, Ohio, GE Aviation establishes a significant presence in Greater Dayton, one of the world's most historical aviation areas, with more than 1,000 employees.

Launching Passport for rarefied air: GE's revitalized corporate jet enterprise, already engaged with Honda, captures a new product segment when Bombardier selects GE to provide the integrated powerplant system, including the new Passport engine, for the Global 7000 and Global 8000 business jets.

The win better positions GE in the ultra-long-range, large-cabin business aviation sector where aircraft can travel nearly 7,000 nautical miles with up to eight passengers. The Passport faces the technical challenge of offering eight percent lower SFC than current business jet engines in the 10,000 to 20,000-pound thrust class, while significantly reducing emissions.

At 16,500 pounds of thrust, the Passport is GE's largest corporate jet engine developed to date and integrates technologies from the company's military and commercial engines, including a composite fan case and unique fifty-two-inch front fan blisk for lower cabin noise and vibration.

The Passport's compression system draws from the GEnx, LEAP, and military demonstrator programs. Nexcelle, the GE and Safran joint venture, provides the propulsion system. The Passport design is completed in 2012, with ground testing beginning in 2013.

✈ *Also in 2010...*

Greenville, South Carolina: Reflecting an expanding commercial engine portfolio, GE Aviation opens an airfoils factory in Greenville, South Carolina.

Auburn, Alabama: GE commits to a new factory in Auburn, Alabama. The plant is established to support GE's JSF engine, which is cancelled the following year. Fortunately, GE's expanding commercial business fills the void. Ultimately, the Auburn plant will also make LEAP components, including fuel nozzle injectors that are produced using additive manufacturing.

F414 for India: GE's military operations continue to grow its international customer base for dependable legacy fighter engine programs. The F414 turbofan is selected to power the second generation of India's indigenous light combat aircraft, the Tejas Light Combat Aircraft.

Also that year, the F414 powers the 'Green Hornet,' an F/A-18 Super Hornet fueled by a 50/50 biofuel blend, marking the first time a US Navy fighter flies with a non-petroleum fuel source.

LEAP secured for Airbus A320neo: Amid launches of Bombardier's P&W-powered C Series aircraft and the LEAP-powered COMAC C919 in China, Airbus moves quickly to freeze the design on an upgraded A320 with more fuel-efficient engines.

At year's end, CFM reaches agreement with Airbus to power the A320neo (neo: new engine option) with the LEAP turbofan. Thus begins the head-to-head competition with P&W's "Purepower" geared turbofan, which is selected earlier in 2010 for the Airbus jetliner. IAE does not have a turbofan offering for the A320neo, thus freezing out the consortium from the next generation of single-aisle jetliners.

Boeing, still evaluating an all-new 737 aircraft design, watches anxiously as the A320neo scores major airline orders. Boeing continues discussions with CFM, P&W, and Rolls-Royce on potential turbofans for a new aircraft design.

2011
The LEAP Summer of Love

LEAP engine surges on A320neo: While competitions between jet engine makers to power certain aircraft can last for decades, the greatest pressure is always at the opening bell. CFM certainly feels it in the first few months of 2011. P&W's geared turbofan is first out of the gate in March as launch engine for the Airbus A320neo and establishes a quick 500-engine sales lead over the LEAP turbofan.

GE and Safran technical leaders must huddle to reevaluate potential LEAP engine shortfalls. To assure better fuel efficiency and improved range for the A320neo, CFM increases the LEAP fan diameter by two inches, adds an extra LPT stage, and takes the engine's bypass ratio to 10:1. In early June, the improvements help the LEAP engine to win a sixty-engine launch order from Virgin America. CFM breathes easier.

With the Paris Air Show two weeks away, GE and Safran prepare for a showdown on aviation's largest stage. Watching from the other side of the Atlantic Ocean is GE Chairman Jeff Immelt. "I had total confidence in our aviation team and the (engine) design they picked, but I still wanted to be subtly paranoid," he

The best-selling LEAP engine on a test stand. CFM's new engine receives an astounding flurry of orders in 2011.

says. "We put a ton of GE money into the LEAP engine right in the middle of the global financial crisis [of 2007–2008], which was not the best timing. So we were all watching what would happen next."[11]

CFM leaders arrive at Paris-Le Bourget Airport with great confidence, because they know that several longtime customers will open their checkbooks to expand their aircraft fleets. When the dust settles at the show, CFM's order book swells to 910 LEAP-1A turbofans for 455 A320neo jetliners, including AirAsia's stunning order of 200 LEAP-powered A320neos. In addition, CFM sells almost 300 additional CFM56 engines for current Boeing 737s and Airbus A320s.

What in the world happened? "There had been a pent-up demand for the CFM product, but airlines were waiting for us to put our best foot forward," says Bill Brown, general manager of CFM marketing. "Once we introduced a final design of the LEAP engine with the larger fan, the floodgates opened. Customers were waiting on us to make that commitment."[12]

While the dramatic orders seem to unfold overnight, this splendid outcome has actually been years in the making. CFM's tradition of outstanding reliability and field support plays a huge role in the stunning affirmation the company received from customers at a critical moment for the new LEAP program. "Nothing sells better with customers than the CFM engine's operating history," says Kevin McAllister, GE's head of commercial engine sales, at the time.[13]

LEAP engine for 737 MAX: However, more is soon to come. The A320neo sales bonanza at Paris forces Boeing's hand. Two months before the air show, Boeing President Jim McNerney says that his team is still evaluating both all-new and upgraded 737 designs, and the all-new design is still his preferred option. Meanwhile, CFM, which reaches an initial agreement with Boeing on a re-engined 737 in 2010 that is later shelved, continues to lobby hard for Boeing leadership to decide sooner rather than later on which aircraft to develop.

"We worked hard to keep the LEAP engine core as close as possible for both Airbus and Boeing," says CFM's Bill Clapper. "We knew the fan size for the two applications would be different, but we were in a great position by 2011 to have an excellent engine for both companies."[14]

By mid-July, brisk A320neo orders and strong interest in the new Airbus jetliner by American Airlines, a long-standing Boeing customer, put into motion another game-changing event for CFM. It begins when Chaker Chahrour, CFM program leader, takes a surprise phone call from Boeing. "I'm asked to fly to Dallas with them to make a deal with American Airlines," Chahrour says. "We [CFM] were locked in with Boeing on an engine configuration, but American needed a personal level of confidence from the engine maker that we could deliver on our fuel burn and maintenance commitments."[15]

After hours of technical briefings in a conference room, Chahrour stands up to join Boeing and American Airlines leaders in a flurry of handshakes. The airline has endorsed Boeing's plans to offer an "upgraded" 737 with the LEAP engine, as opposed to introducing a new aircraft design years later.

From the Dallas airport, Chahrour calls his Safran counterpart, Olivier Savin, and David Joyce, who had already floated financial scenarios with American Airlines. Everyone is elated. Echoing the engine order spree at the Paris Air Show, the CFM56 engine's successful operating history with American Airlines plays an important role in winning confidence for the LEAP engine. "You negotiate for years, and it all comes to this single moment in time," Chahrour recalls.[16]

Boeing's handshake deal on the "upgraded" 737 plays into CFM's technical strategy for the LEAP engine. The 737's lower-wing clearance requires a smaller front fan than engines on the Airbus A320neo. The 68-inch diameter of the LEAP front fan for an upgraded 737 is more than twelve inches smaller than the competing P&W engine and enables Boeing to avoid costly redesigns, including a new landing gear. The CFM focus on jet engine thermal efficiency, as opposed to a dramatic change in engine architecture, pays off. Boeing has its propulsion solution for the upgraded 737, and, better yet, the new engine can be ready in time.

On July 20, American Airlines announces plans to order 460 single-aisle aircraft, including Airbus A320s and Boeing 737s, as well as an additional 100 "upgraded 737s" with LEAP-1B engines. Weeks later, the Boeing board of directors approves the upgraded, LEAP-powered Boeing "737 MAX" program, knowing that a critical airline customer, Southwest Airlines, is waiting in the wings.

The thirty-year Boeing/CFM partnership is affirmed for yet another generation of high-volume, single-aisle Boeing aircraft. A strong relationship between David Joyce and Jim McNerney helps to forge the LEAP sole-source agreement. Additional CFM assurances to Boeing arrive through highly promising results from recent LEAP component and core tests at Safran and GE. The LEAP design is proving a winner.

The brisk sales for LEAP-powered Airbus and Boeing jetliners continue throughout 2011. By November, CFM has booked 2,660 LEAP engines for the Airbus A320neo, the Boeing 737 MAX, and the COMAC C919— the fastest sales rate for any new CFM jet engine.

In December, long-standing Boeing and CFM customer Southwest Airlines makes it official: 150 737 MAX and fifty-eight current CFM56-7-powered 737s. It is one of the largest single CFM/737 orders ever.

IAE consortium transition: While the LEAP engine books orders at a record clip, P&W and Rolls-Royce radically alter the IAE consortium. For decades, the IAE V2500 engine has been the airline industry's second best-selling engine on the popular Airbus A320. Between 1985 and 2011, IAE's V2500 won between 45 and 48 percent of the engine orders for A320s against the CFM56-5. However, re-engining the Boeing and Airbus jetliners without an IAE engine offering changes everything.

In October, P&W agrees to pay $1.5 billion for Rolls-Royce's share in IAE. In addition, P&W will pay Rolls-Royce an unspecified amount for each hour flown on the V2500 fleet already in service for the next fifteen years. In other words, P&W is going it alone for single-aisle jetliners. The deal is disclosed along with plans for P&W and Rolls-Royce to partner on a future commercial engine, but with no details or timetable specified.[17]

The agreement dramatically shifts the competitive landscape between the CFM56-5B and the V2500 for current-generation A320 jetliners. To the surprise of many, sales for current-model A320s (called the A320ceo – current engine offering) stay robust over the next several years as fuel prices decline. However, engine orders for this earlier aircraft model gravitate to the CFM56-5 engine. During 2012-2017, about 900 A320ceos are ordered, with more than 70 percent powered by the CFM56-5.[18]

JSF F136 engine era ends: GE Aviation ends its fifteen-year campaign to compete for the US military's JSF program. In December, the GE Rolls-Royce Fighter Team discontinues self-funding its F136 engine as a competing engine, citing "continued uncertainty in the JSF development and production schedules."[19] The F136 development is almost 80 percent complete.

The decision follows the April vote by US Congress to halt development funding for the F136 engine after more than a decade. Congress cites military budget challenges. Soon after, the US Department of Defense formally terminates the F136 program. In early May, the GE Rolls-Royce team takes an unprecedented move and proposes a self-funded engine program, which is endorsed by the US House Armed Services Committee.

With the Pentagon failing to support the self-funding concept, GE and Rolls-Royce terminate the effort, and the joint fighter engine company is dissolved. Six F136 engines have accumulated more than 1,200 hours of testing. The decision also puts an end to the joint company's campaign to advocate defense acquisition reform by offering unique, fixed-price proposals for F136 engines. The proposal differs from traditional "cost-plus" contracts, which allow contractors to modify the original price offering. P&W's F135 retains a sole-source JSF engine position amid significant engine cost overruns.

Regardless of the setback, GE Aviation has no plans to leave the fighter engine business. On the contrary, GE engineers have been heavily engaged since 2007 in the USAF ADVENT demonstrator engine program, advancing GE's innovations in adaptive-cycle engine technology for next-generation fighters.

"We were never going to give up on the fighter engine business, and the USAF made it very clear that they wanted us in the fighter segment," recalls Jean Lydon-Rodgers, GE's head of military operations. "There was a clear recognition in the Pentagon that GE is developing very unique technologies, and we were strongly encouraged to continue advancing them for future military applications."[20]

In addition to building a fighter engine future with the ADVENT program, GE continues to find international customers for its successful F110, F404, and F414 fighter engines.

GEnx enters service: The GEnx is downselected in 2004 for Boeing's 787, but initially enters operational service on the engine's second aircraft application, the 747-8. Cargolux, a cargo carrier based in Luxembourg, begins operating its first 747-8 in late 2011 several months ahead of the 787. By this time, the GEnx compiles a remarkable order book of more than 1,300 GEnx engines for forty-seven customers across the two Boeing aircraft models.

GEnx-1B goes the distance: GEnx-1B engines power a Boeing 787 to set a record for speed around the world, with a total trip time of forty-two hours and twenty-seven minutes. There was no previous around-the-world speed record for this weight class.

Ellisville, Mississippi: GE selects Ellisville as the site for its second composites plant in Mississippi. The new factory will manufacture composite components for engines and aircraft systems. In 2017, the facility transitions into PG Technologies, a joint venture between Praxair Surface Technologies and GE to specialize in advanced coatings for GE and CFM engines.

Aviage joint venture: GE and AVIC of China form a joint venture company, Aviage, to provide avionics systems for commercial aircraft, with the COMAC C919 as the launch customer.

2012

A technology epiphany

Adding "additive" to the portfolio: GE Aviation's purchase of Greater Cincinnati-based Morris Technologies further drives GE's aggressive entry into the brave new world of additive manufacturing.

Quite simply, additive technology is changing forever the process for designing and manufacturing some of the most complex parts in a jet engine. As David Joyce frequently asks his leadership team at the time, "Do you want to be on the inside, or the outside, of this [additive] revolution?"[21]

Additive manufacturing (also called 3D printing) involves taking digital designs from computer-aided-design (CAD) software and building a component by adding horizontal cross-sections layer by layer. Additive components are typically lighter and more durable than traditional parts, because they only put material where it is needed and require less welding and machining. Freed of traditional restrictions, additive manufacturing dramatically expands design possibilities for engineers, while reducing wasted material.

GE has a long history with additive technology. In the 1980s, the GE Global Research Center (GRC) in Niskayuna, New York, is involved in additive manufacturing research, leading to a dedicated laboratory in 2011. However, GE Aviation's collaboration with Morris Technologies eventually leads to a practical jet engine application, as additive manufacturing is used to solve a production challenge.

GE Aviation first engages Morris Technologies in the 1990s for the rapid prototyping of engine components in early development. By then, Morris Technologies, co-created by Cincinnati brothers Greg and Wendell Morris, along with Bill Noack, is emerging as a world-leading "job shop," where additive manufacturing

Inside the tip of this LEAP engine fuel nozzle is a complex fuel injector produced using additive manufacturing. The process results from years of collaboration with Morris Technologies.

machines produce advanced components for several industries. With factories in the Cincinnati suburbs of Sharonville and West Chester, Morris Technologies becomes one of the world's largest operators of additive machines.

By 2003, GE develops a new fuel nozzle injector (later for the LEAP) with a complex design nearly impossible to produce conventionally because of its elaborate interior geometry and small passages. If produced using conventional casting methods, every nozzle injector inside the fuel nozzle would require at least twenty parts welded and brazed together. That is a daunting and expensive proposition for a high-volume part.

Led by GE combustion engineer Marie McMasters, the company initiates a secret project with Morris to additively produce the complex fuel injector. Morris employees sign proprietary agreements as if it is a classified program, and work continues for years. By 2005, Morris and GE achieve a significant breakthrough: a fuel injector made of the superalloy cobalt chromium. "We used this alloy for dental and medical products," Greg Morris recalls. "GE was not familiar with it, and there was skepticism at first. But it proved highly durable."[22]

By 2012, Morris and GE develop the additive process parameters for mass-producing nineteen fuel nozzle injectors for each LEAP engine. At the same time, Robert McEwan, GE manufacturing leader, and Mohammad Ehteshami, vice president of engineering, advocate for an outright purchase of Morris Technologies. "When I saw what they could do with the nozzle, it was an epiphany," recalls Ehteshami. "I think the first thing out of my mouth was 'Buy them!'"[23] Even when the purchase is disclosed in late 2012, however, GE is mum on the years of secret additive development work on the LEAP fuel nozzle injector.

GE Aviation's additive manufacturing capabilities soon accelerate. GE creates the Additive Technology Center north of Cincinnati. Within six years of the acquisition, GE is mass-producing thousands of LEAP fuel injectors on rows of additive machines in Auburn, Alabama.

"The acquisition of Morris Technologies led us to get into the market and develop our own [additive] machines and powder," says Gary Mercer, vice president of engineering. "This technology is unique and has the promise of lower cost, while being lighter and more efficient. No technical trades—this is a win, win, and win."[24]

GE acquires Avio Aero of Italy: On the heels of the Morris acquisition, GE acquires the historic aviation business of Avio S.p.A, an Italy-based producer of aviation propulsion components and systems for civil and military aircraft. The $4.3 billion deal closes in 2013, and the operation becomes Avio Aero, a division of GE Aviation. Avio operates plants in Rivalta di Torino (Turin), Pomigliano d'Arco (Naples), Brindisi, and Cameri, Italy, as well as a plant in Poland.

A leading GE supplier for almost thirty years, Avio is a key provider of technology, particularly gearboxes and LPT technology, for the GE90 and GEnx, and a significant participant in the CT7/T700 civil and military helicopter programs. Before the acquisition, more than 50 percent of Avio's aviation business involves supporting GE and its partner companies.

GE's plans extend well beyond acquiring an established supplier. GE invests significantly in Avio's European operations, including the advanced engineering centers in Italy and Poland, and enhances Avio production capabilities as a leading supplier to such aerospace companies as P&W and Rolls-Royce. Avio also becomes an important supplier in the power-generation, oil, and the marine and industrial sectors.

Avio strengthens GE's global supply chain capabilities as engine production rates continue to rise. In addition, Avio is extensively engaged in additive manufacturing and bolsters GE's effort into this pioneering technology.

✈ Also in 2012...

CMC joint venture in Japan: With the growing demand for CMC raw material for GE and CFM engines, GE and Safran form the NGS joint venture to produce CMC fibers in partnership with Japan-based Nippon Carbon, a world-leading CMC material supplier. Within two years, the NGS joint venture doubles the size of its CMC factories in Japan to increase CMC fiber output by tenfold to meet the demand for LEAP engine shrouds and for other components across GE's commercial and military engine portfolio.

Next-generation fighter engine progress: GE's long journey to develop an adaptive-cycle engine for next-generation fighters continues. However, the new head-to-head competitor for GE is archrival P&W.

The USAF awards separate contracts to GE and P&W for the Adaptive Engine Technology Development (AETD) program to mature fuel-efficient, high-thrust engines for post-2020, sixth-generation combat aircraft and potential JSF F-35 upgrades. GE, P&W, and Rolls-Royce compete for the contract.

The ADVENT demonstrator program, precursor to the AETD programs, involved separate contracts for GE and Rolls-Royce demonstrator programs. However, Rolls-Royce is not selected for the AETD contract, which is intended to maintain a competing engine technology roadmap for future USAF fighter aircraft.

CT7: Bell Helicopter selects the GE CT7-2F1 engine to power its new Bell 525 "Relentless" Super Medium Transport helicopter.

GEnx-1B enters service on Dreamliner: The GEnx-1B enters service on the 787 Dreamliner after the first GEnx-powered 787 delivery to JAL.

2013
World's biggest jet engine gets bigger

Boeing launches GE9X in grand style: History repeats itself when Boeing selects the GE9X as the sole engine for a 777X twin-engine jetliner entering full-scale development. However, unlike the sole-source selection fourteen years earlier for the GE90-115B, this decision surprises no one.

By 2013, GE90 preeminence on the Boeing 777 family is well-earned. The 777-300ER surpasses all sales projections and becomes the airline industry's most profitable long-haul jetliner. The GE90-115B service entry on the aircraft is arguably the best for any new high-thrust engine, based on its reliability, and its low fuel burn, noise, and emission levels. The GEnx engine also enters service on the Boeing 787 and 747-8 with unique propulsion capabilities that are integral to the GE9X's technology suite.

While Boeing holds a formal engine competition for the 777X, GE has publicly committed to the program for years. GE also put its money where its mouth is. GE9X design begins as early as 2010, and, by the first 777X customer order, "$500 million is already invested in the engine," says Bill Fitzgerald, GE's head of commercial engines.[25]

That order, announced at the Dubai Air Show in November 2013, launches the GE9X in grand style, with Emirates committing to 150 777X aircraft. The deal is one of the largest single commercial engine orders in GE history. By this time, Emirates is already the largest operator of GE90-powered Boeing 777-300ERs and GP7200-powered A380s. GE is involved in establishing Emirates' engine overhaul capability in the Middle East and Asia as well.

Clearly, the GE9X benefits from GE's recent technology advances. "We had come off the GEnx and LEAP developments and could deploy that learning to the

GE9X," Fitzgerald says. "Knowing Boeing's design practices so well would heavily influence our approach in optimizing the GE9X for the aircraft."

"If we had taken the GEnx and scaled it up to 102,000 pounds [of thrust] we would have achieved a five percent improvement [in fuel burn], but we wanted to deliver more, and so we went with additional technologies," says Bill Millhaem, GE90 program manager.[26]

In the 105,000-pound thrust class, the GE9X is designed to achieve 10 percent better fuel efficiency than the GE90-115B and to produce lower emissions and noise. It incorporates several "industry firsts," including aviation's largest-diameter front fan, highest pressure-ratio compressor ever, and CMC core engine components.

Bill Fitzgerald, head of commercial engines, leads the GE9X campaign.

The 133.5-inch fan diameter exceeds the 128-inch fan of the GE90-115B. The fourth-generation carbon-fiber blades are surrounded in a carbon-fiber fan case like the LEAP and GEnx engines. GE9X fan-blade count is reduced to sixteen, compared to eighteen for the GEnx and twenty-two for the GE90-115B.

The eleven-stage compressor's 27:1 pressure ratio, a record for a commercial turbofan, compares to 23:1 for the GEnx and 18:1 for the GE90-115B. By building upon the GEnx and LEAP experience, the GE9X is expected to contribute half of the aircraft's 20 percent fuel efficiency improvement over previous 777 models.

The CMC components comprise the combustor liner, first- and second-stage high-pressure turbine nozzles and first-stage shrouds. The CMCs are matured and validated through extensive GEnx test runs in 2015-2016 using scaled CMCs. As with the LEAP, the GE9X fuel nozzle injectors are produced with additive manufacturing machines.

The technology infusion into the GE9X, from new materials to additive manufacturing, creates "a massive hidden multiplier," Fitzgerald contends. Over time, GE will feed GE9X technology into the company's large base of commercial engines in service.

During the decade of 2010 to 2020, the airframe manufacturers double the airline capacity for long-range, twin-aisle aircraft. The GE90, GEnx, and GE9X turbofans place GE in an enviable position to power these aircraft for decades.

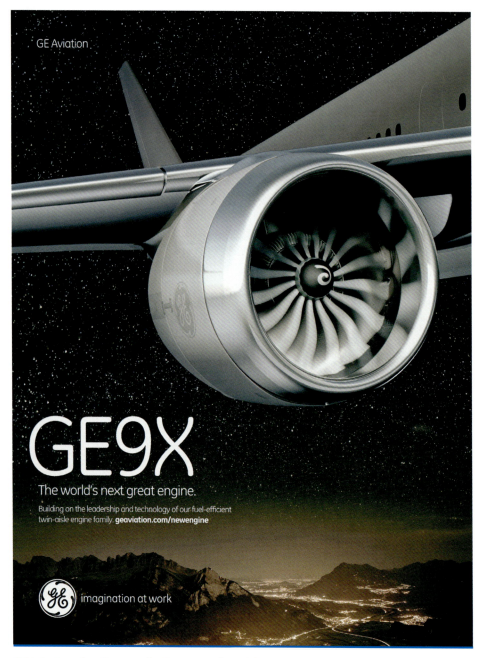

GE Aviation advertisement for the GE9X selected for the new Boeing 777X jetliner. Like its GE90 predecessor, the GE9X introduces several unique technologies.

Temperatures rising: For six years, GE's military team in Evendale has prepared for this day. Tests begin on the ADVENT engine, the world's first fully adaptive (variable) cycle engine for future combat aircraft.

During tests, the engine achieves core temperatures more than 130 degrees Fahrenheit above target, resulting in the highest combination of compressor and turbine temperatures ever recorded. GE's aggressive technology investments in both military and commercial engines fuel the ADVENT effort, including a compressor based on the LEAP design, CMC core components, and additively-manufactured parts.

The end result: a 25 percent improvement in engine fuel efficiency for the next-generation fighter. Dan McCormick, head of GE's adaptive cycle programs, leads an analysis of the engine parts with the USAF, which publicly praises GE's unique technical achievement. "To be in the game for the long haul, we knew we had to make a clear step change in the technology," says Jean Lydon-Rodgers, head of GE's military business.[27]

The ADVENT program, which began for GE in 2007, follows a long history of GE advances in adaptive-cycle (also referred to as variable cycle) technology dating back to the 1960s. The GE YJ101, the first full engine to demonstrate variable-cycle capabilities in 1976, leads to the YF120 variable-cycle engine, which set the world super-cruise record in 1990 for the USAF's Advanced Tactical Fighter (ATF) program. Unlike fixed-cycle engines powering today's aircraft, variable-cycle engines are designed to operate efficiently in conditions across the entire flight envelope, including subsonic and supersonic speeds.

GE's latest ADVENT design also includes a third stream of air that can be used to achieve maximum fuel efficiency and optimal thermal management.

GE's progress in adaptive-cycle technology does not end with ADVENT testing. GE continues to improve the technology through the USAF's next technology phase, called the Adaptive Engine Technology Development (AETD) program, pitting GE against P&W.

✈ Also in 2013...

Embraer E-Jet E2 engine decision: After CF34 turbofans successfully power the fast-selling Embraer ERJ-170 and ERJ-190 regional jets for more than a decade, GE decides not to aggressively compete for Embraer's next-generation E-Jet E2 family of aircraft. The regional jets are launched with P&W PW1000G engines.

GE cannot make the business case to justify the development investment. However, GE does not view this decision as a parting of ways with longtime customer Embraer. "After the decision, I told Fred Curado [Embraer president] that we will continue to be his best engine supplier," GE's Bill Fitzgerald says.[28]

At the time, analysts are forecasting that GE-powered ERJ-170 and ERJ-190 fleets will be largely out of production by the decade's end. However, both aircraft models will continue to experience strong production runs well beyond 2020. Further, Embraer recognizes GE Aviation with a "supplier of the year" award in 2017.

New UK aerostructures site: GE's aerostructures business begins development of a composites production facility at its Hamble, UK, site to support the manufacture of wing components for the Airbus A350 jetliner. The A350 XWB contract is the largest in Hamble's 75-year history, comprising more than 3,000 components from composite panels to complex machined assembles.

Jack Parker passing: A giant in GE's aviation journey, Jack S. Parker dies at age 94. He joined GE in 1950 and soon headed the Aircraft Gas Turbine Division in Lynn. Among his many contributions are turning Lynn into a turboshaft engine powerhouse and committing to GE's return to the large commercial engine business in the late 1960s. He served as GE vice chairman from 1968 to 1980 as a strong advocate for GE's aviation programs.

HF120 certifies: The GE Honda HF120 business jet engine is certified.

Passport testing: The first full engine tests begin for the Passport engine.

CT7-2E1: The advanced civil version of the T700-701D, the CT7-2E1, is certified for the AW189 helicopter.

2014
GE's manufacturing renaissance

Building out production capability: A surging commercial production backlog, exceeding 15,000 engines for GE and its partners by 2014, drives a transformation of GE's supply chain. The number of jet engines in airline service will grow to 39,000 by decade's end. Moreover, the new engines require more sophisticated manufacturing and material processes.

The production tidal wave requires dramatic preparations. From 2011 to 2016, GE Aviation spends $4.3 billion in the US to create new factories and to expand and upgrade existing sites, including $350 million to renovate the Evendale headquarters and add test cells. Another $1.1 billion is invested in international operations. In total, the company is adding two million square feet of manufacturing floor space across its international network of plants.

Colleen Athans, head of the supply chain, feels the challenge firsthand. "Producing the new engines is challenging due to tighter tolerances and new materials systems," she says. "While we ramp up, the flying fleet in service keeps growing and requires more overhauls, repairs, and spare parts. Influencing our factory investments is the need to drive year-over-year productivity through improved processes and automation."[29]

GE's supply chain highlights in 2014, the year peak investments are made, include establishing operations unique to jet propulsion:

- **Auburn goes additive:** The Auburn, Alabama, plant is designated for large-scale additive manufacturing. Within four years, rows of additive machines are installed, producing thousands of fuel nozzle injectors for the LEAP engine. Auburn is also a LEAP component machining shop.
- **Evendale CMC laboratory:** The CMC Fastworks Laboratory opens in Building 700 in Evendale to further integrate CMC production. The factory building that once mass-produced Wright radial engines during World War II now houses a research lab where CMC components are fabricated for the first time in low-rate production.

From Evendale, the innovative fabrication processes will transfer to the CMC lean factory in Newark, Delaware. Jonathan Blank, the lab's first manager, describes the process as "building to a factor of ten." In other words, Evendale creates the roadmap for fabricating a production lot of CMC parts, which, in turn, are produced at ten times that original volume at the Delaware facility, which is also expanded in 2014. From Delaware, CMC fabrication transitions to mass CMC production in Asheville, North Carolina.

- **Asheville CMC factory:** Announced the previous year, the brand new Asheville plant opens in 2014 to produce CMC HPT shrouds for the LEAP, in addition to CMC components for military engines. It is the world's first factory dedicated to large-scale CMC production for jet engines. Investments in GE's CMC sites soar as the company runs CMCs in the cores of LEAP and advanced military engines.

GE Aviation's new engine assembly operation in Lafayette, Indiana, is just one of eight new facilities established by GE Aviation in just a decade.

• Lafayette, Indiana, assembly: A new 300,000-square foot assembly factory is announced in Lafayette, Indiana, near Purdue University, for LEAP final assembly. The facility opens in 2016 to complement LEAP assembly in Durham, North Carolina. Lafayette is also designated as a LEAP maintenance and overhaul shop. Indiana Governor Mike Pence, the future US vice president, is part of the 2014 announcement celebration.

• Peebles, Ohio: In 2014, GE completes a $70 million expansion of the Peebles Test Operation in Adams County, Ohio, following the $90 million expansion in 2007. Peebles now operates eleven test sites, including two large indoor sites. The site handles engine certification and development tests, final acceptance testing before customer delivery, final engine assembly (GE90, GEnx, Passport), and maintenance and repair.

In addition to a larger manufacturing presence, GE also broadens its involvement in the communities where it operates, including more collaboration with area schools and universities, as well as local, state, and federal government officials.

Influenced by GE's campaign earlier in the decade to promote the economic benefits for a competing JSF engine, the company's investment in US manufacturing sites creates a greater political outreach for the future.

GE electrical power for 777X: GE's investment in electrical power and distribution drives the company's success in competing as an electrical power supplier for future jetliners. GE wins a contract for the Boeing 777X's electrical load management system (ELMS), backup generator, and the backup converter.

This win represents GE's first electrical-power generating system for a commercial jetliner after decades of providing electrical power for military aircraft. To handle the higher loads from the 777X's GE9X engines, systems, and large passenger cabin, the ELMS will manage 30 percent higher main and auxiliary power unit generator outputs compared to the 777-300ER system.

GE commissioned the EPISCENTER in Dayton, Ohio, and EPIC site in Cheltenham, England, to model and simulate how the electrical system and components will perform. The ELMS will be handled from Cheltenham, while the backup generator and converter systems are managed at GE's Dayton sites.

GE's avionics site in Grand Rapids, Michigan, provides the common core system for the Boeing 777X, based on the computing system in the Boeing 787, as well as the enhanced airborne flight recorder.

✈ Also in 2014...

Yet another T64 application: GE's venerable T64 engine, first developed in the late 1950s, is selected to power Bell Helicopter's V-280 tilt-rotor demonstrator for the Army Joint Multi-Role (JMR) technology demonstrator.

LEAP and Passport take flight: First flights of the LEAP and Passport engines occur on the GE flying testbed aircraft in Victorville, California.

G3000 (T901) engine tests: With funding through the US Army-managed Advanced Affordable Turbine Engine (AATE) and Future Affordable Turbine Engine (FATE) programs, GE completes initial tests on the GE3000 (later designated the T901) turboshaft engine.

2015
Challenging a turboprop dynasty

GE launches the Catalyst: Just as GE in the early 1950s sparks a turboshaft revolution for helicopters with its T58 engine, Pratt &Whitney Canada in the early 1960s fosters a similar revolution for small propeller-driven airplanes with its PT6 turboprop engine.

New engines tested on GE's 747 flying testbed aircraft in Victorville, California. GE mounts the LEAP engine on the wing of the 747-400 in the foreground. Behind it, the Passport engine flies on the wing of GE's venerable 747-100, one of the first 747s ever built.

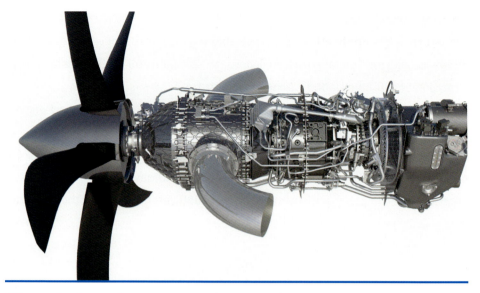

GE's new Catalyst engine represents an important advancement in turboprop technology. Textron's Cessna Aircraft company launches the engine in 2015.

Introduced in 1964 and soon popularized on the Beech King Air aircraft, the PT6 will dominate the civil turboprop airplane landscape for decades, with more than 50,000 engines delivered for more than 130 aircraft models. For a half-century, the PT6 franchise expands without a serious competitive challenge.

That changes in 2015. After months of secret negotiations, Brad Mottier, GE's head of business and general aviation, unveils the Advanced Turboprop Engine (later named "Catalyst") for a new Textron Cessna airplane at the National Business Aviation Association Show in Las Vegas, Nevada.

For Mottier, who established GE's business and general aviation division in 2008, creating a strong competitor to the entrenched PT6 has been a multi-year priority. Step one involves establishing the H80 turboprop engine at GE's operations in Prague, Czech Republic, a move that builds GE's experience in small turboprop engines for general aviation.

However, GE needs a far greater technology disruption to challenge the PT6 preeminence. The Catalyst presents the industry not only with a major advance in turboprop technology, but its control system will also make flying small prop-driven airplanes easier than ever before.

Three years before the Catalyst launch, the GE team engages airplane manufacturers and individual operators to be sure a serious appetite exists for a new, clean-sheet turboprop in the 1,000 to 1,600 horsepower class for both current and future airplane models.

"At first, no one took our program seriously, but, by 2014, people were clearly excited," Mottier says. "Cessna kept pushing us to advance the technology, and that gave us all the encouragement we needed. After all, if we didn't bring something really different and better to the table, why would airframers ever change to the GE engine?"[30] Textron (Cessna's parent company) initiates an engine competition for its new Cessna Denali airplane, and the Catalyst is selected.

While four iterations of the Catalyst are designed and evaluated, GE concurrently introduces the Electronic Engine and Propeller Control (EEPC) system for its H80 H Series turboprop engine. It is general aviation's first single-lever control for engine and propeller operations. The EEPC becomes the proving ground for the Catalyst's system.

The Catalyst EEPC governs engine and propeller pitch with a FADEC. Unlike previous hydromechanical, multi-lever control systems in the cockpit of small prop planes, the Catalyst's single lever simplifies the pilot's job and maximizes performance without overdriving the engine. The EEPC system governs engine and propeller pitch as a single system.

The Catalyst design feeds upon GE's broad technology portfolio. By incorporating 3D aerodynamic design from the GE9X program, the Catalyst has double the pressure ratio of turboprops in its class, which delivers far greater fuel efficiency and power. The titanium compressor, with four axial-flow stages and one centrifugal impeller stage (from the T700 turboshaft engine) feeds air into a reverse flow single-annular combustor. The two-stage HPT blades are made with single-crystal material.

In another sweeping change for GE, the Catalyst is the company's first all-new "European engine," incorporating components designed at Avio Aero sites in Italy and Poland, as well as from GE Aviation's engineering team in Poland. In addition, component and engine design, testing, and final assembly are all performed at the GE Czech complex in Prague.

The Catalyst also has more components designed and produced using additive manufacturing than any previous aviation engine, comprising more than 25 percent of the overall engine. The additive parts reduce engine weight and improve SFC.

GE realizes that such a technology innovation in additive manufacturing requires a significant demonstrator program in advance. In just 18 months, GE secretly assembles and tests a CT7 demonstrator engine with 35 percent of the engine content produced through additive manufacturing. GE completes testing of the "additive CT7 demonstrator" in late 2016, and runs a second demonstrator in 2017.

Most popular commercial turbofans: In 2015, the FlightGlobal Ascend Aircraft Fleet Database ranks the most popular commercial aviation turbofan engines since the dawn of the jetliner age in the mid-1950s. The rankings are based on a sixty-year tally of installed engine deliveries:

1. CFM International: CFM56 family—22,418 engines.
2. P&W: JT8D family—12,049 engines.
3. GE Aviation: CF6 family—6,241 engines.
4. International Aero Engines (IAE): V2500 family—5,774 engines.
5. GE Aviation: CF34 family—5,694 engines.
6. P&W: JT3D family—4,184 engines.
7. Aviadvigatel (Soviet Union): Soloviev DC-30 family—3,260 engines.
8. P&W: PW400 family—2,846 engines.
9. Ivchenko (Soviet Union): Al-25 family—3,260 engines.
10. Rolls-Royce: RB211 family—2,832 engines.

✈ Also in 2015...

Additive R&D in West Chester, Ohio: GE creates the Additive Technology Center in West Chester, Ohio. Initially, the plant consolidates research equipment and additive machines from Morris Technologies facilities acquired in 2012.

"The idea is to co-locate our most forward-thinking engineers in the additive world with R&D equipment, like they do in Silicon Valley or at the automotive headquarters in Detroit," says Greg Morris, the center's first manager.[31] The center works closely with GE Aviation and Avio Aero in Italy in increasing additive components in jet engines, including the Catalyst engine launched in 2015.

Huntsville, Alabama: GE announces plans to establish CMC fiber and tape factories in Huntsville, Alabama. GE will invest more than $200 million to construct a plant to mass-produce silicon carbide (SiC) ceramic fiber, which will be the first high-volume production plant of its kind in the US. An adjacent factory will use the SiC ceramic fiber to make the unidirectional CMC tape necessary to fabricate CMC components. The plants will support not only GE CMC production capability but also the US defense industry.

HF120 enters service: The HondaJet with the HF120 engine enters service. It is certified in Europe the following year.

LEAP-1A certification: The LEAP-1A for the Airbus A320neo receives FAA FAR 33 certification, setting the stage for the engine's entry into service the following year.

2016
GE's future military engines

Key military milestones: Military power is deeply imbedded in GE Aviation's DNA. That is why the company's exit from the JSF program in 2011 only further emboldens the Evendale military team to power the next generation of combat aircraft. At the same time, Lynn's military team is equally dedicated to inventing turboshaft technology for future helicopters.

By 2016, GE's military propulsion efforts coalesce and point clearly to a strong future. For almost a decade, GE teams have immersed themselves in US military-sponsored technology programs to meet aggressive propulsion goals. More than 700 GE engineers transition from commercial engine programs to join their fellow GE engineers engaged in protecting and growing GE's military propulsion future.

"We have a culture where engineers are passionate about advancing very specialized military technologies," says Jean Lydon-Rodgers. "They are very aware that they are creating technologies that their children will work on as production engines. This is a tradition as old as our company."[32]

In both the combat aircraft and helicopter propulsion arenas, government-sponsored, cost-sharing contract awards in 2016 affirm GE's special commitment to military propulsion:

GE executive Jean Lydon-Rodgers leads the military business during a key transition.

The innovative T901 turboshaft engine developed in Lynn.

AETP award: In June, the USAF awards GE Aviation a $1 billion contract running through 2021 to continue advancing its three-stream adaptive-cycle technology through the Adaptive Engine Transition Program (AETP). The USAF considers future applications on an advanced fighter, as well as a potential upgrade for the F-35 JSF program.

With the award, Evendale engineers continue their decade-long efforts on adaptive engine design. GE raises the bar by demonstrating the capability of adaptive engine technology to extend a fighter jet's operating range by 30 percent and to improve fuel consumption by 25 percent, while increasing thrust by more than 10 percent. In addition, GE integrates the first rotating CMC components, LPT blades, which are successfully tested for 500 cycles at high operating temperatures and stresses.

FATE award: The Lynn team demonstrates its turboshaft prowess by running the first full engine in the Future Affordable Turbine Engine (FATE) program for the US Army. The engine is designed to reduce SFC by 35 percent, improve the power-to-weight ratio by 80 percent, and design life by 20 percent, in addition to a 45 percent reduction in production and maintenance costs.

GE's FATE compressor rig records the highest single-spool compressor pressure ratio in GE's history. Needless to say, the late Jack Parker, the founding father of GE's turboshaft franchise in the 1950s, would be amazed by the progress. The FATE combustor incorporates CMC components, and the turbine is built using additive manufacturing.

ITEP award: On the heels of the FATE engine tests, the US Army awards GE a $102 million contract for the preliminary design of the T901 engine (originally the GE3000) for the Improved Turbine Engine Program (ITEP). The T901 is a 3,000-shaft horsepower engine for Army Black Hawk and Apache helicopters.

The T901, designed as a single-spool engine for maintainability, integrates technologies from two Army-sponsored technology programs: the Advanced Affordable Turbine Engine (AATE) and the FATE program. GE's goal with the T901 is to maintain engine simplicity with a modular design and single-spool architecture while improving overall performance.

Bolstered by its large commercial engine portfolio, GE is advancing the use of CMCs and additive manufacturing to benefit military jet engine performance. Lydon-Rodgers and her team often present to military leaders GE's special technology box, which they amusingly call the "Petting Zoo."

The box includes CMC and additive components. "While it is fun to watch generals toss CMC blades in the air with one hand while tossing a heavier metal blade of the same size with the other, in all seriousness, it shows the huge investments GE has made for their future engines," she recalls.[33]

✈ Also in 2016…

Establishing GE Aviation, Digital Solutions: Four years earlier, GE Aviation acquires a forty-employee company in Austin, Texas, which digitally captures and analyzes flight data. For GE, the small company is the start of something big.

Austin Digital, folded into GE Engine Services, reveals new ways to use flight data analysis to optimize customers' flight operations. The acquisition gives GE access to analytical tools for a range of digital services important to airlines and business jet operators.

Among its many benefits, flight data analysis involves trend monitoring to reveal potential risks, while, at the same time, supporting routine maintenance and engineering actions. This analysis can optimize fuel usage, reduce emissions, and improve engine component life, providing an attractive business proposition to aircraft operators. Over the next several years, GE Aviation begins to bring economic benefits to airline customers by marrying GE's vast aviation knowledge base to the fast-evolving tools used for analyzing massive reams of digital flight data.

In 2016, the company's growing digital offerings are consolidated under a single business called GE Aviation, Digital Solutions. Its broad menu of digital products gains traction with airlines worldwide, supported by a global network of digital customer collaboration centers.

GE Aviation, Digital Solutions is well positioned to offer digital services for flight and operational efficiency to a large global customer base. After all, the same digital tools help GE to better understand and forecast the operating characteristics of 35,000 GE and partner company engines in airline service, which are monitored in real time as part of long-term service packages.

In 2017, GE Aviation, Digital Solutions adds to its portfolio the company Critical Technologies, branded AirVault®, a supplier of cloud-based, digital records management. AirVault® has access to mission-critical records across an industrial supply chain network. After the acquisition, the company is managing seven billion aircraft maintenance records with one million new updates per day.

Establishing an additive business: An early adopter of additive manufacturing, GE suddenly becomes a leading provider of the technology when the company boldly acquires two additive firms in Europe.

Arcam AB of Sweden and Concept Laser of Germany become part of a new business, GE Additive, which reports to David Joyce, president and CEO of GE Aviation. Since 2010, GE has invested $1.5 billion in additive technologies across its research laboratories and industrial businesses, and has earned 346 patents in powder metals technologies. With the fuel-nozzle injector on the CFM LEAP engine, GE Aviation introduces the first complex component in a jet engine core produced with additive manufacturing.

Based in Mölndal, Sweden, Arcam AB, inventor of electron beam melting (EBM) machines for metal-based additive manufacturing, is also a leading producer of advanced metal powders. At the time of the acquisition, Arcam already has a relationship with Aero Avio, which is heavily engaged in EBM technology.

Concept Laser, based in Lichtenfels, Germany, pioneered metal additive manufacturing with laser additive machines capable of processing various powder materials, including titanium, nickel-base, cobalt-chromium, and precious metal alloys, as well as hot-work and high-grade steels and aluminum.

Immediately after the acquisitions, GE invests in Arcam AB and Concept Laser operations to bolster their product lines and customer field support. In addition, GE Aviation will leverage the new capability to drive additive opportunities across the jet engine portfolio.

Unique power extraction: GE Aviation expands its electrical power and distribution capabilities by successfully extracting power from jet engines to generate electricity for future aircraft requirements. With support from NASA and the USAF, GE successfully demonstrates a "dual-spool" extraction of one megawatt of power from a F110 fighter engine.

This feat is accomplished by pulling 250 kilowatts from the engine's HPT and 750 kilowatts from the LPT. The electricity is extracted while the engine continues to generate conventional thrust and run at altitude conditions. Typically, power extraction from a jet engine is derived exclusively from the HPT.

In addition, GE focuses on taking large capability and making it smaller, lighter, and cooler. For example, GE is researching silicon carbide transistors. The devices have higher temperature capability and reliability, twice the current-carrying density, and ten times greater switching speeds compared to traditional silicon devices.

These technologies are part of a broader GE effort to advance power conversion, electrical distribution, energy storage, and overall power integration systems, which are required for future hybrid electric and electrical propulsion concepts.

Leaping forward: The LEAP-1B engine for the Boeing 737 MAX receives FAA engine certification. Meanwhile, the LEAP-1A engine enters service on the Airbus A320neo.

Prague, Czech Republic: GE establishes Prague, Czech Republic, as the site for the new development and production center for the Catalyst turboprop engine.

Passport certified: The FAA certifies GE's Passport turbofan for the Bombardier Global 7000 and Global 8000 long-range business jets.

CF34 milestone: The COMAC ARJ21 regional jet, powered by the CF34-10, enters passenger service.

GE9X tests: The first full GE9X engine goes to test.

2017
All eyes on the LEAP engine

Uncharted territory: The CFM LEAP turbofan's production ramp-up and aggressive entry into airline service reach a scale never before seen in commercial aviation.

More than a decade of strong airline growth fuels record orders for single-aisle jetliners. In recent years, most airline orders are for the re-engined Airbus A320neo and Boeing 737 MAX. In addition, earlier versions of these two jetliners continue to sell briskly, and the single-aisle COMAC C919 is making inroads in the Chinese market. The LEAP and CFM56 turbofans are either the exclusive engines or the best-selling engines on these popular jetliners.

As they say: You can do the math. The amazing, if not daunting, CFM statistics speak for themselves.

By 2017, the LEAP turbofan order backlog reaches 14,500 engines and then exceeds 15,500 the following year. That represents seven years worth of engine production waiting in the wings for CFM partners GE and Safran.

LEAP turbofan delivery rates grow from seventy-seven engines in 2016 to 459 in 2017 to approximately 1,100 in 2018—the first year LEAP engine deliveries surpass CFM56 engine deliveries. By 2020, LEAP engine deliveries are expected to reach 2,000 engines.

In twenty-seven months, the first 1,000 LEAP engines are delivered. That triples the rate for initial CFM56-7 and CFM56-5 deliveries.

While LEAP engine production scales up, CFM also delivers in high volume the CFM56 engines for earlier A320s and 737s. Between 2014 and 2018, more than 7,000 CFM56 engines are delivered. In fact, CFM56 deliveries set a CFM record in 2016 at 1,700 engines. These CFM56 models were first introduced in the 1990s for the A320 and 737 jetliner families.

In 2017, total CFM engine deliveries (including both CFM56 and LEAP engine models) surpass 30,000 engines since the formation of the joint venture. However, CFM takes another 3,344 CFM (LEAP and CFM56) orders and commitments that same year. By the end of 2018, the CFM delivery total since initial production in the early 1980s is in the 33,000-engine range.

GE's famed J47 fighter engine of the 1940s and 1950s, formerly the most-produced jet engine ever with more than 35,000 engines delivered, is now looking over its shoulder at the growing CFM engine fleet.

As LEAP and CFM56 engines roll off the GE and Safran assembly lines in the US and France, the joint company moves into overdrive with airline operators to support the rapid deployment of CFM-powered jetliners. "CFM customers range from the world's largest and most experienced airlines to new operators with a handful of planes and a steep learning curve," says Bill Fitzgerald, head of GE's commercial engines. "The customer profiles are wildly diverse and in every corner of the world."[34] By 2017, the technical teams for more than 300 customers are trained to operate and maintain the new LEAP engine.

The LEAP-powered Airbus A320neo enters commercial service with Pegasus Airlines in 2016, followed by the LEAP-powered Boeing 737 MAX in initial service with Malindo in 2017. The LEAP-powered COMAC C919 begins test flights in China that same year. For the tidal wave of new planes entering airline fleets, the CFM focus can be defined in one word: utilization.

CFM manages the fleet introductions through the LEAP engine's inherent reliability, the application of predictive maintenance analytical tools, and the massive support infrastructure of Safran and GE involving 250 field technicians, three call centers, and a global network of eight "quick-turn" engine facilities.

The strategy works. By mid-2018, just two years after the first Airbus A320neo is delivered, more than 400 LEAP-powered Airbus A320neos and Boeing 737 MAX aircraft are in service, flying more than ten hours a day on average. Straight out of the gate, these new LEAP engines are among the most utilized turbofans in airline service, accumulating more than 1.5 million flight hours in two years.

"One percent more aircraft utilization translates into a five percent fuel burn advantage for the airlines," says Allen Paxson, CFM program leader at the 2018 Farnborough Air Show. "The airlines only make money when they are flying passengers. The customers are running the [LEAP] engine all day long and every day."[35]

Still, the unprecedented ramp-up of the LEAP engine challenges CFM. Low first-time yields on certain castings and forgings, along with other concerns, periodically slow production rates. Yet, as 2018 draws to a close, CFM delivery rates closely approach original targets.

While premature shroud coating losses in the HPT lead to some engine removals, the LEAP engine fleet is delivering on projected performance. The LEAP engine in its first two years in operation does not experience any mechanical de-

The fast-selling, LEAP-powered Airbus A320neo.

sign issues. "So far, we haven't had to redesign anything in the engine," Paxson says. "The engine design is stable."[36]

✈ Also in 2017...

GE9X testing: The GE9X large turbofan for the Boeing 777X begins engine certification testing. Veteran GE engineer Ted Ingling leads the program.

Catalyst running: The new Catalyst turboprop engine completes its first full engine tests at GE's turboprop operation in Prague, Czech Republic.

25 years of regional jet power: When the CF34-3-powered Bombardier CRJ100 entered passenger service in 1992, GE Aviation never imagined how successful its regional jet engine franchise would become. In 2017, GE celebrates twenty-five years powering regional jet aircraft with more than 6,500 engines delivered. GE-powered regional jets produced by Bombardier, Embraer, and COMAC operate in 130 countries with 12,000 daily passenger flights.

New MAX variant launched: At the Paris Air Show, Boeing launches the larger-capacity 737 MAX 10 powered by the LEAP-1B turbofan.

Going beyond 65,000: Also at Paris, GE Aviation announces that more than 65,000 commercial and military jet engines from GE and its partner companies are powering aircraft worldwide. Between 2016 and 2020, GE and its partners expect to deliver an additional 10,000 engines to commercial and military customers.

2018
CMCs: GE's bold technology odyssey

Creating a new material system: At the grand opening of a unique production complex in Huntsville, Alabama, a confident Mike Kauffman approaches the microphone. "GE Aviation and our partners have cracked the code on mass producing CMC [ceramic matrix composite] material," he says on a warm May morning. "The impact will be felt around the globe."[37]

On the surface, his comments smack of hyperbole. After all, GE Aviation's CMC supply chain leader is speaking before a crowd of smiling politicians, community leaders, and reporters who are viewing GE's two sparkling, new factories, which will produce CMC raw material and hire hundreds of area workers.

Before the crowd, Kauffman also cites an Institute for Defense Analysis report from 2001 warning that "there may be more pigs flying than ceramics in the future," which reflects a common industry view at the time on the prospect for CMCs in jet engines.[38] "Not that I'm keeping score, but we beat the pigs to the air," Kauffman says.[39]

Indeed, GE Aviation's CMC initiative, among the most aggressive technology efforts in the company's history, is living up to the hype by 2018. CMC turbine shrouds are now successfully operating in the hottest section of the best-selling CFM LEAP turbofan, which is powering hundreds of commercial jetliners. CMC components are benefiting GE's military designs, including a demonstrator engine that achieved the highest jet-engine temperatures ever. GE has successfully tested CMC rotating parts.

At the Huntsville grand opening, GE Aviation celebrates another CMC milestone: a decade-long investment to establish America's first fully-integrated CMC supply chain, which includes a network of four interrelated GE production sites. In fact, three months after the Huntsville grand opening, GE Aviation's new CMC component-assembly plant in Asheville, North Carolina, produces its 25,000[th] CMC turbine shroud. The plant also successfully fabricates five different CMC hot-section components for the GE9X high-thrust engine.

With more than $1.5 billion invested, CMC technology is a centerpiece of GE's jet propulsion strategy for the twenty-first century. There is no turning back.

It has been a long odyssey. CMCs are made of SiC, ceramic fibers and ceramic resin, manufactured through a sophisticated process and further enhanced with proprietary coatings. CMCs are one-third the density of metal alloys and one-third the weight. Because they are more heat resistant than metal alloys, CMCs require less air from the flow path of a jet engine to be diverted to cool the hot-section components. By keeping more air in the flow path instead of cooling parts, the engine runs more efficiently at higher thrust. In total, CMCs bring better fuel efficiency, lower emissions, and greater durability.

During jet propulsion's history, the average rate of increase for turbine engine material temperature capability is about 50 degrees Fahrenheit per decade. With CMCs, GE increases jet engine temperatures by 150 degrees Fahrenheit in one decade. As CMCs further populate the core of GE engines, they are expected to increase engine thrust by 25 percent and improve fuel burn by 10 percent.

While the benefits are attractive, industrializing CMCs has posed a huge challenge to private industry for decades. Difficult to fabricate, CMCs also have brittle properties. The US government has funded CMC research since the early 1970s,

At the Huntsville, Alabama plant, technicians create ceramic matrix composite (CMC) raw material for commercial and military applications. By 2018, GE Aviation establishes a fully integrated supply chain network for producing CMC components.

and GE scientists have wrestled with the technology ever since then. In the 1980s, GE pursued CMCs for large ground-based gas turbines and filed for its first CMC patent in 1986. Within twenty years, the company successfully ran CMC turbine shrouds in multiple industrial gas turbine applications.

By the mid-2000s, GE's Global Research Center (GRC) began to shift its CMC focus to jet engines. "There was a steering of the ship to jet engines as we progressed the technology," recalls Sanjay Correa, GRC's former head of Energy and Propulsion Technology, and, later, head of GE Aviation's CMC program. "Because they reduce weight, CMCs held even greater potential for flying engines."[40]

A corresponding effort unfolds at GE Aviation, both in demonstrating CMCs in engines and in building the supply chain. By 2018, the company has CMC sites in Evendale, Ohio (component development); Newark, Delaware (low-rate production); Asheville, North Carolina (full-rate production); and Huntsville, Alabama (raw materials). GE and Safran's joint venture with Nippon Carbon of Japan, a leading producer and innovator of CMC raw material, is instrumental in establishing the Huntsville site.

The last of GE's CMC production sites, the Huntsville complex is comprised of two factories on 100 acres. One produces SiC ceramic fiber, the first high-volume production operation in the US. Supported by USAF funding, this plant increases US capability to produce SiC ceramic fiber capable of temperatures of 2,400 degrees Fahrenheit. The adjacent factory uses SiC ceramic fiber to make unidirectional CMC prepreg, a reinforcing fabric that has been pre-impregnated with the resin system necessary to fabricate CMC components.

The Huntsville operation begins delivering raw material in late 2018. At the same time, the CMC demand for GE and CFM engines has grown twentyfold over the course of a decade. And that is just the beginning. The six tons of CMC raw material produced in Huntsville's first full year of operation is likely to grow tenfold by 2028.

"We are able to do coatings and infiltration technology at scale and at rate," Kauffman tells *Aviation Week & Space Technology* in late 2018. "With the fiber and matrix, we have solved the ability to coat the fiber in large quantities and to put on chemical vapor deposition coatings in a way that allows us to do it at scale. We can do it in a fiber format that can be made into a tape [prepreg], which can then be laid out. That's one of the huge technical hurdles we have overcome."[41]

With an established supply chain, GE Aviation continues to increase CMC production rates and improve shop-floor productivity, both key factors in driving down the overall cost curve at a rapid rate. GE's advancements in CMC production, castings, and coatings will facilitate a greater CMC presence in new engines, as well as in replacement parts for the massive GE and CFM base of jet engines in commercial and military service.

In the same way digital analytics is driving jet propulsion efficiencies, the same technology is refining GE's CMC production processes, says Jonathan Blank, CMC leader at the Evendale lab. "We will institutionalize our learning, further develop the robustness of the material and process models, and drive digital tools deeper into our processes to make analytics a way of life for this vertically integrated technology," Blank says.[42]

GE's CMC story parallels the historic aviation narrative. The continuous advancement of materials dates back to the Wright Brothers with the first powered-aircraft comprised of wood, steel, and canvas. Faster and more capable airplanes drove the introduction of metal alloys, such as aluminum, titanium, and other high-temperature metals.

In the jet propulsion industry, GE has introduced some of the world's most advanced metal alloys, including single-crystal alloys, inside the jet engine core. "Both the chemistry and processing of new materials are stepping-stones for advancements in thermal efficiency, fuel burn, and emissions," says Gary Mercer, vice president of engineering.[43] During the 1990s, when GE introduced carbon-fiber composite fan blades for the GE90 turbofan, aircraft manufacturers more aggressively pursued large composite structures to reduce aircraft weight and increase durability.

With CMCs, GE's journey will extend beyond the jet engine to support broader aerospace requirements, including space travel, where operating environments can be most extreme. These developments will "rocket" GE Aviation into the role of world-class CMC provider for a fast-evolving aerospace environment well into the twenty-first century.

"We are at generation one with CMCs," says Mercer. "As you think of the future of flight, light and hotter are two constants. With the reemergence of supersonic, hypersonic, and reusable space vehicles, it is easy to see how CMCs will add value to future propulsion and airframes alike."[44]

✈ Also in 2018...

Further progress for future fighter engine: GE gains further momentum in its quest to power future USAF combat aircraft when the USAF awards a $437 million contract modification for propulsion risk reduction on the company's adaptive-cycle combat engine.

The contract bolsters an eleven-year effort by GE and the USAF to mature technologies for adaptive-cycle engines through the successful ADVENT, AETD, and AETP technology demonstration programs. Between 2007 and 2018, GE successfully designs and tests multiple three-stream adaptive fan configurations, an advanced compressor rig, two full-scale core engines, and a full three-stream, adaptive-cycle technology demonstrator engine.

An Affinity for SST: GE completes initial design of its Affinity turbofan engine, the first civil supersonic engine in decades, for the proposed Aerion AS2 supersonic business jet. The Affinity engine is being studied as a dual-spool, dual-fan turbofan with the highest bypass-ratio of any supersonic engine. In addition to GE, Aerion is collaborating with Honeywell and Lockheed Martin on the proposed business jet.

Landmark T901 win: GE submits its final Engineering and Manufacturing Development (EMD) proposal to the US Army for the T901-GE-900 turboshaft engine for the competitive ITEP program. Then, in early 2019, the US Army selects the T901 engine for the EMD phase, another landmark victory for GE's Lynn turboshaft engine team. The US Army plans to re-engine its AH-64 Apache and UH-60 Black Hawk helicopter fleets, which have been T700-powered for four decades. T901 technologies position the new engine to deliver enhanced capability to the US Army for yet another four decades. From its large military and commercial engine portfolio, GE invested $9 billion in advanced technologies applicable to the T901 (such as advanced materials and additive manufacturing) and more than $300 million on turboshaft-specific technologies. The US Army also expects the ITEP engine to meet Future Attack Reconnaissance Aircraft requirements for Future Vertical Lift aircraft.

Tony Mathis, head of military systems at GE Aviation.

The T901's single-spool design is a key technology feature for reducing engine weight and complexity, while assuring a modular configuration, says Tony Mathis, head of GE military systems. "What the US Army loves most about the [predecessor] T700 is its simplicity, its ease of maintenance, and the ability to fix it in the field, all driven by its modularity of design," Mathis tells *Aviation Week & Space Technology* magazine at the 2018 Farnborough Air Show. The higher-capable T901 can be fixed in the field as well. "You just pull the module," Mathis says. "Instead of shipping the whole engine back, you put a new module on, and you put it back in the helicopter."

Entering 100 years with an eye to the future: With the close of 2018, GE Aviation enters its 100-year anniversary with the most significant presence it has ever experienced in commercial and military aviation.

GE Aviation and its partners have far-and-away the largest jet engine fleet in service in aviation history. With more than 80 facilities around the world, GE Aviation is advancing aviation in every corner of the globe.

More importantly, GE Aviation is intensely focused on the future, broadening its product offerings beyond jet engines, and advancing technologies for future generations of aircraft. From CMCs and additive manufacturing to hybrid electric power and new engine architectures, GE Aviation will continue to reimagine the future of flight for decades to come. ✈

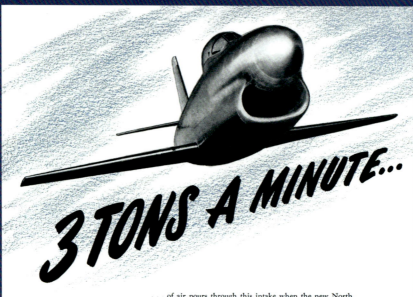

Epilogue

GE Aviation enters its second century in a fabulous position to further push the boundaries of aviation. With more than 65,000 engines in service and still growing, GE Aviation and its partner companies have built the world's largest operational fleet and established a firm business foundation.

GE's innovative portfolio of new civil engines introduced already for this century is extensive and ambitious: the high-thrust GEnx and GE9X families for large twin-aisle jetliners and freighters, the CFM LEAP family of turbofans for single-aisle aircraft, the GE Honda HF120 and Passport business jet engines, and the Catalyst turboprop.

In the military arena, GE's next-generation fighter jet engines and advanced turboshaft engines are setting propulsion performance records while bringing greater capability to future aircraft designs.

Dramatic progress in real-time trend monitoring and flight data analysis will further benefit aircraft operators as GE better understands what the massive reams of digital flight data reveal about its engine fleet in service.

Future jet propulsion systems will be driven by traditional requirements: better fuel efficiency and reliability, more thrust at lower engine weight, and reduced emissions, noise, maintenance, and operating costs. GE is attacking these demands on several fronts, including new engine architectures currently being secretly evaluated in the laboratory.

GE's impressive gains in new material systems (most notably CMCs) and additive manufacturing are beginning to revolutionize the industry. The era of super lightweight and heat-resistant components is upon us. In addition, additive manufacturing is turning the engineering discipline on its head, freeing designers of manufacturing restraints and creating a clean palette on which to work. Hundreds of individual engine parts are being consolidated into single, more reliable and durable components.

What will future aircraft look like? As always, the sky is the limit. However, we know the demand for greater electrical capability will be unrelenting. GE is advancing core computing systems and electrical power and distribution, including the extraction of electrical power from turbine power at unprecedented levels. These advances will also propel future hybrid-electric propulsion systems still in their infancy.

With more than eighty facilities, GE Aviation will continue to operate on the world stage and advance aviation in every corner of the globe. Proud of its rich heritage and heavily invested in its future, GE Aviation is ready to reimagine the future of flight for another 100 years.

The GE Aviation Propulsion Hall of Fame Members

Few companies invest in establishing and preserving their own Hall of Fame. For GE Aviation, this tradition involves no ego. Rather, it recognizes that aviation is the ultimate team sport, and when you succeed in pushing the aviation boundaries, you change the world.

The GE Aviation Propulsion Hall of Fame pays tribute to a select group, many of whom worked side by side for years, over the past century. They contributed to the company's unique place in the aviation industry today. However, each member would tell you that supporting them were thousands of GE Aviation employees devoted to the same cause. (The date represents their induction year.)

Arthur P. Adamson
1989

In an engineering career spanning almost half a century, Art Adamson's expertise and creativity touched numerous development programs from turboshaft engines and CF6 turbofans to the revolutionary Unducted Fan engine of the 1980s. Among his colleagues, Adamson was Yoda.

P. Arthur Adinolfi
1997

Art Adinolfi's leadership and commitment to customer service contributed significantly to GE's reputation as a world leader in propulsion for business jets, commercial helicopters, and commuter aircraft.

Richard W. Albrecht
2016

During a GE career of forty-one years, Rick Albrecht helped to advance many of GE's most technically challenging engine programs, including the CF6, GE90, F136, and YF120 variable-cycle engine. He was awarded thirty-one patents on various turbomachinery components.

Pierre Alesi
Honorary Member 1999

A founder of CFM International, Pierre Alesi was a longtime Snecma leader and friend of GE. He supervised development of CFM's first CFM56-2 engine and played a huge role in the joint company's early success.

Joseph S. Alford
1984

During his half-century engineering career, Joe Alford contributed to numerous GE programs from turbosuperchargers to 1980s turbofans. He earned twenty-seven US patents and mentored countless GE engineers. He also advocated the hiring of a young Gerhard Neumann.

Bernard J. Anderson
1997

Bernard Anderson's engineering contributions touched several important jet engines, including the J85 turbojet, the TF34 turbofan, the GE4 supersonic transport engine, and the YJ101, precursor to the F404 fighter jet engine.

William L. Badger
1984

A materials engineering pioneer, Bill Badger's long GE career as a chemist and metallurgist extended from turbosuperchargers to early small aircraft engines of the 1950s.

Donald W. Bahr
1995

During his thirty-eight years at GE, Don Bahr became a leading gas turbine combustion technology innovator. He helped to put GE at the forefront of NOx emission technology for jet engines.

Edward C. Bavaria
1999

One of GE's most important airline sales leaders, the charismatic Ed Bavaria, a former USAF fighter pilot, played a critical role in the dramatic sales success of the CF6 and CFM56 engines during the 1980s.

Dr. M.J. Benzakein
2005

Mike Benzakein's engineering expertise helped to make GE the world's leading producer of commercial jet engines. Among his accomplishments, he led CFM56 engineering through several certification programs, as well as the GE90 certification program.

Donald C. Berkey
1985

During four decades with GE, Don Berkey contributed to several engine product lines. Most notably, Berkey was the project manager for the game-changing TF39, the world's first high-bypass turbofan engine.

Walter S. Bertaux
1986

Walter Bertaux made significant technical and managerial contributions during a long GE career, including leading the T58 turboshaft program during its formative years of the 1950s. A decade later, he was the TF39 project manager.

Louis A. Bevilacqua
2003

During his GE career, Lou Bevilacqua was best known for his seventeen years as the creative leader of the T700 turboshaft program, which became the best-selling engine for turbine-powered helicopters worldwide.

John W. Blanton
1991

John Blanton's many career achievements involved both jet propulsion and community service. He led the X370 demonstrator engine program in the late 1950s, which pioneered advances in hollow blades, supersonic compressors, and low-emission combustors.

Melvin Bobo
1993

Known as "an engineer's engineer," the personable Mel Bobo dedicated more than forty years supporting several key GE development programs. From 1985 to 1991, he was the company's chief engineer.

O.R. (Bud) Bonner
1989

Bud Bonner contributed to aircraft engine manufacturing productivity during his first eighteen years with GE and spent the next twelve years expanding the marine and industrial portfolio.

Henry J. Brands
1997

Hank Brands advanced jet engine technology, including several turbine innovations. He led the F101 engine project for the B-1 bomber and F101 "Derivative Fighter Engine" project, which resulted in the successful F110 fighter engine. He was program manager of the F118 engine for the B-2 bomber.

Brian Brimelow
1999

A former Royal Air Force pilot, Brian Brimelow's GE career included key contributions to compression system design, including features that led to the stall-free performance of the F110 fighter jet engine. He was an important figure in GE's "Great Engine War" F110 success of the 1980s and 1990s.

Thomas A. Brisken
2016

Like father like son. Son of Walter Brisken, also a GE Propulsion Hall of Fame member, Tom Brisken made several contributions to commercial and military engines over a long career. As the first GEnx general manager, he helped the engine become GE's fastest-selling, high-thrust turbofan.

Walter Brisken
1985

During his four-decade engineering career, Walter Brisken became known as "Father of the LM2500" for spearheading development of this highly successful industrial and marine aeroderivative engine.

Fred I. Brown, Jr.
1989

During his long GE career, Fred Brown held several engine design positions before leading the marketing organization. He helped to launch GE's cooperative programs with Snecma in the late 1960s. GE's very close relationship with Snecma led to the creation of CFM International.

Bruno W. Bruckmann
1984

Bruno Bruckmann spent sixteen years advancing GE's aircraft engines, including leadership of the J47 engine and the X211 nuclear propulsion project. His greatest contributions were on the J93 for the XB-70 and the GE4 for the US Supersonic Transport program.

Bruce O. Buckland
Honorary Member 1985

Joining GE in 1923, Bruce Buckland became a technical leader in the Steam Turbine Division in Schenectady, New York. He influenced the company's early axial flow compressor designs. These designs helped to establish GE as a jet engine leader.

Neil Burgess
1985

One of GE's most important jet propulsion engineers, Neil Burgess left his creative imprint on the J35, J47, J73, and J79 military engines as project manager. Elected a company vice president, he was also honored as a co-recipient of the prestigious Collier Award for his work on the J79 engine.

Kenneth N. Bush
1984

Even though he began his GE career a decade before the company ran its first jet engine in 1942, Ken Bush managed manufacturing for Lynn's small aircraft engine department and helped to drive the success of the J85 turbojet for Northrop's T-38 and F-5 aircraft.

Frank Byrd
2005

Frank Byrd began his career as a technologist, but gravitated to commercial engine sales and marketing. He and his sales teams sold almost 3,300 commercial engines. Working with Ed Bavaria, he was a key leader during

GE's remarkable rise in commercial aviation in the 1980s.

David L. Calhoun
Honorary Member 2019
As president of GE Aviation during the 9/11 terrorists attacks of 2001, Dave Calhoun successfully led the company during several tumultuous years in commercial aviation. His commitment to jet propulsion proved unwavering as he advocated aggressive engine investments, such as the GEnx engine. He founded the Brian H. Rowe Learning Centre at the Evendale headquarters.

Vincent M. Cardinale
2003
During his long GE career, Vince Cardinale advanced aeromechanical design technology. He contributed to the success of several key Lynn engines, including the TF34, T700, F404, and F414.

Corbett D. Caudill
2008
Corbett Caudill held leadership roles in military, commercial, and product engineering before becoming vice president of engineering in 1994. The engines that he influenced included the F101, F110, and GE90. He became the key technical "GE90 troubleshooter" in the mid-1990s.

Charles L. Chadwell
2008
Chuck Chadwell's long GE career included such leadership roles as sourcing, supply chain, and human resources. Heading commercial engines in the difficult mid-1990s, he fought for key engine programs, such as the CF34-8 and GE90-115B, which positioned the company for decades. Without Chuck Chadwell, GE Aviation would look radically different today.

Stephen J. Chamberlin
1993
During thirty-five years at GE, Steve Chamberlin made lasting technical and managerial contributions, particularly with small aircraft engines. He helped to ensure extended engine production runs and new applications.

Peter A. Chipouras
1999
Peter Chipouras made significant contributions to several of Lynn's most important engines, including the TF34 and the F404, one of GE's most successful fighter jet engine programs.

William S. Clapper
2016
During an exceptional four-decade career, Bill Clapper held leadership roles in engineering, commercial marketing, business planning, and market development. During his long tenure as CFM program leader, the joint company took orders for almost 10,000 engines. He was awarded France's Chevalier of the Legion of Honor. Clapper was an architect of the agreement that extends the GE/Safran partnership in CFM International to 2040.

David Cochran
1985
David Cochran devoted his career to advancing technology, ranging from turbosupercharger metal temperature measurement and nuclear heat exchanger development for naval vessels to the creation and management of new jet engine development facilities.

Dorothy M. Comassar
2005
As general manager for manufacturing and quality technology, Dottie Comassar drove advancements in inspection and quality technology, leading to significant productivity and cost improvements. Comassar understood as

well as anyone what customers wanted from their jet engines.

Robert Conboy
2012
GE's key contact with leading aircraft manufacturers, Bob Conboy developed deep relationships with Boeing and Airbus, along with Snecma and other GE partners. Widely outspoken with regards to GE's product planning, his greatest achievement was leading the daily negotiations resulting in the GE90-115B launch on longer-range Boeing 777s. It would become one of GE's most important strategic aviation wins.

Calvin H. Conliffe
1995
Cal Conliffe initiated several engine technology innovations and held positions as a design engineer, project engineer, and program manager. For several years, he was manager of commercial engine advanced technology programs. Conliffe's commitment to technical expertise was only matched by his devotion to the community where he lived.

Nicholas J. Constantine
1986
Nick Constantine was a major contributor to GE's success in selling military engines to the US Air Force and the US Department of Defense as a key contact with the Pentagon.

Dr. Thomas Cooper
2012
For two decades, Tom Cooper was the face of GE Aviation in Washington, D.C. to politicians, staffers and government officials. His technology experience was only matched by his warm humor. He had a major influence on several GE military programs, including the F118, CFM56-2, T700, and F404. Without Cooper, GE may have never succeeded in placing the F110 engine on the F-16.

Laurence "Bill" Craigie
Honorary Member 1986
Lieutenant General (USAF) Bill Craigie was the first military officer to fly the Bell XP-59A, powered by the GE l-A engine, on October 2, 1942. His honorary membership in the GE Aviation Hall of Fame recognizes his distinguished military aviation career.

William J. Crawford III
1993
Bill Crawford was widely recognized for his major contributions and leadership in the advancement of small turboshaft and turboprop engines during his long GE career. He exerted a huge impact on the highly successful T700/CT7 family of gas turbines.

Walter F. Cronin
1987
Walt Cronin spent most of his thirty-nine years with GE in building and sustaining viable business relationships with many of the world's leading aircraft manufacturers dating back to Boeing and the B-17 Flying Fortress bomber.

Clarence E. Danforth
1984
Clarence Danforth's GE career began in 1943 and was marked by his efforts in analytical and experimental development of aeromechanics for turbomachinery blading. His work was instrumental in providing an understanding of cyclic fatigue phenomena in engine components.

Samuel H. Davison
2003
During thirty-nine years with GE, Sam Davison worked on several military, commercial, and marine and industrial engines. His most significant accomplishment was the first production FADEC on the CFM56-5A engine. The engine, in concert with the fully electronic A320 aircraft, was a bold step forward in aviation.

Robert D. Desrochers
1991
Bob Desrochers played a key role in decisions regarding new product development and market penetration, which positioned GE to attain its stature as a major engine supplier and a leading profit-maker for GE.

Thomas F. Donohue
1995
Tom Donohue devoted his more than thirty years at GE on the cutting edge of jet engine technology, designing and developing new concepts for higher performance engines to power both military and commercial aircraft.

Perry T. Egbert
1984
One of GE's great jet engine pioneers, Perry Egbert contributed to the design and development of the J47 and J73 engines. He managed the MX2118 Project, which ultimately became the J79.

Fredric F. Ehrich
1995
Fred Ehrich's long and diverse engineering career included contributing to the GE12, precursor of the T700/CT7 family of engines; the GE15, which evolved into the YJ101 and the F404 fighter engine; and the TF34 turbofan.

Pierre Fabre
Honorary Member 2019
As a longtime Safran (Snecma) executive, Pierre Fabre forged significant relationships with GE leaders. During his five years as CFM International president, the joint company's installed base of engines in service grew by 4,000. Fabre was a key member of the GE/Safran team that created the technology roadmap for the successful LEAP engine.

Leander J. Fischer
1986
Lee Fischer was a pioneer in centrifugal compressors for turbosuperchargers. In the area of axial flow compressors, he was part of the team that designed the compressor for the GOL-1590 demonstrator, predecessor to the highly successful J79 engine fighter engine.

Nicholas F. Frischhertz
1987
Nicholas Frischhertz played a key role in GE's becoming a leading jet engine manufacturer. After GE established J47 assembly operations in 1948 in Evendale, Ohio, Frischhertz managed several key assignments at the plant. He served for many years as J79 project manager.

Frederick W. Garry
1989
Fred Garry retired as a corporate vice president of engineering and manufacturing in 1988 after a distinguished career devoted primarily to the design, development, and program management of GE's most important jet engines.

Robert J. Gerardi
1995
The colorful and devoted Bob Gerardi left his mark on GE's aviation business in several areas, including evaluation engineering and test operations, project management, and product support and service.

Dr. Christopher C. Glynn
2016
A holder of sixty-seven patents, Chris Glynn played a key role in the design of almost every GE aircraft engine developed between 1985 and 2015. He was the engineering design manager for a diverse portfolio of engines, including the GE90, the small HF118 business jet, and the H80 turboprop.

Bruce J. Gordon
2001

Bruce Gordon's career included program leadership across several important GE engines. He ran small commercial engines and oversaw the wildly successful CF34 launch on Bombardier's early regional jets. He was instrumental in GE's return to the commercial engine business in the 1960s and was a key figure in that business during the last four decades of the 20th century.

Robert Griswold
2013

A celebrated technologist during his long GE career, Bob Griswold also made significant contributions as a calm and steady leader in the military engine business, including serving as F110 project manager and program manager for the F136 fighter engine.

Robert C. Hawkins
1991

Bob Hawkins advanced propulsion across several key GE engine programs. He served as manager of Evendale engineering operations, general manager of Evendale product engineering, and general manager of advanced technology operations.

Daniel Heintzelman
2019

A technology leader and executive for several GE businesses, Dan Heintzelman led the fast-growing services business of GE Aviation for several years. He also managed assembly operations in Evendale, Ohio, and was plant manager in Rutland, Vermont. As a corporate vice chairman, Heintzelman was a strong advocate for GE's expanding aviation enterprise.

Martin C. Hemsworth
1987

Marty Hemsworth's engineering excellence spanned almost a half-century from the first jet engines of the early 1940s to the Unducted Fan engine of the 1980s. He helped to design the J53, J73, J79, X211, J93, and CJ805 engines. He also headed engineering efforts for the TF39 and CF6 engines. In 1948, he was among the original Lynn managers to establish the GE jet engine operations at the Evendale, Ohio, complex.

J. Walter Herlihy
1985

Walt Herlihy devoted more than two decades of his long GE career to establishing and managing aircraft engine facilities in Vermont and New Hampshire. His colleagues affectionately knew him as "Mr. GE in New England."

Frederick C. Herzner
2008

Fred Herzner spent a long career in turbomachinery design and systems engineering leadership before becoming the company's chief engineer. His most lasting accomplishment was in driving titanium material cleanliness standards, an achievement recognized by the US Federal Aviation Administration (FAA). For many years, Herzner was GE's most respected voice with the FAA.

Paul Joseph Hess
2003

Paul Hess made lasting contributions as an aerodynamicist, performance engineer, aircraft-engineering manager, and educator. He tutored several future GE leaders in both aerodynamics and system engineering concepts.

Richard W. Hevener, Jr.
1987

Richard Hevener served in several engineering design and management positions during a successful four-decade career dating back to the late 1940s. He influenced the design of such key engines as the J47 and TF39.

James W. Heyser
2001

One of GE's leading propulsion engineers, Jim Heyser was responsible for all production engine fan designs for many years. Among his many management roles, he served as the company's chief engineer.

Frank R. Homan
1993

Frank Homan's GE career advancing jet propulsion technology culminated in his successful management of CFM56 engine programs during the growing 1980s for CFM International. He was awarded France's Chevalier of the Legion of Honor.

Edward E. Hood, Jr.
1995

Ed Hood was a significant player during GE's rise in airline propulsion in the late 1960s as manager of commercial engine programs. He served as a GE vice chairman and executive officer for the corporation for fourteen years as a huge advocate for the company's aviation enterprise.

Ned A. Hope
1989

Ned Hope made major contributions to propulsion technology on several GE engines, including the J79, TF39, CF6, and several marine and industrial aeroderivative engines.

Walter B. Houchens
1997

GE's preeminence in jet engine high-pressure turbine cooling technology was strongly influenced by Walt Houchen's innovations throughout a long career beginning in the late 1940s.

Henry Hubschman
Honorary Member 2012

The charismatic Henry Hubschman served as general counsel and led the business development team during the challenging mid-1990s for GE's jet engine business. In 1997, he became the president of GE Capital Aviation Services, the commercial aircraft financing and leasing arm of GE.

Walter "Pete" Hutto
2012

Pete Hutto developed the F110 control system for the single-engine F-16. His philosophy of backup systems and flawless integration of the fuel control and engine operability made great strides in single-engine aircraft safety. He contributed significantly to the remarkable F110 success.

Michael Idelchik
2019

A leading technologist across several GE businesses, Michael Idelchik led advanced technology programs for GE Global Research and served as managing director for GE's China Technology Center. Idelchik was a key advocate of technology advances for the growing aviation business.

Robert B. Ingraham
1984

An exceptional engineer with a long GE career, Bob Ingraham made key engineering contributions to the J79, the J93, and the X211 engines and also headed the T64 growth engine development program.

John W. Jacobson
1987

John Jacobson's leadership and technical expertise brought GE to the aviation industry forefront in small engine controls, including directing development of the first GE electronic control on the J47 afterburning engine.

Louis P. Jahnke
1985

In his twenty-five years at GE, Lou Jahnke contributed significantly to the company, including the development of the superalloy René 41 and the application of fracture mechanics in primary design technology.

Freeman James
2005
During a long GE career, Freeman James touched many commercial and military engines, though he was best known for his leadership of the F110 fighter jet engine with a special focus on operational safety.

Kenneth O. Johnson
1987
K.O. Johnson made significant technological contributions for engines across aircraft and marine and industrial applications over a twenty-year period. His patent for the basic Unducted Fan propulsion system was a career highlight.

Lee Kapor
1995
Lee Kapor combined engineering knowledge and business acumen to become a major player in GE's aviation rise in the 1970s and 1980s. He contributed to GE's most popular engines from the J79 and CF6 to the GE90. He ultimately led the company's commercial engine and support operations during the booming 1980s.

Peter G. Kappus
1986
Pete Kappus was recognized for novel engine configurations, especially those utilizing high-bypass-ratio principles. He contributed to the CJ805-23 and the CF700 aft fan engines, and led the design innovation of the tip-turbine-driven fan for the XV-5A fan-in-wing research vehicle.

Donald F. Keck
1995
Don Keck gained industry-wide recognition for his knowledge and technical leadership in the integration of the aircraft engine into a total propulsion system including the nacelle and associated instrumentation.

Everett J. Kelley
1986
During his long GE career, Ev Kelley contributed to the art of contract negotiation with the government customer. He established strong relationships with government counterparts based upon mutual trust and integrity.

Robert B. Kelly
2001
Bob Kelly delivered effective financial and contractual leadership to GE's growing military engine business. From 1966 to 1986, he led all financial and contractual activities for military engine operations.

John F. Klapproth
1985
During twenty-eight years with GE, John Klapproth's technical achievements touched numerous engines, including the design and development of the TF39 fan and compressor.

Lester H. King
1995
During forty-four years with GE, Les King's name became synonymous with the phenomenal state-of-the-art improvements made in jet engine compressor efficiency and reliability.

W. George Krall
1995
George Krall made management contributions to both product engineering and manufacturing capabilities, particularly during the massive buildup of military, commercial, and marine and industrial engines during the 1980s.

James N. Krebs
1989
The career of engineer Jim Krebs is felt across all GE engine families. Early on, he managed mechanical design for the GOL-1590 demonstrator engine, which led to the successful J79 engine. He managed the J85, CJ610, and CF700 projects. He later identified market opportunities for the TF39, T700, F404, CFM56, and CF6 engine families. Krebs is in the rarified air of GE leaders.

Vincent LaChapelle
2003
Vince LaChapelle began work in the field of accident investigation in 1952 and spent most of his long career in the pursuit of mishap root cause identification, along with the advancement of the investigative art and the promotion of flight safety.

C.W. "Jim" LaPierre
1984
In the early 1950s, Jim LaPierre formulated plans that made the Aircraft Gas Turbine Division not only a jet engine developer but also a leading engine producer. He expanded GE's Evendale plant and established the famous outdoor test operation in Peebles, Ohio.

G. William Lawson
1985
A true jet pioneer, Bill Lawson joined GE in 1941 and devoted forty years to the new jet engine industry. He touched such key programs as the J35 and J47 turbojets. He was part of the original T58 turboshaft design team.

William P. Lear
Honorary Member 2019
Unique inventor, self-taught electrical engineer, and aviation pioneer, Bill Lear created great excitement for commercial aviation by introducing the Lear Jet business aircraft in the early 1960s. The sleek jet was powered by GE's innovative CJ610 turbojet. Baby boomer music lovers experienced Lear's creativity through another of his wild inventions: the eight-track tape player.

Dean J. Lennard
1997
Dean Lennard's career covered a full spectrum of technical and managerial contributions to successful large aircraft engines. Building on his work on advancing engine components, Dean led engine programs, most notably the CF6 engine family. Lennard's special personality inspired many to achieve for the company.

Harry LeVine, Jr.
1984
During his twelve years as general manager of the company's Congressional relations office in Washington, D.C., Harry LeVine led key efforts to acquire funding for GE aircraft engine programs, including the F404 and F110 engines.

Samuel J. Levine
1984
Sam Levine experienced a diverse and successful career at GE. His most lasting impact was leading the marine and industrial department that developed the LM1500 and LM2500 for a range of US Navy and international defense ships.

Dennis Little
2005
Starting at GE as a performance engineer, Dennis Little rose through the company to hold several management roles. He ran the marine and industrial division and military engine operations. He also drove a global expansion of GE military engines, as well as new applications for aeroderivative products.

Fred O. MacFee, Jr.
1984
During forty years at GE, Fred MacFee served the jet engine business in roles ranging from

laboratory assistant to lead executive. His diversity of assignments was unique as an engineer, engineering manager, and project manager. His greatest legacy was working on the "building block" GE1 demonstrator, which created the foundation for several successful GE engines.

Jackson R. McGowen
Honorary Member 1991
After Jack McGowen retired from Douglas Aircraft, he approached GE with the idea of re-engining DC-8s with the CFM56-2 engine to provide better fuel economy, and lower noise and emissions. The concept ultimately launched the first engine program for CFM International.

John T. Moehring
1999
After several years as a successful GE engineer on such programs as the J93, J79, and GE4, John Moehring distinguished himself as the longtime leader of the company's flight safety organization.

Dr. Sanford A. Moss
1984
GE's journey into aviation begins with Sanford Moss, who spent a career advancing turbosuperchargers and gas turbines. He led the demonstration of GE's turbosupercharger at Pikes Peak in 1918, leading to the first high-altitude flights with the device in 1919. His technology influenced the outcome of World War II by enabling high-altitude bombers and fighters. The turbosupercharger led to GE building America's first jet engine.

Robert E. Neitzel
1993
Colleagues called Bob Neitzel "Mr. Preliminary Design," a title earned by his contributions to GE engine designs for more than four decades. He influenced the J79, F101, F404, F110, and TF39 engines. He also led the GE13 design concept, precursor to the CFM56 turbofan.

Anthony J. Nerad
Honorary Member 1995
Tony Nerad was a key player in the early Jet Age, pursuing combustor technology for GE's turbojet successors to the l-A, the first US jet engine. He developed a combustion liner for the l-14 and the TG-100/T31 engine, known as the "Nerad Combustor."

Gerhard Neumann
1983
Gerhard Neumann left a lasting impact on GE's jet engine business as one of its most dynamic leaders. His key technical invention was the variable-stator compressor. After becoming top executive of the jet engine business, he initiated the "building block" concept of engine design, leading to the launch of several critical GE engines, including the TF39 and F101. Neumann is a founder of CFM International. He helped to lead GE back into the airline business in the late 1960s and 1970s. For good reason, a street at the Evendale plant bears his name.

Timothy J. Noonan
2008
Tim Noonan rose through several manufacturing leadership roles, ultimately leading all East Coast manufacturing operations. His lasting contribution was lean manufacturing. He championed single-piece flow lines, which reduced engine assembly cycle times and eliminated waste.

Morrough P. O'Brien
Honorary Member 1984
Mike O'Brien became a GE consultant in 1949 and brought his knowledge and experience as an academician. Among his many key decisions, he advocated using the game-chang-

HALL OF FAME

257

ing variable stator design for the GOL-1590 demonstrator engine and J79 turbojet.

Jack S. Parker
1983
A giant of GE's jet engine business, Jack Parker established Lynn's small engine business in the 1950s and diversified GE's portfolio to include commercial and military engines. He led the creation of the T58, J85, and T64 programs. As a GE corporate officer, Parker helped to lead the jet engine division's charge back into the airline industry in the late 1960s.

Ralph E. Patsfall
1989
Ralph Patsfall enriched the science of manufacturing and aircraft engine production technology. Combining his education in metallurgical engineering with a law degree, he made outstanding contributions to the production of aircraft gas turbines.

Frank E. Pickering
1995
Frank Pickering devoted his engineering creativity and leadership to major technology advancements. After leading T64 and TF34 engineering, Pickering managed engineering for all Lynn products, and, ultimately, for the entire jet engine operation.

Dr. Cyril M. Pierce
2005
Dr. "Sonny" Pierce's career included advancing manufacturing technologies such as laser drilling and inertia welding. He started the turbine airfoils plant in Madisonville, KY, and led the creation of the Turbine Airfoils Center of Excellence.

Roy E. Pryor
1986
For years an ace GE test pilot, Roy Pryor flew the J79 engine in 1955 in a modified, single-engine XF4D. As a part of Evendale's marketing team, he used his pilot experience to drive sales for several military engines.

General René Ravaud
Honorary Member 1982
As president of Snecma, General René Ravaud was a founder of CFM International. His foresight, patience, and determined attitude helped establish what has become one of the most successful international aviation joint ventures.

Jacques Renvier
Honorary Member 2012
Throughout his long Snecma career, Jacques Renvier fostered team unity within the highly successful CFM International. His association with CFM began in 1974, and he contributed to the joint company across four decades while forging strong relationships with GE leadership.

James Rhoda
2005
During a long GE career, James Rhoda contributed to fan and compressor design for military, commercial, and industrial engines. His contributions included applications development, certification, and qualification.

Theodore J. Rogers
1985
Ted Rogers became a jet pioneer working on the GE I-A, America's first jet engine. He was one of three land-borne "pilots" who escorted two I-A engines from the East Coast to California for America's first jet flight in the Bell XP-59A in October 1942.

Jeanne Rosario
2019
Jeanne Rosario led the engineering team that delivered on the largest portfolio of new engines in the company's history, including the GEnx, LEAP, GE9X, GE38, and Passport. Un-

der her leadership, GE Aviation also incorporated new technologies such as ceramic matrix composites and advanced combustion technologies. She initiated numerous organizational improvements and fostered better working relationships between engineering and the global supply chain.

Brian H. Rowe
1995

Among the most beloved executives in GE's aviation enterprise, Brian Rowe led the jet engine business for fourteen years. During that period, GE became the world's largest designer and producer of engines for military and commercial aircraft as well as marine and industrial applications. A creative engineer, Rowe moved up the ranks, leading the CF6 program and the commercial engine operation. The GE90 was his signature engine. Appropriately, the Learning Centre at GE Aviation's headquarters is named after him.

M. Robert Rowe
1985

Bob Rowe's aviation career spanned more than forty years, including twenty years advancing and supporting GE engines. Known as GE's top commercial engine troubleshooter, he headed the CF6-6 and CF6-50 projects.

Georges Sangis
Honorary Member 2003

Georges Sangis held numerous leadership roles in a long career at SNECMA, including sales and marketing, business operations, and military operations. As an executive vice president, he played an important role in the success of CFM International.

Dr. Robert E. Schafrik
2016

During a seventeen-year GE career, Bob Schafrik and his team led the company through numerous challenges with respect to the cost and production of high temperature alloys. Among his many achievements, he helped GE to introduce intermetallic titanium aluminide for low-pressure turbine blades in the GEnx engine.

Jan C. Schilling
2016

Jan Schilling's impact on jet propulsion will be felt for many years to come. From his time as a program engineer in advanced programs design through his tenure as the chief engineer, his strong voice and evangelical devotion to jet propulsion shaped the future of GE's aviation business as a technology powerhouse.

William E. Schoenborn
2001

Bill Schoenborn was among the pioneering experts in the field of gas turbine compressor mechanical design. His work led to the successful integration of mechanical and aerodynamic design criteria.

Larry A. Scott
1997

Larry Scott's commitment to customer satisfaction was a hallmark of his career supporting GE commercial engines in operational service. Long associated with the CF6 engine, Scott became the first president of the GE-P&W Engine Alliance.

Roger Seager
2019

During a distinguished career in aviation, Roger Seager led GE's military engine marketing team in Lynn before managing the CF6 program. After leading the global sales team for several years, he served as lead executive for the aviation business in China, where he forged lasting relationships with the Chinese aviation industry.

Bert E. Sells
1989

Bert Sells contributed his engineering expertise to aircraft gas turbine technologies from turbosuperchargers to the F101, CF6, and CFM56 engine families.

James E. Sidenstick
2001

During a long GE career, Jim Sidenstick's greatest contribution was developing advanced cooling schemes for high-temperature turbines, which helped the TF39 high-bypass turbofan change the world of aviation.

R. Leroy H. Smith, Jr.
1995

Roy Smith was a key contributor in the design and development of fans and compressors during his forty years at GE. He received worldwide recognition for innovative work in fluid mechanics.

Richard B. Smith
1991

Dick Smith contributed across GE's commercial engines in engineering, flight testing, marketing and product support, project management, and business planning. He was GE's CFM56-2 project manager during the launch of this critically important engine for CFM International.

Robert J. Smuland
1999

After earning twelve patents as a turbine designer, Bob Smuland played a key role in the CF6 engine success. As head of the marine and industrial division, he helped to define applications for GE's aeroderivative engines.

Russell Sparks
2016

Russ Sparks left his mark on both commercial and military engines during a memorable four-decade career. A celebrated design engineer early in his career, Sparks led the GE90 program in the mid-1990s through development and certification. His legacy leading the military business is reflected in an annual military award given each year at GE Aviation's Leadership meeting.

Robert L. Sprague
1999

Bob Sprague introduced materials and processing advancements that helped GE to compete successfully in the "Great Engine War" of the 1980s and to achieve preeminence in the commercial engine market.

Michael J. Stallone
1995

Mike Stallone became an industry leader in the development of technologies that increased the knowledge of engine vibrations, structural dynamics, and blade aeromechanics during a forty-year GE career.

Richard Stanley
2019

During a thirty-six year career at GE, Rick Stanley led engineering with passion and vision. As head of engineering at GE Aviation, he influenced the growth of the CF34 and GE90 engines, and helped to launch the GEnx family.

Eugene E. Stoeckly
1984

Beginning his GE career in 1934, Gene Stoeckly became an integral part of the turbosupercharger organization. He is credited with directing design and construction of Lynn's supercharger and gas turbine test facilities.

Dale D. Streid
1985

During forty years at GE, Dale Streid innovated technology in turbosuperchargers as well as in the early jet engines. He was project engineer for the l-40/J33 turbojet, GE's first complete engine design.

Theodore T. Thomas, Jr.
2003

After joining GE in 1966, Ted Thomas spent three decades improving turbine aerodynamic codes, teaching and mentoring young engineers, turning concepts into practice, and advancing turbine designs for several commercial and military jet engines.

Louis V. Tomasetti
1997

During his long GE career, Lou Tomasetti produced consistently outstanding results in areas as diverse as industrial products, aerospace, and international sectors as well as in the aircraft engines business. His expertise touched numerous GE engines, including the J85, TF34, and T700.

Robert C. Turnbull
1995

Bob Turnbull impacted GE's aviation business with technical innovations and strong management of the military engine business. His engineering prowess influenced several GE engines, including the T700, F110, and CFM56.

Walter E. Van Duyne
1993

Walt Van Duyne's commitment to customer satisfaction with aircraft engines was foremost in his career of more than fifty years in aviation. In the late 1970s and early 1980s, he helped to establish GE's commercial product support department, which was critical to the company's wide success.

Irving W. Victor
1993

During his four-decade career, Irv Victor became a recognized expert in engine cycle analysis. His expertise was particularly relevant in performing altitude analysis on GE's supersonic engines as well as other advanced military engines.

George H. Ward
1991

George Ward was a major contributor to GE's success in the military engine business. His long GE career culminated with the selection of the F110 engine for the USAF F-16 and the US Navy F-14 fighter programs in the early 1980s.

Donald F. Warner
1984

A true jet engine pioneer, Donald "Truly" Warner was a design engineer in the supercharger department when GE was selected to produce America's first jet engine. The chief designer for the GE I-A and I-16 engines, he worked with drawings and components of the original Whittle engine design, making extensive changes to add strength to the compressor impeller vanes and turbine blades.

Glenn B. Warren
Honorary Member 1985

After joining GE in 1919, Glenn Warren quickly began solving technical problems facing the company's rapidly expanding and troubled steam turbine business. Under his leadership, GE steam turbines prospered, setting world standards of excellence. He retired a company vice president and a holder of forty-nine patents.

Virgil L. Weaver
1984

In the late 1940s, recognizing that the final proof of a jet engine was flying it, Virgil Weaver envisioned a flight test center to provide GE's design and installation engineers with test data that could not be obtained in the factory. He founded the GE Flight Test Center at Edwards Air Force Base.

Barry Weinstein
1999

During a long GE career, Barry Weinstein made lasting contributions to combustor and augmentor design. He provided leadership that fostered the technology development of new and derivative engines for the Lynn product line.

Sir Frank Whittle
Honorary Member 1982

Today's turbojet and turbofan engines trace their lineage to the inventions of Sir Frank Whittle, the propulsion pioneer whose development of the jet engine in Britain beginning in the late 1920s changed the face of aviation. With the support of General H.H. Arnold and the US Army Air Corps, a Whittle engine was shipped to GE in 1941 for developing the first US jet engine, the I-A.

James C. Williams
2003

During ten years in GE's aviation business, Jim Williams brought several key materials programs to fruition. He piloted several turbine material programs, including two generations of single-crystal blade alloys, a powder disk alloy, and thermal barrier coatings.

David Wisler
2012

Dave Wisler's career at GE Aviation and the GE Global Research Center spanned forty years. His work to improve airfoil shapes and to understand the complex flow fields in rotating components has been instrumental in improving stall margin and performance.

Edward Woll
1984

One of GE's most important aviation leaders, Ed Woll is regarded as the "father" of Lynn's small military engine programs—the T58, J85, T64, TF34, T700, F404—and their commercial derivatives. As head of engineering in the 1970s, he contributed outstanding leadership across the entire product and technology spectrum, including forging a strong relationship with Snecma as CFM International was being formed.

James E. Worsham
1993

For more than forty years, Jim Worsham advanced aviation. For the first thirty years, he was a leading engineer and executive in GE's jet engine business. He headed several engine programs and later became general manager of the military and commercial engine operations. He left GE in the early 1980s to become president of the Douglas Aircraft Company of McDonnell Douglas.

Endnotes

1892–1940 • Into Rarefied Air

1. Hickman Powell, "He Harnessed a Tornado," *Popular Science*, June 1941, p. 68.
2. Major George Hallett, "Superchargers and Supercharging Engines," *Aviation & Aeronautical Engineering*, January 15, 1920, p. 533.
3. *Eight Decades of Progress: A Heritage of Aircraft Turbine Technology*. Cincinnati, Ohio: GE Aircraft Engines, 1990. Sanford Moss's early career is detailed in the book.
4. Donald Sherman, "Hill Climb," *Air & Space Smithsonian*, June 2001, p. 22.
5. Dr. Sanford A. Moss, "General Electric Turbo Supercharger for Airplanes," *Aviation & Aircraft Journal*, March 15, 1920, p. 147.
6. Hallett, "Superchargers and Supercharging Engines," p. 535.
7. Ibid.
8. Moss, "General Electric Turbo Supercharger for Airplanes," p. 147.
9. Charles M. Ripley, "Lifting of Censorship on War-Time Inventions Reveals Yankee Genius," *Indianapolis Star*, July 27, 1919, p. 66. The Ripley article appears in newspapers in the US and Europe. His article publicly reveals for the first time the maiden flight of GE's turbosupercharger.
10. Moss, "Superchargers and Supercharging Engines," p. 149.
11. "McCook Man Marvels at His Escape," *Dayton Daily News*, February 28, 1920, p. 1.
12. "From New York to San Francisco in Nine Hours Believed Possible," *Great Falls Tribune*, October 23, 1921, p. 1.
13. "Boeing will build new super bombers," *Dayton Daily News*, January 1, 1936, p. 15.
14. "Safer flying in all weather is predicted," *Dayton Daily News*, December 28, 1937, p. 9.
15. Ibid.
16. "Flying Fortress Spans Nation in Record 9 ¼ Hours," *Chicago Tribune*, August 2, 1939, p. 3.
17. Dedication Program: Wright Cincinnati Plant, Wright Aeronautical Corporation, June 12, 1941.
18. "Wright selects Lockland for Giant Engine Factory," *Cincinnati Post*, July 27, 1940, p. 1.
19. "Fossil Tusk is Unearthed," *Cincinnati Enquirer*, February 20, 1941, p. 13.

1941–1964 • Fast Jets

1. David M. Carpenter, *Flame Powered: The Bell XP-59A Airacomet and the General Electric I-A Engine*. Jet Pioneers of America, 1992 p. 12. Carpenter's book is a comprehensive study of the I-A and the early European turbojets.
2. Handwritten entry into the original I-A engine test logbook, April 18, 1941. GE Aviation, Evendale, Ohio.

3. Robert Playfair, "Mystery Man at Statler Held Jet Plane Secret," *Boston Globe*, October 1, 1944, p. 1.
4. Carpenter, *Flame Powered, op. cit.*, p. 21.
5. Howard W. Blakeslee, "Jet Propulsion Engine Simple; Supercharger is Key to Power," *Minneapolis Star Tribune*, December 17, 1944, p. 23.
6. Carpenter, *Flame Powered, op. cit.*, p. 43.
7. Powell, "He Harnessed a Tornado," p. 67.
8. GE newspaper advertisement, "The Turbo-Supercharger," *The Courier* (Louisville, Kentucky), June 3, 1943, p. 8. Advertisement appears in many publications in 1943.
9. "Dr. Sanford Moss to be Honored Next Week," *Dayton Herald*, December 8, 1937, p. 1.
10. "GE Leases Plant," *Cincinnati Enquirer*, June 29, 1948, p. 18.
11. Steve Hoffman, "Retiree Helped Bring GE to Life in Evendale," *Cincinnati Enquirer*, September 2, 1986, p. B–13.
12. Mike Boyer, "GE Marks 50 Years of Powering Jet Aircraft," *Cincinnati Enquirer*, October 11, 1988, p. 1.
13. Hoffman, "Retiree Helped Bring GE to Life in Evendale," p. B–13.
14. "Businesswoman Only Now Sees Difficulties," *Lafayette Journal and Courier*, October 29, 1976, p. 1.
15. Frank Ruhl, "Air Force Accepts First Jet Power Engines Made at GE's Lockland Plant," *Cincinnati Enquirer*, March 1, 1949, p. 22.
16. General Electric news release, February 9, 1951, GE Aviation archives, Evendale, Ohio.
17. Ibid.
18. Gerhard Neumann, *Herman The German*. New York: William Morrow and Company, 1984, p. 207.
19. GE advertisement, "Jet City U.S.A.," *Aviation Week*, May 2, 1952, p. 52.
20. "GE Experts praise British Jet Engines," *Aviation Week*, November 16, 1953, p. 9.
21. Richard A. Leyes II and William A. Fleming, *The History of North American Small Gas Turbine Aircraft Engines*. Washington D.C.: Smithsonian Institution and AIAA, 1999, p. 245.
22. "Gas Turbine Designed for Helicopters by GE," *Hartford Courant*, February 22, 1954, p. 17.
23. Jack Dudley, "Pogo Tests in Adams Area," *Cincinnati Enquirer*, December 18, 1954, p. 1.
24. Jack Dudley, "Versatile, This GE Executive!" *Cincinnati Enquirer*, June 19, 1955, p. 62.
25. "GE Reorganizing Engine Programs," *Aviation Week*, August 22, 1955, p. 12.
26. *Eight Decades of Progress: A Heritage of Aircraft Turbine Technology, op. cit.*, p. 95.
27. Jack Parker, *Have We Done Everything We Came Here To Do?* Scottsdale, Arizona: Scottsdale Multimedia Inc., 2011, p. 54.
28. Boyer, "GE Marks 50 Years of Powering Jet Aircraft," p. 22.
29. Brian H. Rowe with Martin Ducheny, *The Power to Fly: An Engineer's Life*. Reston, Virginia: AIAA, 2005, p. 25.
30. Jack Parker, *Have We Done Everything We Came Here To Do?, op. cit.*, p. 52.
31. Harold Watkins, "Jet Fleet Gives Rexall Great Flexibility," *Aviation Week & Space Technology*, September 13, 1965, p. 30.
32. Jack Parker, *Have We Done Everything We Came Here To Do?, op. cit.*, p. 60.
33. Brian H. Rowe with Martin Ducheny, *The Power to Fly, op. cit.*, p. 46.
34. Ibid, p. 25.

1965–1986 • Chasing Jetliners

1. Gerhard Neumann, *Herman The German, op. cit.*, p. 228.
2. Michael Yaffee, "8-1 Bypass Ratio Marks Design of GE's C-5A Engine," *Aviation Week & Space Technology*, March 14, 1966, p. 35–36.
3. Glenn Varney, interview with Rick Kennedy, August 2018.
4. Ibid.
5. Ibid.
6. Emil Dansker, "GE Joins in History's Grandest Air Project," *Cincinnati Enquirer*, January 1, 1967, p. 1.
7. "Area will share in GE prize," Cincinnati Enquirer, January 1, 1967, p. 1.
8. Gerhard Neumann, *Herman The German, op. cit.*, p. 229.
9. Ibid., p. 30.
10. Richard A. Leyes II and William A. Fleming, *The History of North American Small Gas Turbine Aircraft Engines, op. cit.*, p. 330.
11. Michael L. Yaffee, "GE Sets Airbus Engine Design, Cost," *Aviation Week & Space Technology*, September 27, 1967, p. 28–29.
12. Guy Norris and Mark Wagner, *Giant Jetliners*, Osceola, Wisconsin, Motorbooks, 1997, p. 23.
13. Brian H. Rowe with Martin Ducheny, *The Power to Fly, op. cit.*, p. 47.
14. Frederick Ungeheuer, "They Make Good Things for Flying," *TIME*, May 5, 1988, p. 55.
15. Bob Brumfield, "Huge 'Airbus' Proclaimed," *Cincinnati Enquirer*, July 24, 1970, p. 1.
16. Brian H. Rowe with Martin Ducheny, *The Power to Fly, op. cit.*, p. 51.
17. Robert Drewes, *The Air Force and the Great Engine War*. Washington D.C.: National Defense University Press, 1987, p. 10.
18. Robert Drewes, *The Air Force and the Great Engine War, op. cit.*, p. 31.
19. Guy Norris and Felix Torres, *CFM: The Power of Flight*. Wilmington, Ohio: Orange Frazer Press, 2016, p. 75.
20. Gerhard Neumann, *Herman The German, op. cit.*, p. 234.
21. Ibid.
22. Robert Webb, "Senate Vote 51-46 to Kill SST; 1500 Face Layoff At GE," *Cincinnati Enquirer*, March 25, 1971, p. 1.
23. "Reviving the SST at Higher Cost Has Even Greater Reason to Fail," *San Antonio Express*, May 14, 1971, p. 8.
24. "GE announces layoffs; Evendale is included," The Journal News (Hamilton, Ohio), July 22, 1971, p. 23.
25. Jack Parker, *Have We Done Everything We Came Here To Do?, op. cit.*, p. 76.
26. "T700 Aims at Low Combat Maintenance," *Aviation Week & Space Technology*, January 28, 1974, p. 45.
27. Guy Norris and Felix Torres, *CFM: The Power of Flight, op. cit.*, p. 126.
28. "GE Will Supply France with F101 Core Technology," *Aviation Week & Space Technology*, June 11, 1973, p. 25.
29. Ibid.
30. Guy Norris and Felix Torres, *CFM: The Power of Flight, op. cit.*, p. 153.
31. Fred Smith, public remarks at the Brian H. Rowe Tribute, March 6, 2007, Steven F. Udvar-Hazy Center, Washington, D.C. Remarks recorded by Rick Kennedy.

32. "CFM-56 Aimed at Transports," *Aviation Week & Space Technology*, July 22, 1974, p. 49.
33. Michael Yaffee, "GE Increased Thrust in Engine for F-18," *Aviation Week & Space Technology*, September 8, 1975, p. 37.
34. Brian H. Rowe with Martin Ducheny, *The Power to Fly, op. cit.*, p. 57.
35. Michael London, "GE to make engines for 767, not P&W," *Hartford Courant*, November 11, 1978, p. 1.
36. Private memo from Gerhard Neumann to Jack Parker, January 8, 1979. David Joyce collection.
37. Chuck Chadwell, interview with Rick Kennedy, October 16, 2018.
38. Jamie Jewell, interview with Rick Kennedy, April 2017. Jewell interviewed Dick Smith for the book, *CFM: The Power of Flight*.
39. Gerhard Neumann, *Herman The German, op. cit.*, p. 237.
40. Robert Drewes, *The Air Force and the Great Engine War, op. cit.*, p. 84.
41. Brian H. Rowe with Martin Ducheny, *The Power to Fly, op. cit.*, p. 73.
42. Ibid., p. 75.
43. Wayne Buckhout, "GE Grabs Lion's Share of Giant Engine Order," *Cincinnati Enquirer*, February 4, 1984, p. 1.
44. Robert Drewes, *The Air Force and the Great Engine War, op. cit.*, p. 138.
45. Guy Norris and Felix Torres, *CFM: The Power of Flight, op. cit.*, p. 366.
46. Richard A. Leyes II and William A. Fleming, *The History of North American Small Gas Turbine Aircraft Engines, op. cit.*, p. 260–261.
47. Brian H. Rowe with Martin Ducheny, *The Power to Fly, op. cit.*, p. 133.

1987–2006 • Big Fans

1. Bill Carley, "How Pratt & Whitney Lost Jet-Engine Lead to GE After 30 Years," *Wall Street Journal*, January 27, 1988, p. 1.
2. *Eight Decades of Progress: A Heritage of Aircraft Turbine Technology, op. cit.*, p. 314.
3. Brian H. Rowe with Martin Ducheny, *The Power to Fly, op. cit.*, p. 75.
4. "Canadair Seeks 50 Firm Orders, *Aviation Week & Space Technology*, May 16, 1988, p. 67.
5. Bill Sweetman, "The Short, Happy Life of the Prop-Fan," *Air & Space Smithsonian*, September, 2005, website edition.
6. Robert Weisman, "Rolls-Royce goes for bigger piece of jet-engine market," *Hartford Courant*, November 11, 1989, p. D–4.
7. Mike Boyer, "GE Tries to Lap Competitors with New Engine," *Cincinnati Enquirer*, January 17, 1990, p. E–6.
8. Stanley W. Kandebo, "Pratt & Whitney, GE Team To Study HSCT Propulsion," *Aviation Week & Space Technology*, October 15, 1990, p. 53.
9. Rick Kennedy, notes from Robert Turnbull media interviews, November 1991.
10. Mike Boyer, "GE Aircraft Still Flying High After ATF Loss," *Cincinnati Enquirer*, April 24, 1991, p. E–4.
11. "Engine would put $2 billion in local hands," *The Palm Beach Post* (West Palm Beach, Florida), April 21, 1991, p. 1.
12. Boyer, "GE Aircraft Still Flying High After ATF Loss," p. E–4.
13. GE Aircraft Engines press release, May 11, 1993.

14. Karen West, "Southwest Airlines OKs Purchase of New Boeing Jet," *Seattle Post-Intelligencer*, November 19, 1993, p. 1.
15. Chuck Chadwell, interview with Rick Kennedy, October 16, 2018.
16. Brian H. Rowe with Martin Ducheny, *The Power to Fly, op. cit.,* p. 143.
17. Bill Carley, "Engine Trouble Put GE Behind in Race to Power New 777s," *Wall Street Journal*, July 12, 1995, p. 1.
18. Barbara Nagy, "Pratt Gets Big Role in Joint Venture," *Harford Courant*, September 2, 1996, p. 1.
19. Bruce Hughes, interview with Rick Kennedy, October 17, 2018.
20. Jim McNerney, first public meeting with the GE Aircraft Engines executive team, Building 800 auditorium, GE Evendale facility, August 1993. Rick Kennedy archive.
21. Bruce Hughes, interview with Rick Kennedy, October 17, 2018.
22. Chuck Chadwell, interview with Rick Kennedy, October 16, 2018.
23. Article with Jack Welch's handwritten note is provided to Rick Kennedy in 1998, Evendale, Ohio. Rick Kennedy archive.
24. Robert Conboy, interview with Rick Kennedy, August 14, 2018.
25. Rick Kennedy recorded discussion between Jim McNerney and Chuck Chadwell, July 3, 1999, Building 100, GE Evendale complex. Rick Kennedy archive.
26. Recorded comments at Boeing/GE press conference, Rockefeller Center, New York City, July 12, 1999. Rick Kennedy archive.
27. Chaker Chahrour, interview with Rick Kennedy, October 29, 2018.
28. Robert Conboy, interview with Rick Kennedy, August 14, 2018.
29. GE Aircraft Engines press release, July 7, 1999.
30. Brian H. Rowe with Martin Ducheny, *The Power to Fly, op. cit.,* p. 145.
31. Chris Kraul, "Big Bet on Small Planes Pays Off for Brazil," *Los Angeles Times*, July 25, 1999, p. C-1.
32. Gail Makinen, "The Economic Effects of 9/11: A Retrospective Assessment," *Congressional Research Service*, September 27, 2002.
33. Mike Boyer, "GE Battered by Airline Downturn," *Cincinnati Enquirer*, October 4, 2001, p. D-1.
34. Ibid.
35. Jeff Immelt, interview with Rick Kennedy, October 26, 2018.
36. 2001 General Electric Company Annual Report.
37. Lynn J. Lunsford and Kathryn Kranhold, "GE, Rolls-Royce Gain Boeing Deal," *Wall Street Journal*, April 7, 2004, p. 1.
38. David Joyce, interview with Rick Kennedy, January 6, 2018.
39. Ibid.
40. Jeff Immelt, interview with Rick Kennedy, October 26, 2018.
41. David Calhoun, interview with reporters, April 8, 2004.
42. Tom Brisken, interview with Rick Kennedy, October 14, 2018.
43. Muhammad Al-Lamadani, comments recorded by Rick Kennedy, February 2005. Rick Kennedy archive.
44. Jeanne Rosario, interview with Rick Kennedy, October 19, 2018.
45. Jeff Immelt, interview with Rick Kennedy, October 26, 2018.
46. Brian Ovington, interview with Rick Kennedy, August 20, 2018.

2007–2018 • Wider Horizons

1. Harry Nahatis, interview with Rick Kennedy, October 21, 2018.
2. Ed Birtwell, interview with Rick Kennedy, October 22, 2018.
3. Ibid.
4. Robert McEwan, interview with Rick Kennedy, December 15, 2010.
5. Alexander Coolidge, "GE Aviation Sees Blue Skies," *Cincinnati Enquirer*, May 22, 2007, p. 1.
6. Richard Ostrom, interview with Rick Kennedy, October 20, 2017.
7. Bill Clapper, interview with Rick Kennedy, June 13, 2018.
8. David Joyce, interview with Guy Norris, July 13, 2008.
9. Lynn J. Lunsford and Daniel Michaels, "Jet-Engine Makers Launch New War," *The Wall Street Journal*, July 14, 2008, p. 7.
10. Vic Bonneau, interview with Rick Kennedy, June 24, 2018.
11. Jeff Immelt, interview with Rick Kennedy, October 26, 2018.
12. Bill Brown, interview with Rick Kennedy, November 2, 2018.
13. Guy Norris and Felix Torres, *CFM: The Power of Flight, op. cit.*, p. 596.
14. Bill Clapper, interview with Rick Kennedy, June 13, 2018.
15. Chaker Chahrour, interview with Rick Kennedy, October 29, 2018.
16. Ibid.
17. Mara Lee, "Rolls-Royce to form partnership with Pratt," *Hartford Courant*, October 13, 2011, p. 14.
18. CFM International internal sales tallies based on public announcements, 2012–2017.
19. Mara Lee, "GE, Rolls Abandon Engine: Big Victory for P&W," *Hartford Courant*, December 4 2011, p. 4.
20. Jean Lydon-Rodgers, interview with Rick Kennedy, October 23, 2018.
21. David Joyce, remarks at GE Aviation Leadership Council meeting, January 8, 2017.
22. Greg Morris, correspondence with Rick Kennedy, July 12, 2018.
23. Mohammad Ehteshami, correspondence with Rick Kennedy, July 22, 2017.
24. Gary Mercer, correspondence with Rick Kennedy, October 29, 2018.
25. Bill Fitzgerald, interview with Rick Kennedy, August 10, 2018.
26. Charles Alcock, "GE Pushes Envelope with GE9X for new Boeing 777," *AINonline*, June 16, 2013.
27. Jean Lydon-Rodgers, interview with Rick Kennedy, October 23, 2018.
28. Bill Fitzgerald, interview with Rick Kennedy, August 10, 2018.
29. Colleen Athans, correspondence with Rick Kennedy, May 15, 2018.
30. Brad Mottier, interview with Rick Kennedy, May 12, 2018.
31. Greg Morris, interview with Rick Kennedy, June 19, 2018.
32. Jean Lydon-Rodgers, interview with Rick Kennedy, October 23, 2018.
33. Ibid.
34. Bill Fitzgerald, interview with Rick Kennedy, August 10, 2018.
35. Allen Paxson, CFM press briefing, Farnborough Air Show, July 14, 2018.
36. Ibid.
37. Hanno van der Bijl, "GE opens new $20M manufacturing facility in Alabama," *Birmingham Business Journal*, May 10, 2018.
38. Lisa C. Veitch and William S. Hong, "Will Pigs Fly Before Ceramics Do?" *Institute for Defense Analyses*, Alexandria, Virginia, January 2001.

39. Michael Kauffman, remarks at GE Huntsville factory grand opening, May 10, 2018, Huntsville, Alabama.
40. Sanjay Correa, interview with Rick Kennedy, October 2015.
41. Guy Norris, "CMC Ramp-up Is Key Element of Production Readiness for GE9X," *Aviation Week & Space Technology*, October 15–28, 2018, p. 61.
42. Jonathan Blank, correspondence with Rick Kennedy, October 31, 2018.
43. Gary Mercer, interview with Rick Kennedy, October 2018.
44. Ibid.

Bibliography

A Century of Progress: The General Electric Story. Schenectady, New York: Hall of History Foundation, 1981.

Carpenter, David M., *Flame Powered: The Bell XP-59A Airacomet and the General Electric I-A Engine.* Jet Pioneers of America, 1992.

Carpenter, David M., *NX-2 Convair Nuclear Propulsion Jet.* Jet Pioneers of America, 2005.

Carpenter, David M., *River Works: A City Within a City.* Jet Pioneers of America, 2000.

Dedication Program: Wright Cincinnati Plant, Wright Aeronautical Corporation, June 12, 1941.

Drewes, Robert W., *The Air Force and the Great Engine War.* Washington D.C.: National Defense University Press, 1987.

Egan, Louise, *Thomas Edison: The Great American Inventor.* Hauppauge, New York: Barron's Educational Series, 1987.

Eight Decades of Progress: A Heritage of Aircraft Turbine Technology. Cincinnati, Ohio: GE Aircraft Engines, 1990.

Garvin, Robert, *Starting Something Big: The Commercial Emergence of GE Aircraft Engines.* Reston, Virginia: AIAA, 1998.

Grant, R.G., *Flight: The Complete History of Aviation.* London: DK Publishing, 2017.

Heiman, Grover, *Jet Pioneers.* New York: Duell, Sloan, and Pearce, 1963.

Johnson, Mary Ann, *McCook Field 1917–1927*, Dayton: Landfall Press, 2002.

Leyes II, Richard A. and William A. Fleming, *The History of North American Small Gas Turbine Aircraft Engines.* Washington D.C.: Smithsonian Institution and AIAA, 1999.

GE Aviation Press Release archive, 1981–2018.

Neumann, Gerhard, *Herman The German.* New York: William Morrow and Company, 1984.

Newhouse, John, *Airbus versus Boeing.* New York: Vintage Books, 2007.

Newhouse, John, *The Sporty Game*, New York: Knopf Doubleday Publishing Group, 1982.

Norris, Guy and Felix Torres, *CFM: The Power of Flight.* Wilmington, Ohio: Orange Frazer Press, 2016.

Norris, Guy and Mark Wagner, *Airbus.* Osceola, Wisconsin: MBI Publishing, 1999.

Norris, Guy and Mark Wagner, *Boeing.* Osceola, Wisconsin: MBI Publishing, 1998.

Norris, Guy and Mark Wagner, *Douglas Jetliners.* Osceola, Wisconsin: MBI Publishing, 1999.

Norris, Guy and Mark Wagner, *Giant Jetliners*, Osceola, Wisconsin, Motorbooks, 1997.

Parker, Jack Steel, *Have We Done Everything We Came Here To Do?* Scottsdale, Arizona: Scottsdale Multimedia Inc., 2011.

Proving Ground: Flight Propulsion Laboratory Department, General Electric Company, 1959.

Rowe, Brian H. with Martin Ducheny, *The Power to Fly: An Engineer's Life*. Reston, Virginia: AIAA, 2005.

Seven Decades of Progress. Cincinnati, Ohio: General Electric Company, 1979.

Twenty five years of Jet Flight, General Electric Jet Times. Special 1967 employee publication.

Index

A

A-10 Thunderbolt, 103, 142
A-12, 145
A300, 93-94, 105, 120, 125, 136
A310, 109-110, 120, 136
A320, 120-125, 134, 137-138, 144, 147, 149-150, 155, 199, 209, 212-213, 236, 251
A320neo, 209-212, 231, 235-236, *237*
A321, 138, 149
A330, 134, 138, 142, 151, 174
A340, 133-134, 140, 144, 146, 149, 161
A350, 184, 222
A380, 161-162, 173-174, *175*, 180, 193, 202
AAH (Advanced Attack Helicopter), 101
Adamson, Art, 78, 94, 122, *127*, 166, 247
Adaptive Engine Technology Development (AETD) program, 217-218, 221, 242
Adaptive Engine Transition Program (AETP), 232, 242
Adaptive Versatile Engine Technology (ADVENT), 197, 203, 206, 213-214, 218, 221, 242
Additive Technology Center, 216, 230
Adinolfi, P. Arthur, 247
Advanced Affordable Turbine Engine (AATE), 227, 232
Advanced Manned Strategic Aircraft (AMSA) program, 95, 97
Advanced Tactical Fighter (ATF) program, 143, 221
Aerion AS2 supersonic business jet, 242
Aero Commander, 74
AgustaWestland EH101, 182
AH-64 Apache, 101, 109, 243
AirAsia, 210
Airborne Command Post E-4A Nightwatch, 103
Airbus, 93-94, 105, 108-109, 120-121, 124-125, *132*, 133-134, 136-138, 140, 142, 146-147, 149, 153, 161-162, 173-174, 184, 193, 198-199, 203, 209-212, 222, 231, 235-237, 251
Airbus Industrie, 93, 120
Air China, 203
Air China Southwest, 126
Aircraft Nuclear Propulsion Department, 50, 56
Air Force One, 125, 145, *168*, 169
Air France, 124, 137, 164, 173
AirVault, 234
Albert Kahn Associated Architects and Engineers, 22
Albrecht, Richard W., 247
Alesi, Pierre, 247
Alfa Romeo Avio, 150
Alford, Joseph, 20, 44, 247
Al-Lamadani, Muhammad, 175, 184
AlliedSignal, 128
Allis Chalmers plant, 30, 36
Allison Engine Company, 35, 151
All Nippon Airways (ANA), 180
Alternate Engine Program, 151, 158
American Airlines, 62, 67, 90-92, 100, 109, 137, 211-212
American Supersonic Transport (SST), 98, 100
Andersen, Lars, 166
Anderson, Bernard J., 247
Anderson, Dick, 124

Appalachian Mountains, 21, 58
Arcam AB, 234
ARJ21 program, 175-176, 181, 235
Armstrong, Neil, *113*
Arnold, H.H. "Hap", 29-30, 262
Athans, Colleen, ix, 223
Auger, Claude, 42
Austin Digital, 233
Aviadvigatel, 230
Aviall, 159
Aviation Week & Space Technology
    coatings and infiltration technology, 241
    GE90-94B compressor and, 163
    Lear Jets and, 77
    Lockland plant and, 54
    Tony Mathis interview and, 243
AVIC I Commercial Aircraft Company (ACAC), 175, 214
Avio Aero, 216-217, 229-230
Avio S.p.A, 216
AW189 helicopter, 222
axial-flow engines, 35-41, 57, 65, 125, 229

B
B-1, 86, 95, 97, 103, 106, 112, 117, 249
B-2 stealth bomber, 47, 86, 120-121, *138*, 249
B-17, *17*, 19-20, *21*, 24, 36, 85
B-24 Liberator, 30, 36
B-25 Mitchell, 24
B-29 Superfortress, 24, 36
B-32 Dominator, 24
B-45 Tornado, 49, 61
B-47 Stratojet, 49
B-52 bomber, 55, 62-63, 90
B-58 Hustler bomber, 56, 63, 68, 71, 76, 95, 115
Bachelet, Eric, *199*
Badger, William L., 248
Bahr, Donald W., 248
Barbour, Haley, 202
Bavaria, Edward C., 137, 248
Beech King Air aircraft, 228
Bell 525 "Relentless" Super Medium Transport helicopter, 218
Bell Aircraft, 32

Bell Helicopter, 218, 227
Bell, Larry, 32
Bell P-59 aircraft, 34
Benzakein, M.J., 248
Berger, "Doc", *15*
Berkey, Donald C., 84, 248
Bertaux, Walter S., 248
Bevilacqua, Louis A., 248
Birtwell, Ed, ix, 195-196
Blank, Jonathan, ix, 223, 241
Blanton, John W., *73*, 248
Bobo, Melvin, 248
Boeing 7J7, 128, 134, 136
Boeing 707, 62, 112-113, 116, 123, 125
Boeing 727, 78, *127*, 128, 134, 140
Boeing 737, 116, 120, 125-126, 137, 146, 160, 182, 199, 212, 235-237
Boeing "737 MAX" program, 211-212, 235-238
Boeing 747-8, 173, 182, 214, 218
Boeing 747, 87, 90-91, 103, 107-108, 125, 139, 141, 145, 155, 161, 169-170, 173, 182, 214, 218, 227, 243
Boeing 747-200, 107, 145
Boeing 747-500X, 155, 161, 173
Boeing 757, 110, 116, 128
Boeing 767, 109-110, 125, 136, 138-139, 178
Boeing 777, 139-141, 144, 150, 153-155, 158, 161, 163, *164*, 165-166, 169-170, 176-178, 180-182, 184, 218-219, 226
Boeing 777-200 model, 140, 144, 154, 180
Boeing 777-300ER, 165-166, 169-170, 176-177, 181-182, 184, 218, 226
Boeing 777X, 207, 218, *220*, 226, 238
Boeing 787, 173, 177-180, 182, 184-185, *192*, 193, 203, 214, 218, 226, 243
Boeing 2707 airframe, 86-87
Boeing Model 299 ("Flying Fortress"), 16, *17*, 19, 24, 251
Boeing XB-47 Stratojet, 37
Bombardier, 134-136, 151, 153, 167, 169, 177, 198, 207, 209, 238, 253
Bombardier CRJ100, 238
Bombardier Global 7000, *207*, 208, 235
Bombardier Global 8000, *207*, 208, 235

Bonneau, Vic, ix, 206
Bonner, O.R. (Bud), 248
Boschung Global AG, 203
Boston Globe, description of Frank Whittle and, 32
Brands, Hank, ix, 124, 248
Brian H. Rowe Learning Centre, 160, *180*, 181
Brimelow, Brian, ix, 124, 249
Brisken, Tom, ix, 124, 173, 184, 249
Brisken, Walter, 60, 95, 249
Bristol Siddeley Engines, 79, 97
British Air Ministry, 29
British Airways, 144, 153
Brown, Bill, ix, 210
Brown, Jr., Fred I., 249
Brown University, 46
Bruckmann, Bruno W., 60, 249
Büchi, Alfred, 8
Buckland, Bruce O., 249
Burgess, Neil, 35, *40*, 56, *69*, 70, 249
Burnham, Frank, *33*
Bush, Kenneth N., 249
Business Week, Marion S. Kellogg and, 47
Byrd, Frank, 137, 249

C

C-5A Galaxy, 87, 93, 168
C-5B Galaxy aircraft, 123
C-5 Galaxy, 90
C-47 transport, 24
C-141 transport, 74
Calhoun, David L., *171*, 173, 179, 181, 185, 250
Campini, Secondo, 29
Canadair, 135
Canadair Challenger 601, 117, 123
Canadair Challenger 604, 154
Canadair Challenger business jet, 134
Canadair Regional Jet (CRJ100), 146, 151, 238
Canadair Regional Jet (CRJ), 135-136, 146, 153
Canadair Regional Jet (CRJ700), 151, 153, 174
Caravelle SE210, 112
Cardinale, Vincent M., 250
Cargolux, 182
Carter, Jimmy, 97, 112, 117, 126

CASA CN-235 aircraft, 121
Catalyst engine, 227, *228*, 229-230, 235, 238, 245
Cathay Pacific, 166, 182
Caudill, Corbett, 124, 154, 250
CDB Leasing Company, 203
Celebrity Cruises, 163
CELMA, 158
Ceramic Composite Products, 196
ceramic matrix composite (CMC) components, 196-197, 200, 203, 206, 217, 219, 221, 223, 230-233, 238-239, *240*, 241-242
Cessna Aircraft company, 228-229
Cessna Denali airplane, 229
CF6-50, 93-94, 98100, 103, 105, 107, 109, 112, 125, 134, 166, 259
CF6-80A, *109*, 110, 117, 125, 136
CF6-80C2, 110, 124-125, 128, 134, 136-137, 139, 145, 151, *168*, 169-170, 179-180
CF6-80E1A3, 174
CF6-80E1, 134, 137, 142, 151
CF6 turbofan, 75, 89-90, *91*, 92-94, 98, 100, 102-103, 105, 107, 109-110, 112, 114, 117, 124-125, 128, *132*, 13-134, 136-137, 139, 142, 145, 151, 154-155, 159-160, 166, *168*, 169-170, 174-175, 179-180, 182, 188, 197, 230, 247-248, 253-256, 259-260
CF34-3, 134-136, 146, 151, 238
CF34-8C, 151-152, *153*, 167, 174
CF34-8E, 167, 177
CF34-10, 175-176, 186, 235
CF34-10E, 167, 177, 186
CF34 engine, 115, 117, 123, 134-136, 146-148, 151, *152-153*, 154, 167, 169, 171, 174-177, 186, 197, 221, 230, 235, 238, 250, 253, 260
CF700, 71, 77, 79, 88-89, 105, 115, 117, 255-256
CFAN, 149
CFE738 commercial turbofan, 122, 128, 155, 194
CFM56-4, 120
CFM56-5, 236
CFM56-5A, 134, 137, 251
CFM56-5B, 144, 147-149, 155, 213
CFM56-5C, 133-134, 144, 146, 149
CFM56-7, 146, *147*, 152, 161, 163, 168, 182, 189, 212, 236

CFM56 engine, 97, 103-105, *106*, *111*, 112-117, *119*, 120, 122-126, 133-134, 137-138, 144-146, *147*, 148-152, 154-155, 158, 160-161, 163, 168, 171, 173, 175, 180, 182, 186, 188-189, 200-202, 210-213, 230, 235-236, 247-248, 251, 254, 256-257, 260-261

CFM International, x, xviii, 105-106, 112, 131, 150, 161, 199, 230, 247, 249-250, 252, 257-260, 262

CH-53A Sea Stallion, 79

CH-53K, 122, 194, *195*, 196

Chadwell, Chuck, ix, 112, 151, 162, 165, 250

Chahrour, Chaker, ix, 165-166, 211

Chamberlin, Stephen J., 250

Chemical and Industrial Corporation, 77

Chevrolet Motor Division, 37

Chidlaw, B.W., 33

China Eastern, 203

China Eastern Yunnan, 126

China Southern Airlines, 158, 203

Chinese Air Force, 45

Chipouras, Peter A., 101, 250

Cincinnati Art Museum, 172

Cincinnati Enquirer, Pogo Tests in Adams Area and, 59

Cincinnati Gas & Electric Company, 76

CJ610 engine, 71, 74, 76-77, 89, 115, 117, 256

CJ805 engine, 62-63, *67*, 71, 73-75, 83, 92, 108, 169, 253, 255

Clapper, Bill, ix, 186, 198, *199*, 211, 250

Cleveland, Grover, 158

Cochran, David, 57, 250

Cochran, Jackie, 55, 57, 78, 250

Collier Trophy, 41, 69-70

COMAC C919, 202-203, 209, 212, 214, 235-236

Comair, 169

Comassar, Dorothy M., 250

Commercial Aircraft Corporation of China (COMAC), 202

Committee for Aviation Strategy, 55-57

Conboy, Robert, ix, 165, 251

Concept Laser, 234

Concorde, 86, 97, 141

Conliffe, Calvin H., 251

Consolidated Vultee XP-81, 38-39

Constantine, Nicholas J., 251

Continental Airlines, 154, 182

Convair 880, 62-63, 71, 73, 108

Convair 990, 67, 71, 73, 75

Convair B-36, 49

Cooper, Thomas, ix, 158, 251

Cornell University, 7-9

Correa, Sanjay, ix, 240

County NatWest Securities, 143

Craigie, Laurence C., 33, 251

Crawford, Bill, 101, 251

Critical Technologies, 234

Cronin, Walter F., 251

Cross, Carl, 88

CT7-2F1, 218

CT7-8, 168, 177, 182

CT7, 101, 115-116, 121, 126, 159, 168, 177, 182, 217-218, 222, 230, 251-252

Curado, Fred, 222

CX-HLS (Experimental Cargo/Heavy Logistics System), 83

D

Danforth, Clarence E., 251

Dassault, 112

Dassault-Breguet Mercure jetliner, 104

Dassault Falcon 20, 77

Dassault Falcon, 77, 79, 194

Dassault Falcon 2000, 128

David, George, 179

Davison, Samuel H., 251

Dayton [Ohio] Herald, on Sanford Moss and, 41

DC-8, 62, 111-113, 120

DC-9, 78, 120

DC-10, 90, *91*, 92-93, 100, 107, 110, 134

DC-10-30, 93, 107, 134

DDG-51 Aegis destroyer program, 177

de Havilland Company, 61, 74, 79

Delta Air Lines, 62, 71, 109-110, 112-113, 169

Demler, Marvin, 83

Denver, John, 71

Department of Defense, 21, 42, 60, 123, 143, 145, 149, 158, 185, 213

Depp, Herb, 165
Desert Storm, 86, 131, 142-143
Desrochers, Robert D., 252
Deutschendorf, Henry, 71
DH 106 Comet, 61
DHC-4, 74
Donnelly, Scott, 185-186, 195-197, 200
Donohue, Thomas F., 252
Doolittle, Jimmy, *38*
Dorchester Hotel, 198
Dowty Propellers, 193
Dreamliner, 177-178, 180, 184, 218
Dubai Air Show, 218
Duncan, William, 128
Durand, William, *8*, 9

E

E-3A Airborne Warning and Control System (AWACS) aircraft, 116
eCore program, 201
Edison Illuminating Company, 5
Edison, Thomas A., *4*, 5, 7
Edwards Air Force Base, 33, *54*, 70, 90, 136, 261
Egbert, Perry T., 252
EGT, 148, 150
Ehrich, Fredric F., 252
Ehteshami, Mohammad, ix, 216
electrical load management system (ELMS), 226
Electrical Power Integrated Systems Research & Development Center (EPISCENTER), 206-208, 226
Electrical Power Integration Centre (EPIC), 207, 226
Electric Auto-Lite Corporation, 25, 42
electron beam melting (EBM), 234
Electronic Engine and Propeller Control (EEPC), 229
Embraer E-Jet E2 engine, 221
Embraer ERJ-170, *167*, 177, 221-222
Energy Efficient Engine (E3), 108, 125, 140
Engine Alliance, 155, *156*, 158, 161-162, 173-175, 178, 202, 259
ERJ-190, 167, 186, 221-222
ETOPS certification, 138, 141
European Aviation Safety Agency (EASA), 196
Evendale plant, ix, *44*, 50, 54, 58, 63-65, 67-68, 71-73, 75-76, 82, 85, 100, 105, 109, 112, 114, 117, 123, 126, 139, 148, 153-154, 160, 163, 168, 173, 176, 179, *180*, 201, 203, 221-223, 231-232, 240-241, 250, 252-253, 256-258
Extended Twin Operations (ETOPS), 136, 138, 141, 154

F

F-4 Phantom, 68, 73, 88, 92, 95, 115, 175
F-5, 69-70, 77, 88, 94, 137, 249
F-14 Tomcat, 95, 97, 114, 124, 149, 261
F-15 Eagle, 95, 97, 114, 117, 123, 149, 159, 176, 202
F-16, 107, 114, 117, 123-124, 142, 149, 158, 170, 175, 251, 254, 261
F-22, 143, 145, 194
F-35, 194, 217, 232
F-84 Thunderjet, 37, 42
F-86H fighters, 48, 55
F-86 Sabre, 44, 49, 55
F-100, 55
F100 engine, 95, 101, 103, 107, 114, 123-124, 158
F101 Derivative Fighter Engine program, 114
F101 engine, 86, 95, *96*, 97-98, 101, 103-104, 106, 112, 114, 117, 121, 123, 126, 137, 149, 155, 200, 249-250, 257, 260
F-104 Starfighter, *54*, 56, 63, 68-70, 78, 87-88, 115
F108 engine, 115-116
F110 engine, 97, 121, 123, *124*, 126, 138, 142, 145, 148-149, 152, 158-159, 170, 176, 182, 197, 202, 214, 234, 249-251, 253-257, 261
F110-GE-100, 124, 126
F110-GE-129, 124, 138, 142, 149, 159, 176, 182, 202
F110-GE-132, 170
F-117, 86, 120, *121*, 142
F118 engine, 86, 97, *120*, 121, 126, 137, *138*, 149, *150*, 170, 249, 251
F118-GE-100, 126
F119 engine, 155
F120 engine, 155, 158
F136 engine, 185, 203, 213, 247, 253
F401 engine, 95

F404 engine, 101, 107-108, 110, 114, 120, *121*, 126, 128-129, 137, 142, 145, 163, 176, 182, 214, 248, 250-252, 256-257, 262

F412, 145

F414 engine, *144*, 145-146, 151-152, 155, 170, 202, 208-209, 214, 250

F/A-18E/F Super Hornet, *144*, 145-146, 155, 209

F/A-18 Hornet, 107, *108*, 209

Fabre, Pierre, 252

Falcon 2000, 155, 194

Farnborough Air Show, 57, 128, 135, 136, 176, 198, 200, 237, 243

Farson, Max, 181

Fastworks Laboratory, 223

Federal Aviation Administration (FAA), 70, 74, 76, 79, 112, 136, 141, 150, 181, 231, 235, 253

FedEx, 105

FIAT, 63, 121-122

FiatAvio, 141, 150

Firestone, Neil, 71

First American Volunteer Group, 45

Fischer, Leander J., 252

Fitzgerald, Bill, ix, 218, *219*, 222, 236

FlightGlobal Ascend Aircraft Fleet Database, 230

Flying Tiger Line, 112-113

Flying Tigers, 45, 98

Ford Motor plant, 36

Forecast International, 143

Foster, Everett, 42, 54

Franus, David, 143

Frischhertz, Nicholas F., 252

full-authority digital electronic control system (FADEC), 124, 194, 229, 251

Future Affordable Turbine Engine (FATE), 227, 232

Future Attack Reconnaissance Aircraft, 243

Future Vertical Life aircraft, 243

G

GAM-72 Green Quail missile decoy, 63

Gardner, David, 139

Garrett Aviation Services, 186

Garry, Frederick W., 101, 252

GE1 "building block" demonstrator engine, 74-75, 83, 93-94, 97, 101, 114, 257

GE4 turbojet, 74, *85*, 86-87, 89-90, 98, 100, 248-249, 257

GE9 demonstrators, 97

GE9X engine, 201, 218-219, *220*, 226, 229, 235, 238-239, 245, 258

GE12 demonstrator, 88, *89*, 101, 252

GE13 turbofan, 98, 257

GE15, 94, 101, 252

GE27 demonstrator, 122, 128, 194

GE38, 122, 194, *195*, 258

GE90-92B, 158

GE90-94B, 163-164, 166, 170, 180, 163

GE90-115B, 160, 163, *164*, 165-167, 169-171, 173-174, 176, *177*, 180-182, 184, 218-219, 250-251

GE90 engine, xvii, 100, 108, 131, 138-141, 144, 147-155, 158, 160-167, 169-171, *172*, 173-177, 179-182, 184-185, 188, 197, 217-219, *220*, 226, 242, 247-248, 250-252, 255, 259-260

GE3000, 227, 232

General Dynamics, 102-103, 107, 126, 145

General Electric Company (GE)
    Additive Technology Center and, 216, 230
    advertisement for the F101 engine and, *96*
    Aircraft Programs and, 165, 193, 201
    Aviation Propulsion Hall of Fame and, 247-262
    Canadian Airlines International, 134
    Capital Aviation Services, 203, 254
    Committee for Aviation Strategy and, 55-57
    Digital Solutions, 233-234
    dramatic wartime advances and, 34-36
    eCore program and, 201
    Engine Services and, 144, 154, 158-160, 162, 186-187, 198, 233
    Flight Propulsion Division, 68, 71, 74, 93
    Flight Test Center, 54, 90, 261
    founding of, 5-6
    Global Research Center and, 185, 207, 215, 240
    Great Engine War and, 123-125
    helicopter challenge and, 88-89

installed engine deliveries and, 230
lift-fan propulsion system and, 78, *79*
Modern Technology Demonstrator Engine (MTDE) program and, 122
OnPoint campaign and, 186-187
The Proving Ground and, 58-59
secret "stealth" propulsion and, 84-87
Steam Turbine division and, 30, 249
turbosupercharger and, xxi, 8-10, *11*, 12, 14, 17-19, *21*, 30-31, 35-36, *38*, 41, 43, 257

General Motors, 35, 37
GEnx-1B, 177, 182, 184, 214, 218
GEnx engine, 148-149, 167, 173, 177, *178*, 179-182, *183*, 184-185, 194, 197, 200-201, 203, 208, 214, 217-219, *220*, 226, 245, 249-250, 258-260
Gerardi, Robert J., 252
Gloster E.28/39, 29
Gloster Meteor, 38
Glynn, Christopher C., 252
Gnome & Rhône, 39
GOL-1590 engine, 51, *52*, 56, 252, 256, 258
Gordon, Bruce J., 253
GP7200 engine, 155, *156-157*, 161-162, 171, 173-174, *175*, 176, 180, 202, 218
Graceland, 108
Gray, Harry, 133
Great Depression, 16, 20
Great Miami River, 9, 206
Greenwich Air Services, 159
Griffith, Alan Arnold, 66
Griswold, Robert, 253
GTS William M. Callahan cargo transport, 95
Guinness Book of World Records, GE90-115B engine and, *177*
Gulfstream, 206
Gulf War, 142

H

H80, 196, 203, *204*, 228-229, 252
Hainan Airlines, 203
Hallett, George, *15*
Hamilton Standard, 150
Hartford Courant, Great Engine War and, 123

Hawker-Siddeley Harrier V/STOL aircraft, 79
Hawkins, Robert C., 253
Heathrow Airport, 162
Heinkel Aircraft Company, 18
Heinkel He 178, *28*, 29
Heintzelman, Daniel, 253
Hemsworth, Marty, 42-43, 73, 84, 108, 253
Herlihy, J. Walter, 253
Hertemen, Jean-Paul, 198
Herzner, Frederick C., 253
Hess, Paul Joseph, 253
Hevener, Jr., Richard W., 253
Heymann, Nicholas, 143
Heyser, James W., 254
HF118, 181, 188, 252
HF120 turbofan, *188*, 189, 222, 231, 245
Hickock, Dick, 122
Hinkle, Robert, 42
Hispano-Suiza, 98
Homan, Frank R., 145, 254
Honda Aero Engines, 180-181, *188*
Honda Aircraft Company, 188
HondaJet, 181, *188*, 189, 231
Honda Motor Company, 180
Honeywell, 128
Hood, Ed, 89, 92-94, 117, *127*, 254
Hooksett plant, 88
Hope, Jack, 104
Hope, Ned A., 254
Horner, Chuck, 142
Hotel Statler, 32
Houchens, Walter B., 254
Houseman, Kenneth, 42-43
Hubschman, Henry, 254
Hughes, Bruce, 158, 161
Hughes, Howard, *62*, 63
Huntsville, Alabama plant, 230, 238-239, *240*, 241
Hush-Hush Boys, 29-30
Hutto, Walter "Pete", 254

I

I-16 turbojet, 34, 39, 261
I-40 cutaway engine, *34*, 35

I-A program, 29-35, 51, 54-55, 258, 261-262
Idaho Test Station, 59
Idelchik, Michael, 254
Immelt, Jeffrey R., ix, 170-171, 173, 179, 185, 201, 209
Immelt, Joseph, 173
Improved Performance Engine (IPE), 138, 142
Improved Turbine Engine Program (ITEP), 232, 243
infrared (IR) emissions, 85
Ingersoll Rand, 129
Ingling, Ted, 238
Ingraham, Robert B., 254
Institute for Defense Analysis, 238
International Aero Engines (IAE), 121-122, 133, 198-199, 209, 212, 230
International Civil Aviation Organization (ICAO), 136
Inter Sinex AG, 203
Irwin, Walter, 69
Ishikawajima-Harima Heavy Industries, 63-64, 152, 167
Ivchenko, 230

J

J31 engine, 34
J33 engine, 34-37, 39, 41, 261
J35 engine, 36-37, 39-42, 47, 249, 256
J47 turbojet, 39-42, *43*, 44, *45*, 47-51, 55-56, 59, 61, 63, 236, 249, 252-254, 256
J57 turbojet, 51, 55-56, 62
J73 engine, 48, 55, 249, 252-253
J79 engine, 52, 54, 56, *58*, 59, 61-64, 67-71, 73-74, 76, 78-79, 83, 92, 95, 97, 107, 115, 161, 249, 252-258
J85 turbojet, 63, 69-71, 77-78, 83, 94, 101, 137, 174, 248-249, 256, 258, 261-262
J93 turbojet, *65*, 74, 78-79, 84, 86-87, 95, 249, 253-254, 257
J97 turbojet, 94
J101 engine, 94, 101-102, 105, 107
Jacobson, John W., 254
Jahnke, Louis P., 254
James, Freeman, ix, 124, 255

Japan Aero Corporation, 121-122
Japan Airlines (JAL), 166, 169-170, 182, 184, 218
JAS 39 Gripen, 137, 145, 163
Johnson, Howard, 69
Johnson, Kelly, 35, 63, *69*
Johnson, Kenneth O., 255
Joint Multi-Role (JMR) technology demonstrator, 227
Joint Strike Fighter (JSF) program, 143, 151, 155, 158, 185, 203, 208, 213, 217, 226, 231-232
Joint Technology Demonstrator Engine (JTDE) program, 105
Jones, Reginald, 112
Joyce, David, ix, xix, 140, 176, 178-179, 181, 198, *199*, 200, *201*, 211-212, 214, 234
JT3D engine, 68, 78, 230
JT3 turbojet, 62
JT8D-200, 116
JT9D, 87, 107, 109
JTF14E turbofan, 84

K

Kapor, Lee, 133, 255
Kappus, Peter, 60, 75, 78, 255
Katana high-speed yacht, 129
Kauffman, Mike, ix, 238-239, 241
KC-135 tanker, 55, 62, 115-116
Keck, Donald F., 255
Kelley, Everett J., 255
Kellogg, Marion S., 46, *47*
Kelly, Robert B., 255
Kelsey, Harold D., 41-42, 44
Kennedy, John, 73
King, Dennis, 202
King, Lester H., 255
Klapproth, John F., 255
KLM, 91, 93, 107, 110, 154
Knies, Robert D., 59
Korean Helicopter Program, 189
Korean War, 36, 41, 47, 49-50
KralI, W. George, 255
Krapek, Karl, 155
Krebs, Jim, 74, 84, 101, 124, 256
KSSU, 93

L

L-1011, 91, 100
LaChapelle, Vincent, 256
Lafayette, IN (GE Aviation) plant, *224-225*, 226
LaPierre, Cramer W. "Jim", 47, 49, *50*, 51, 256
Lawson, G. William, 256
LEAP-1A, 210, 231, 235
LEAP56 program, 185-186
LEAP engine, 148-149, 167, 198-203, 208-209, *210*, 211-212, *215*, 216-219, 221, 223, 226-227, 231, 234-239, 245, 252, 258
Lear, Bill, 76-77, 193, 256
Lear Jet, 76, *77*, 88, 256
Lear Siegler Holdings Corp., 193
Leis, Dale, 77
Lennard, Dean J., 256
LeVine, Jr., Harry, 256
Levine, Samuel J., 256
Liberty engine, 9-10, *11*, 12
Light-Weight Fighter (LWF) competition, 102
Little, Dennis, 256
LM100, 70, *75*
LM1500, 70, 73, 76, 256
LM1600, 129
LM2500, 95, 163, 177, 249, 256
LM6000, 189
LMS100, 189
Lockheed P-38, 36
Lockheed P-80 Shooting Star, 33, 35-36, *37*, 41
Lockland, Ohio complex, 20-21, *22-24*, 25, 42-43, *44-45*, 46-51, 54, 56, 84
Lufthansa, 107, 110, 146
Lufthansa CityLine, 146
Luftwaffe, 29
Lunken Airport, 77
Lydon-Rodgers, Jean, ix, 213-214, 221, *231*, 233
Lynn River Works, xiii-xiv, xxi, 5, 6, 7, 9, 16-17, 19-20, 30, *31-32*, 34-36, 38, *40*, 41-44, 46-47, 50-51, *55*, 56-58, 61, 63-64, 70, 88-89, 92, 101, 114, 122, 126, 129, 145, 148, 163, 194, 196, 222, *232*, 242, 250, 253, 258-259, 262

M

M56 design, 98, 106
M601 turboprop, 196, 203
MacFee, Fred, 75, 110, 256
Mach 2 engine, 51, 56, 76, 95
Macready, John, *xii*, 14, *15*
Maintenance Cost Per Hour (MCPH), 154, 160
Malaysia Airlines (MAS), 160
Marine & Industrial (M&I) Division, 75-76
Martin B-51 Bomber, 49
Martin XB-48 bomber, 37
Mathis, Tony, *243*
Maxwell, Tom, 124
MB-1 bomber, 15
McAllister, Kevin, 171, 211
McCook Field, 9, 11-12, *13*, 14, 19
McCormick, Dan, 124, 221
McDonnell Douglas, 75, 91-93, 95, 107-108, 112, 120, 125, 128, 132, 134, 140, 144-145, 155, 159, 193, 262
McEachern, Angus, *33*
McEwan, Bob, ix, 197, 216
McGowen, Jackson R., 257
McMasters, Marie, 216
McNerney, Jim, ix, *159*, 160, 163, 165-166, 173, 211-212
MD-11, 125, 134, 140
MD-80, 128, 134, *135*, 136
Mercer, Gary, ix, 216, 242
Messerschmitt Me 262, 29
Miami-Erie Canal, 24
MiG-15 fighters, 49
Millhaem, Bill, 219
Mississippi State University, 202
Mitchell, Billy, 15
Mitsubishi Zero, 45
Modern Technology Demonstrator Engine (MTDE) program, 122
Moehring, John T., 257
Montgomery, John B., 66
Morgan, J.P., 5
Morris, Greg, ix, 215-216, 230
Morris Technologies, 214, *215*, 216, 230
Morris, Wendell, 215
Moss, Sanford, xxi, 6, *7*, 8-9, 41, *10*, 11-12, *13*, 14, *15*, 16, 19, *38*, 41, 257

Mottier, Brad, ix, 176, 228-229
Mount Washington, 40
MTU, 94, 121-122
Mulally, Alan, 176
Muroc Dry Lake, 33
Murphy, Gene, 148, 160
Museum of Modern Art (MoMA), 172, 181-182

N

N-156F Freedom Fighter, 69
Nahatis, Harry, ix, 194, 196
National Aeronautics and Space Administration (NASA), 8, 79, 88, 104, 108, 124-125, 140-141, 234
National Business Aviation Association Show, 181, 228
National Defense Program, 20
Neitzel, Robert E., 257
Nerad, Anthony J., 257
Neumann, Gerhard, 44-46, 50-51, *52*, 61, *69*, 70-72, 74, 76-78, 83, 87-89, 92-93, 98, *99*, 100-101, 110, 112, 114, 161, 200, 247, 257
Nexcelle, 202-203, 208
NHIndustries NH90, 182
Nichols, Paul, 42
Nippon Carbon, 217, 240
Nippon Cargo Airlines, 182
Nixon, Richard, *69*, 103, *104*
Noack, Bill, 215
Nomura Securities, 139
Noonan, Timothy J., 257
Northrop, 18-19, 37, 47, 49, 69-70, 77, 86, 94, 101-103, 107, 120-121, 126, 138, 143, 155, 249
Northrop F-89 Scorpion, 37
Northrop Gamma, *18*, 19
Northrop, Jack, 19
Northrop YB-49A Flying Wing, 37
NX-2 bomber, 59

O

O'Brien, Morrough P., 257
Office of Strategic Services (OSS), 45
On-Wing Support Network, 162-163, 169, 187-188, 200

Operation Paper Clip, 60
Ostrom, Dick, ix, 197
O.T. Falk & Partners, 18
Ovington, Brian, ix, 187

P

P-7, 194
P-600 design, 102
Pacific Gas Transmission Company, 129
Pan American Airways, 62, 90
Paris Air Show, 90, 93, 120, 128, 138, 167, 185, 203, 209, 211, 238
Paris-Le Bourget Airport, 210
Parker, Jack, *55*, 56-57, 61, 63, 68, 72, 74, 75, 77, 87, 101, 110, 112, 114, 125, 222, 232, 258
Passport engines, 167, 201, *207*, 208, 222, 226, *227*, 235, 245
Patsfall, Ralph E., 258
Paxson, Allen, ix, 237-238
PB-2A fighter, 17
Peebles Test Operation, xviii, 58-59, 90, 148, 150, 174, 177, 197, 226, 256
Pence, Mike, 226
Pentagon, 103, 149, 170, 213-214, 251
Peter, Paul, and Mary, 71
Petitcolin, Philippe, *199*
Petting Zoo, 233
PG Technologies, 214
Pickering, Frank, 125, 258
Pierce, Cyril M., 258
Pikes Peak, 9, *10-11*, 257
Pompidou, Georges, 98, 103, *104*
Popular Science, GE's turbosupercharger and, 35
Power Jets Ltd., 18
Pratt & Whitney (P&W), 16, 30, 55-56, 60, 62, 66, 68, 74, 78, 83-84, 87, 90-92, 95-98, 101, 103, 107-110, 112-117, 119-124, 133, 136, 140-141, 143-144, 149, 154-155, 158-159, 161-162, 165-166, 170, 176, 178-179, 185, 194, 198-200, 209, 212-213, 217, 221, 227, 230, 259
Praxair Surface Technologies, 214
Presley, Elvis, 108
Proxmire, William, 100

Pryor, Roy E., *48*, 61, 258
PT6 turboprop engine, 227-228
PW1000G engine, 221
PW2037 engine, 110, 122
PW4000 turbofans, 122, 140, 155

Q

Qantas, 173
Qatar Airways, 175
Quiet Clean Short-haul Experimental Engine (QCSEE) program, 104-105

R

RA-4C jets, 115
Rateau, Auguste, 8
Ravaud, René, 98, *99*, 258
RB211-535, 128
RB211 engine, 100, 110, 128, 154, 230
Reagan, Ronald, 97, 117, 126
Renvier, Jacques, 258
Republic Aviation XP-84B, 41-42
Republic F-84 Thunderjet, 37, 42
Republic of Korea Air Force, 176
Republic P-47, 36
Rexall Drug and Chemical Company, 77
Rhoda, James, 258
Rice, Donald, 143
Riemer, Burt, 107
Ripley, Charles M., 12
RJ500 engine, 122
RM12 engine, 137, 145, 163
Rocky Mountains, 21
Rogers, Theodore J., *33*, 258
The Rolling Stones, 203
Rolls-Royce, 56, 66, 91, 97, 100, 108, 110, 120-122, 128, 133, 140-141, 144, 151, 154, 158, 161-163, 165-167, 170, 173, 179-181, 184-185, 194-195, 197-199, 203, 206, 209, 212-213, 217-218, 230
Rolls-Royce Conway engine, 62, 67
Rolls-Royce Welland turbojet, 38
Roosevelt, Franklin D., 20
Rosario, Jeanne, ix, *183*, 185, 258
Roundhill, John, 165-166

Rowe, Brian, ix-x, 61, 72, 75, 78-79, 89, 91-93, 105, 109, 114, 117, 123, 126, *127*, 128, 133, 137-140, 144, 148, 160, 167, 180-181, 197, 200, 250, 259
Rowe, M. Robert, 259
Royal Air Force (RAF), 18, 32, 249
Royal Caribbean International, 163
Royal Danish Navy, 134
Royal Dutch Airlines, 110
Royal Saudi Air Force, 202
Ruegg, Dick, 146
Ryan Aeronautical Corporation, 78-79
Ryan Aeronautical FR-1 "Fireball", 39
Ryan drone aircraft, 94

S

S-3A Viking antisubmarine aircraft, 93, 103
Saab 340, 116, 121, 126, 159
Saab Gripen demonstrator aircraft, 202
Sadi-LeCointe, Joseph, 14
Safran Aircraft Engines, xviii, 81, 186, 198-203, 208-209, 211-212, 217, 235-237, 240, 250, 252
Samsung Techwin, 189
Sangis, Georges, 259
Saudi Arabian Airlines, 175
Saugus River, 6
Savin, Olivier, *199*
Scandinavian Airlines, 93
Schafrik, Robert E., 259
Schenectady Steam Turbine Works, 38
Schilling, Jan, ix, 181, 200, 259
Schoenborn, William E., 259
Schroeder, Rudolph "Shorty", 11-14
Scott, Larry, 155, 259
Seager, Roger, 259
Sells, Bert E., 260
Service Life Extension Program (SLEP), 182
Shaw, Dave, 84
Shoults, Roy, *33*
Sidenstick, James E., 260
Sidewinder missiles, 70, 85
Sikorsky Aircraft, 194
Sikorsky CH-53K King Stallion, 122, 194, *195*, 196

Sikorsky HSS-1F, 66
Sikorsky S-61 helicopter, 73
Sikorsky S-92 helicopter, 168, 182
Sikorsky SH-3A, 76
Sikorsky UH-60A Black Hawk, 101, 106, 110, 142, 182, 202, 232, 243
Sikorsky YCH-53A, 79
silicon carbide (SiC) ceramic fiber, 230
Simmerman, George, 42
Sims, Paul, 124
Sinatra, Frank, 76
Singapore Airlines, 166, 173
Singapore Air Show, 155
Small Aircraft Engine Division, 56-57
Smith, Fred, 105
Smith, Jr., R. Leroy H., 260
Smith, Richard B., 113, 260
Smiths Aerospace, 192-193
Smithsonian Air & Space Museum, 137
Smuland, Robert J., 260
Snecma, 39, 81, 94, 97-98, *99*, 102-103, *104*, 105-106, *111*, 112, 126, 141-142, 146, 148-149, 171, 186, 247, 249, 251-252, 258-259, 262
Sollier, Jean, 106
Southwest Airlines, 116-117, 125, 146, 154, 161, 189, 212
Sparks, Russ, ix, 124, 154, 173, 195, 203, 227, 260
Spear, Ed, 124
Sprague, Robert L., 260
SR-71 spy plane, 96
Stallone, Michael J., 260
Standerwick, Reginald, 20, 32, *34*
Stanley, Bob, 33
Stanley, Richard, 178, 260
Steam Turbine division, 30, 249
Steinmetz, Charles P., 7
Stoeckly, Eugene E., 44, 260
Streid, Dale D., 260
Strother Field, 51
Sud Aviation, 112
Super-Fan engine, 133
Sutter, Joe, 109
Swissair, 93, 110

T

T31 engine, 30, 36, 38-39, 48, 257
T-38 Talon, 69-70, 88, 137, 174, 249
T58 turboshaft engine, 57-58, 61, 63-64, 66, 68, 70, 75-76, 88-89, 125, 129, 227, 248, 256, 258, 262
T64 engine, *64*, 65, 74, 79, 88, 93, 129, 194-195, 227, 254, 258, 262
T406, 195
T407, 194
T408 engine, 122, 194, *195*, 196
T700 engine, 88, *89*, 101, 106, 109-110, 115-116, 121-122, 126, 129, 150, 159, 177, 182, 189, 194, 202, 217, 222, 229, 243, 248, 250-252, 256, 261-262
T700-701D, 182, 222
T700/CT7, 159, 182, 251-252
T700-GE-401, 101
T700-GE-701, 101
T700-GE-701D, 202
T901, 227, *232*, 243
TECH56 demonstrator program, 171, 186
Tejas Light Combat Aircraft, 209
Textron, 200, 228-229
TF30 engine, 124
TF34 turbofan, 92-93, 103, 115, 134, 136, 142, 248, 250, 252, 258, 261-262
TF39 engine, 59, 65, 79, *82*, 83-84, 87, 89-90, 92-93, 95, 123, 126, 139, 168-169, 248, 253-257, 260
TG-100 engine, 30, 36, 48, 257
TG-180 turbojet, 36
Thiokol Chemical Corporation, 76
Thomas, Jr., Theodore T., 261
Thompson, E.S., *40*
Thompson, Lloyd, ix, 151, 153, 173
Thomson, Elihu, 5, 7
Thomson-Houston Electric Company, 5-6
Thrush 510 crop duster, 203
Tomasetti, Louis V., 261
Tomlinson, D.W. "Tommy", *18*, 19
Trabert, Archie, 42
Trabert, Tony, 42
Trans World Airlines (TWA), 18-19, 62-63, 71, 73

Trent 1000 engine, 180
Tritle, Ed, *33*
TRUEngine, 201
Truman, Harry S., 48
Tupolev Tu-144, 86
turbosupercharger, xxi, 8-10, *11*, 12, 14, 17-19, *21*, 30-31, 35-36, *38*, 41, 43, 257
Turkish Aerospace Industries, 126
Turnbull, Bob, ix, 101, 142, 261
Tusas Engine Industries (TEI), 126
TWA, 18-19, 62-63, 71, 73
Twin-Annular Pre-Swirl combustor (TAPS), 171, 180
Twin Towers, 170

U

U-2, 149, *150*
Unducted Fan (UDF) engine, 122, *127*, 128, 134, *135*, 136-137, 139-140
Unison engine components factory, 208
United Airlines, 62, 91-92, 109, 112-113, 166
United Arab Emirates, 170, 174, *175*, 182, 202, 218
United Technologies, 133, 159, 179
University of California, 7
University of Dayton, 206
University of Göttingen, 18
USAir, 116, *119*
US Airways, 177
US Army Air Service, 9, 11-13
US Atomic Energy Commission, 50
US Defense Advanced Research Projects Agency (DARPA), 176
US House Armed Services Committee, 213
US National Advisory Committee for Aeronautics, 8, 30
US Navy Bureau of Aeronautics, 57
US Signal Corps, 9
UTA, 93
UTTAS (Utility Tactical Transport Aircraft System), 101

V

V-22 Osprey, 195
V280 tilt-rotor demonstrator, 227

V2500 engine, 122, 124-125, 212-213, 230
Van Duyne, Walter E., 261
Varney, Glenn, ix, 85-86
Ventre, Marc, 198
Victor, Irving W., 261
Vietnam War, 85, 88, 95
Virgin Atlantic, 173
Volvo Aero, 141
von Ohain, Hans, 17-18, 28-29, 60
Vough-Hiller-Ryan XC-142 tilt-wing aircraft, 74
V/STOL aircraft, 78-79

W

Walker, Chapman, *52*
Walker, Joseph, 88
Wall Street Journal
    competition for the much-anticipated Boeing 787 and, 177-178
GE90 program and, 154
    storied engine battle and, 133
Walter Engines, 196
Ward, George, 124, 261
Warner, Donald "Truly", 20, 31, 44, 55, 261
Warren, Glenn B., 261
Weaver, Virgil, *48*, 261
Weinstein, Barry, 262
Welch, Jack, 116, 159, 163-165, 167, 170
Welsch, Ron, 140
Westinghouse, 30
White Mountains, 40
Whittle, Frank, 17-18, 29, *30*, 31-32, 35, 66, 261-262
Whittle W.1X turbojet, 30
Whittle W.2B, 30-31
Wilbur Wright Field, 9
Williams, James C., 262
Wilson, Charles E., 47
Wilson, Woodrow, 8
Wings Club, 57
Wisler, David, 262
Woll, Ed, 40, *41*, 63, 70-71, 101, 262
Woolard, Frank, 181
World Trade Center, 170
World War I, 8-9, 11, 15, 19, 29, 41

World War II, 15, 17-18, 22, 24, 27, 29, 36, 38-39, 44, 46, 60, 66, 85, 98-99, 193, 196, 223, 257
Worsham, Jim, 75, 262
Wright Aeronautical, 16, 20-21, *22-23*, 30, 42-43, *44*, 181
Wright Brothers, 3, 241
Wright Cyclone piston engine, 19, *24*
Wright Field, 9, 16-17, 19
Wright, Orville, 9, *24*, 206
Wright, Wilbur, 9, 206
Wright-Patterson Air Force Base, 9, 42, 49, 86, 88, 95
Wright-Patterson Air Force Base Museum, 88, 95
WS-125 nuclear-powered aircraft, 64

X

X-15, 88
X-45B Unmanned Combat Air Vehicle (UCAV), 176
X211, *60*, 64, 66, 73, 249, 253-254
X353-5 lift-fan, 78, 83
X370 demonstrator, *73*, 97, 248
XB-47 Stratojet bomber, 37, 47
XB-70 Valkyrie, *65*, 78-79, 84, 87-88, 95, 97, 100, 249
XF4D aircraft, 61, 258
XJN140E, 73
XP-59A jet aircraft, x, 32, *33*, 251, 258
XT901-GE-900, 242
XV-5A Vertifan flight research vehicle, 78-79, 255

Y

YB-17, 16, 19
Yeager, Chuck, 48
YF-16, 103, 107
YF-17 fighter, 94, 101, 103, 107
YF119, 143
YF120, 143, 145, 221, 247
YJ101, 221, 252